MW00484451

Luminos is the open access monograph publishing program from UC Press. Luminos provides a framework for preserving and reinvigorating monograph publishing for the future and increases the reach and visibility of important scholarly work. Titles published in the UC Press Luminos model are published with the same high standards for selection, peer review, production, and marketing as those in our traditional program. www.luminosoa.org

Precarious Claims

Precarious Claims

*The Promise and Failure of Workplace Protections
in the United States*

———

Shannon Gleeson

UNIVERSITY OF CALIFORNIA PRESS

University of California Press, one of the most distinguished university presses in the United States, enriches lives around the world by advancing scholarship in the humanities, social sciences, and natural sciences. Its activities are supported by the UC Press Foundation and by philanthropic contributions from individuals and institutions. For more information, visit www.ucpress.edu.

University of California Press
Oakland, California

© 2016 by Shannon Gleeson

This work is licensed under a Creative Commons CC-BY-NC-ND license. To view a copy of the license, visit http://creativecommons.org/licenses.

Suggested citation: Gleeson, Shannon. *Precarious Claims: The Promise and Failure of Workplace Protections in the United States.* Oakland, University of California Press, 2016. doi: http://doi.org/10.1525/luminos.19

Library of Congress Cataloging-in-Publication Data
Names: Gleeson, Shannon, 1980- author.
Title: Precarious claims : the promise and failure of workplace protections in the United States / Shannon Gleeson.
Description: Oakland, California : University of California Press, [2017] | Includes bibliographical references and index. | Description based on print version record and CIP data provided by publisher; resource not viewed.
Identifiers: LCCN 2016021065 (print) | LCCN 2016019951 (ebook) | ISBN 9780520963603 (ebook) | ISBN 9780520288782 (pbk. : alk. paper)
Subjects: LCSH: Working class—California, Northern—Case studies. | Work environment—California, Northern—Case studies. | Work environment—Law and legislation—United States. | Labor laws and legislation—United States. | Industrial safety—United States.
Classification: LCC HD8066 (print) | LCC HD8066 .G54 2017 (ebook) | DDC 344.7301—dc23
LC record available at https://lccn.loc.gov/2016021065

25   24   23   22   21   20   19   18   17   16
10   9   8   7   6   5   4   3   2   1

CONTENTS

ACKNOWLEDGMENTS

This book is the culmination of so many support networks, intellectual and beyond.

The project began when I first arrived as a faculty member in the Department of Latin American and Latino Studies at the University of California, Santa Cruz. My colleagues in LALS and Sociology, and the UCSC Center for Labor Studies and Chicano Latino Research Center, provided the initial intellectual support for this project, and the best place I ever could have started my career. Financial support for the study was provided generously by the UCSC Committee on Research, the UCSC Chicano Latino Research Center, the UCSC Hellman Fellows Program, the UC Center for New Racial Studies, the UC Institute for Mexico and the United States, the UC Global Health Initiative Center of Expertise on Migration and Health, the Ford Foundation, and the American Sociological Association Fund for the Advancement of the Discipline.

This research was made possible by a team of research assistants, including Annie Lin, Brian Jimenez, Jimmy Chiu, Hannah Fishman, Anel Flores, Joe Garcia, Claudia Medina, Iris Casanova, Mariela Rodriguez, and Claudia Lopez. Several fierce legal advocates referred me to their clients and provided feedback along the way, including Marisol Escalera Durani, Mike Gaitley, Jenna Grambourt, Henry Martin, Adriana Melgoza, Patty Salazar, Marci Seville, Ruth Silver-Taube, Daniela Urban, Florencia Valle-Miller, and Nick Webber. I thank also the California Division of Workers' Compensation, including Etna Borrero and Esther Pangelina.

My research and analysis benefited tremendously from feedback at several convenings, including those held by the American Sociological Association, the Latin American Studies Association, the Law and Society Association, the Population

Association of America, the Labor and Employment Relations Association, and the Pacific Sociological Association. I thank also the University of Pennsylvania, the USC School of Social Work Immigrant Health Initiative, the Global Labour Research Centre at York University, and the UCSC Departments of Psychology and Sociology for inviting me to present on early findings from this research and for providing excellent feedback. Since arriving at Cornell, I have also learned a great deal from discussions with my colleagues at the Cornell Worker Institute Precarious Workforce Initiative and the Cornell Center for the Study of Inequality. I thank all the scholars who organized these panels, provided remarks, presented alongside me, and asked probing questions.

My analysis developed further following discussions at a range of workshops, including those hosted by the Tepoztlán Institute for the Transnational History of the Americas, the UCLA Labor Center, the UCLA César E. Chávez Department of Chicana/o Studies, the UCLA International Institute Program on International Migration, the San Jose State University Immigration Symposium, the Pennsylvania State University Center for Global Workers' Rights, the UC Center for New Racial Studies, the UC Irvine School of Law, the UCSD Center for Comparative Immigration Studies, the Stanford Center on Poverty and Inequality, the Rice University Baker Institute's Latin America Initiative Immigration Research Project, the COEMH Summer Institute on Migration and Global Health, the UC Humanities Research Initiative, and the Critical Race Theory and Empirical Methods Working Group.

Writing is hard. Rewriting is harder. I've benefited extensively from the support of other writers who have read through draft after draft and pushed me to rethink and refine. Several scholars, mostly women, have taken the time to read and comment on my work, and help me through the often lonely and distracting process of writing. Amada Armenta, Els de Graauw, and Cristina Mora have been my constant cheerleaders. Marcel Paret pushed me to think hard about the factors shaping precarity, Kate Griffith provided the sharp eye of a legal scholar, and Anthony Ocampo helped me storyboard and hopefully do justice to these workers' lives. Cristina Mora, Cybelle Fox, and Laura López-Sanders provided some of the most critical early support. The ILR Women's Writing Group and the UC Berkeley Framing Immigrant Rights Writing Group provided interdisciplinary critique and encouragement as the project came to fruition. Colleagues from the National Center for Faculty Development and Diversity, including Miriam Boesch and Sue Maguire, as well as Sonja Poole and Elise Murowchick, checked in with me regularly and helped keep me accountable.

Throughout the project, several colleagues offered additional insight, including Leisy Abrego, KT Albiston, Xóchitl Bada, Carolina Bank-Muñoz, Annette Bernhardt, Ellen Berrey, Irene Bloemraad, Kristin Bumiller, Sébastien Chauvin, Jennifer Chun, Alex Colvin, Ileen Devault, Allison Elias, Anna Haskins, Tanya

Golash-Boza, Ruth Gomberg-Muñoz, Erin Hatton, Ming Hsu Chen, Lisa Martinez, Steve McKay, Ruth Milkman, Cristina Morales, Genevieve Negrón-Gonzales, Caitlin Patler, Veronica Terriquez, Kim Voss, and Pat Zavella.

I thank my family for their love, and the incessant wondering "how's the book going?" including Mom, Dad, Danny, Tom, Carol, Papa, Estela, Sav, Aunt Steph, Uncle Michael, Ry, Er, Jack, Ez, and the many other cousins and tías. Several friends have played the hardest role of encouraging me through the minutiae of daily writing (or attempting to write), and reminding me of the important things in life. My dear friends Rhonda Campbell, Shelly Grabe, Sylvanna Falcón, Milton Magaña, Chris Sullivan, and Leslie Wang supported me through my transition to Ithaca, long before, and long since. Ramon Rodriguez and Javier Bidho, also talented artists, provided friendship and inspiration. BYCI gave me community in Ithaca. Since arriving in my new home, Veronica Martinez-Matsuda, Mike Matsuda, Lucia Matsuda, Joaquín Matsuda, and Oscar Matsuda welcomed me with open arms and have provided me with friendship, much-needed grounding, and social eating. Finally, Gabriel Carraher, Hyacinth, Chahta, Paco, and even Wax also kept me fed and loved.

I thank Jose Ortiz, a talented Salinas-based artist and founder of Hijos del Sol, for permission to use his art on the cover. At UC Press, Maura Roessner has been a supportive editor, and I appreciate also the work of Jack Young and Chris Sosa Loomis. Early discussions with Fran Benson at Cornell/ILR Press also have proven to be so useful. Matt Seidel provided expert editing services before submission, and Lindsey Westbrook assisted with copy editing, as did Barbara Roos with index preparation. Most importantly, I thank the workers who gave me access to their lives and granted me the privilege of hearing and telling their stories.

Introduction

Over the last century, workers in the United States have come to enjoy an expanding array of workplace protections. The minimum wage has continued to increase, albeit sporadically, and several state and city regulations now outpace stagnant federal protections. Workplace safety standards cover more workers than ever, and our modern ability to track occupational injuries, illnesses, and fatalities has helped to inform crucial policy change. Owing to the long struggles waged by civil rights and feminist leaders, employers can no longer fire workers solely on the basis of their race, gender, or religious preference without running the risk of the government holding them accountable. Organized labor has enormous influence in progressive political circles, and key union victories have gone a long way to change industry standards. In short, the fruits of decades of labor organizing are undeniable.

The government apparatus that has sprung up to enforce these protections is also impressive. The Department of Labor enforces 180 federal laws covering 10 million employers and 125 million workers (US Department of Labor 2015a). One of President Barack Obama's goals was to grow the agency by more than 4 percent (Miller and Dinan 2015). Moreover, the Equal Employment Opportunity Commission's strategic plan has yielded some of the highest settlements in history, with the largest verdict to date in 2013 awarding $240 million to thirty-two men in the meat processing industry who suffered horrific discrimination and abuse at the hands of their employer (US Equal Employment Opportunity Commission 2013). As these and other examples demonstrate, workers have made significant strides.

And yet, despite the proliferation of protections, expanding enforcement bureaucracies, and high-profile victories, there has nonetheless been a "rise in polarized and precarious employment systems" over the last four decades (Kalleberg

2011). These so-called "bad jobs," Arne L. Kalleberg argues, are characterized by poor job quality in both economic and non-economic terms, including pay, benefits, and worker power (9–10). Many of these bad jobs have little effective government oversight (Bernhardt et al. 2008), are rarely unionized, have unpredictable schedules, and offer little upward mobility. These characteristics encompass what Marc Doussard (2013) refers to as "degraded work," an employment trend fueled in large part by small and local businesses who are fighting to compete in tough economic environments. "Degraded" workers become disposable bodies as well as indispensable assets that allow companies to compete in the global economy (Uchitelle 2007). The precarious position of US workers is also tied inextricably to the even more egregious disposability of workers across the world, who stand waiting in the wings as industries relocate to find the cheapest and least protected labor source in a race to the bottom (Bales 2012).

Several categories of these "marginal workers" (Garcia 2012a), to use another term for them (for example undocumented immigrants, women, and racial and sexual minorities), face particular challenges in realizing their rights under US labor and employment law. Undocumented workers have limited remedies for injustices under the law and live under the constant threat of deportation. Women not only experience a higher incidence of pay inequity, discrimination, and sexual harassment but also shoulder a substantial burden of reproductive labor responsibilities that impact—and are impacted by—their work lives. Underrepresented racial minorities, including some immigrants, have poorer economic outcomes, are more likely to be in unprotected job categories, and face distinct challenges during the workplace grievance claims process. LGBT workers also continue to lack complete federal protection against discrimination at work. Each of these populations is subject to discriminatory practices that are the result of long-standing institutional inequalities.

Previous studies have examined this widespread workplace inequality, but they have tended to focus on what goes wrong at work or on why aggrieved workers never come forward. This emphasis reflects the undeniable reality that few workers actually manage to claw their way up what William L. F. Felstiner, Richard L. Abel, and Austin Sarat (1980) call the dispute pyramid: the three-part process of "naming, blaming, and claiming." And when social scientists *do* look at the cases where workers engage in a sustained fight, we tend to highlight the valiant efforts of collective worker mobilizations or dramatic individual litigation sagas. However, the vast majority of employment laws offer worker protections through mundane administrative bureaucracies. This machinery predictably receives less attention, in part because it is less rousing, though no less important, than the chants coming from picket lines or the pleas of eloquent attorneys.

Although the vast majority of workplace violations never materialize into a formal claim, this book offers a unique perspective on the experiences of the choice few who do come forward. Their stories provide insight into power relations at the workplace *and* within the rights bureaucracies intended to regulate them. I pose a series of questions in this study from the outset: What propels a worker to come forward and file a claim, given all we know about the barriers to claims-making? What is the role of social networks in educating workers about their rights? How do they learn lessons about when to come forward, how far to push, and when to back down? I then examine the bureaucracies of labor standards enforcement from the perspective of workers on the ground. When does the system work for these courageous claimants? And, alternatively, why, even in the best of circumstances, do workers sometimes lose out in spite of the law's good intentions?

This book is not an ethnography of the system from the perspective of the key actors who run it. Unlike numerous other scholars, I don't interrogate the decisions that judges, bureaucrats, and attorneys make to adjudicate cases. I don't cull data from hours of administrative hearings (though I did spend time in several such sessions), nor are my claims based on interviews with those stakeholders and experts who shape the claims-making process. There are, to be sure, many works covering these important perspectives (see for example Cooper and Fisk [2005], Cummings [2012], and Epp [2010], to name a few). Rather, this is a story, told from the perspectives of individual workers themselves, about how they experience the journey to justice: their plodding path through multiple agencies, appointments, medical visits, and reams of paperwork. Rather than asking how and why the labor standards bureaucracy operates as it does, I focus on how workers navigate its seas. What makes them decide to see their journey through, or, conversely, abandon ship?

PRECARITY AND POWER IN A GLOBAL ECONOMY

We live in a new global economy marked by innovation, ever-evolving technologies, and exponential concentrations of wealth accumulation. Global firms such as Apple, Facebook, Google, and Twitter have become the household names that GM and Chrysler once were. Yet apart from the multiplying tech campuses and the explosion of high-end real estate, this new economy has also given rise to a low-wage workforce producing the goods and services that we have all come to expect—indeed, demand—cheaply and quickly. Industries such as construction, domestic work, food service, and retail are the pillars of the postindustrial societies; pay is low, conditions are often dangerous, and workplace violations run rampant. Therefore, while low-wage workers enjoy some of the most expansive formal rights in history, they also toil in a state of extreme precarity.

This is not to say that precarity is a novel phenomenon. Historically, the basic concessions of food stamps and cash assistance, and the promise of a modest income and access to health care in old age, were beyond the scope of imagination in the United States (Cohen 1991). There were important developments, most notably with the dawn of equal opportunity legislation during the civil rights and feminist movements. But these new laws did not, and could not, single-handedly erase centuries of racial and gendered subjugation of precarious workers (Lucas 2008).

While hailed as a unique marker of the modern economy, globalization— including the export of capital and the import of goods and labor—has cast a long historical shadow. For centuries, migrant workers have crossed oceans to reach the United States and elsewhere only to earn pitiful wages and endure conditions that are akin to, and in some cases are actually, indentured servitude. The informal economy, including what we refer to now as day labor, was once even more widespread than it is today, a means of economic survival for workers (both immigrant and native-born) as well as their employers (Higbie 2003; Valenzuela 2003).

The modern era also does not have a monopoly on exclusionary immigration policies rooted in racial and class-based xenophobia. Long before the emergence of post-9/11 nativism, the early twentieth century ushered in racist immigration rubrics. Former leader of the Knights of Labor Terence Powderly served as the first US commissioner general of immigration from 1898 to 1902. Despite the relatively progressive agenda of the Knights of Labor, his vision was squarely on the path of exclusion. Later, some of this early labor organization's most revered leaders, such as Samuel Gompers, president of the American Federation of Labor from 1886 to 1924, also became champions of Asian exclusion and other restrictionist policies (E. Lee 2003). The Immigration Act of 1965, which proponents initially thought would increase predominantly European migration, horrified many labor leaders as Latinos and Asians came streaming in. Furthermore, labor advocates stridently opposed guest worker programs and would later support employer sanctions under the 1986 Immigration Reform and Control Act (Fine and Tichenor 2012).

Has nothing changed, then, after more than a century of such exclusionary sentiments and weak to nonexistent workplace protections? To be sure, we are decades removed from a time when there was no minimum wage or occupational safety and health standards, and when workers lacked any formal right to organize. Tragedies such as the 1911 Triangle Shirtwaist disaster in New York and the 1914 massacre of striking miners in Ludlow, Colorado, are seemingly behind us. But the pace and the reach of globalization have multiplied exponentially, as has the gap between capital and workers, and the gains of the New Deal and Progressive Era have been steadily disappearing. Such conditions have produced lived realities for today's workers that resemble the exploitative nature of earlier eras, while involving new forms of repression. New consumer markets have come to expect quick and constant product adaptation; industry, in turn, demands a flexible workforce. Transportation and communications technologies now provide the means to create, and perpetuate, a low-wage workforce under constant threat.

For those industries that rely on a domestic workforce, the decimation of union representation and new forms of "flexible" employment that effectively evade employer liability give rise to a situation in which a worker's rights are often theoretical. The illusory nature of workers' rights, a fortified police state in an era when immigration enforcement budgets far exceed those of any other federal law enforcement agency (Meissner 2009), and relatively meager labor standards enforcement budgets combine to create a perfect storm of precarity that deters effective attempts to empower and mobilize immigrant workers. In sum, despite the proliferation of new laws and protections, the political will and practical ability to enforce them is often insufficient to address the rampant abuses the most vulnerable workers must confront.

The political sociologist Saskia Sassen has written an invaluable study for understanding the nature and impact of the current economic and political era in which we live. In *Expulsions: Brutality and Complexity in the Global Economy* (2014), she details a series of predatory systems that disadvantage low-wage workers and that define the "brutal" logic of contemporary capitalism (4). What makes this system work so well is the illusion, and practical reality, that within the system there is no one at the helm and thus no one to be held accountable. As a result, even fair and well-meaning employers may engage in labor practices that, while firmly within the bounds of labor and employment law, are nevertheless exploitative. Moreover, as she shows, these practices then become the industry standard for any business owner hoping to turn a profit and stay competitive. While labor advocates have rallied for "high-road employment" that eschews such tactics, and there is ample evidence that worker-friendly practices can enhance productivity and coexist with profitable enterprise, it is also true that success stories are atypical (Milkman 2002). Unfortunately, low-road practices are the norm.

There has been much debate regarding the state of precarity in the modern era and what Guy Standing (2011, 2014) has labeled the "precariat," a social class whose employment is marked by informality and increased insecurity.[1] This state of precarity can be explained by several factors. In the United States, union membership has precipitously declined since the late 1970s, eroding worker protections. More recently, an economic recession sent unemployment rates soaring to 10 percent and triggered a housing crisis that disproportionately impacted communities of color. The US Bureau of Labor Statistics finds that one in ten workers in 2014 was jobless for ninety-nine weeks or longer, with African Americans being the hardest hit (Kosanovich and Theodossiou 2015).

While the United States has begun to emerge from the recession, research on the "under-employed" casts doubt on even cautious descriptions of an economic recovery, especially for part-time workers of color (Shierholz 2013). Beyond the added income, full-time employment often provides important benefits that a subset of low-wage workers have come to rely on, such as health insurance and retirement accounts. Public benefits provide the only alternative for the rest of these low-wage workers. However, the last two decades have also ushered in a dismantling of the welfare state, which also largely excludes noncitizens (Park 2011) as well as other categories of "undeserving" workers, such as certain ex-prisoners (Travis 2005). The current reality therefore is that if one were to lose his or her job, even an undesirable one, there are few support systems on which to rely.[2]

Nonstandard employment relationships (Kalleberg 2000) and the continued erosion of the social contract (Katz 2010; Quinn Mills 1996) have dovetailed with a perceived explosion of foreign-born workers in the US labor force. While immigrants represented only 4.7 percent of the US population in 1970, this number rose to 13.1 percent in 2013 (Zong and Batalova 2015). However, looking back at the history of US immigration reveals an even higher proportion of foreign-born people at the turn of the twentieth century: 13.6 percent in 1900 versus 12.9 percent in 2010 (Migration Policy Institute 2015). Nevertheless, the recent increase has fueled the perception of an immigrant invasion, with a particular preoccupation with the southern border and a fear that immigrants are "stealing American jobs." Ample research has debated the merits of this claim, with a focus on the complementarity versus substitutionality of immigrant workers. Restrictionists argue that any economic gains from immigration are limited and overstated (Borjas 2013), while recent evidence suggests that the inflow of foreign-born workers actually modestly increases wages for native-born workers (Greenstone and Looney 2012, 2010). In the legal arena, the courts continue to contemplate the rights of undocumented immigrants (Brownell 2011), and immigration debates have become increasingly inflammatory during the 2016 presidential campaign.

But if we shift our focus from the economy and immigration policies to the well-being of these individual workers, another set of key questions emerges. Rather than ask whether low-wage workers have contributed to the degradation of work in the United States—a question that Ruth Milkman (2006) has shown is much more complex than most histories allow—it seems more timely to ask how the exploitation of undocumented workers in particular is the canary in the coal mine for a global system built on precarity. Immigrant workers face particular challenges in the United States and across the world (Costello and Freedland 2014; Garcia 2012a). Immigrant labor is a symptom, not a cause, of domestic *and* global inequality.

To be sure, many foreign-born workers are engineers and doctors in the "high-skilled" workforce. But the contemporary US immigration flow is characterized by a "split personality" (Waldinger and Lichter 2003, 4); that is, although there are some high-skilled workers coming in, many more immigrants possess low levels of human capital, have limited proficiency in English, and are concentrated in low-wage service and production industries. Undocumented workers, who represent 5.4 percent of the national civilian workforce, are especially concentrated in precarious positions: a quarter of all workers in food processing, a third of all those in construction, and, depending on whose estimates you believe, anywhere from 50 to 80 percent of all farm labor in the United States (Passel 2006). These low-wage and conventionally "unskilled" immigrant workers possess key assets that employers in the secondary labor market covet, namely pliability. As Roger D. Waldinger and Michael I. Lichter (2003) write, "The best subordinates are those who know their place. . . . And where employers understand jobs to be demeaning . . . they have reasons to assign the task to a worker already unrespected. . . . Thus, jobs that require willing subordinates motivate employers to have recourse to immigrants" (40).

Undocumented workers occupy a paradoxical position in the US labor market. On the one hand, they are deportable "aliens," and employers who hire them are subject to fines and criminal prosecution. On the other hand, they are a critical part of the workforce, and as easy targets for abuse, they also are an important outreach priority for labor standards enforcement agencies and advocates (Gleeson 2012a). The government then is at once responsible for policing *and* aiding undocumented workers. Yet increased immigration enforcement both at the worksite and in local communities fuels employer abuse (Menjívar and Abrego 2012). Along with at-will employment relationships, the threat of deportation creates a pliable workforce and discourages undocumented workers from speaking up. Immigrant workers are in a sense victims twice over. In a cruelly ironic twist, they are often blamed for the "spiraling crisis of global capitalism" that necessitates them leaving their communities of origin in the first place, then subsequently criminalized in their often hostile receiving communities (Robinson and Santos 2014; Milkman 2011). Nevertheless, as the data in this book reiterates, these workers are also agentic actors who are able and willing to mobilize their rights under the right conditions.

Precarious Claims examines how immigration enforcement efforts and at-will employment relationships jointly fuel the disposability of undocumented workers. I argue that, as with rosy presumptions about the post–civil rights era of workplace discrimination, legal equality for undocumented workers often veils deep-seated institutional inequalities. As such, I contend that undocumented status is a "precarity multiplier" that worsens workplace conditions (occupational segregation, pay differentials, lack of workplace safety); affects claimants' experiences in the legal bureaucracy (lack of access to legal counsel, linguistic and cultural barriers, limited remedies); and limits access to a social safety net that already largely excludes undocumented immigrants.

THE REGIME OF INDIVIDUAL WORKERS' RIGHTS

The system that shapes workplace protections in the United States dates back decades. Federal laws and agencies such as the National Labor Relations Act (1935), the Fair Labor Standards Act (1938), Title VII of the Civil Rights Act (1964), and the Occupational Safety and Health Administration (1970) were all products of intense worker mobilizations and legislative debates. These arenas of protection—collective bargaining, wages and work hours, discrimination, and health and safety—compose a confusing matrix of bureaucracies that cover various statutes and geographic jurisdictions. For example, Alabama has no state minimum wage statute, while workers in Washington are currently entitled to $9.47 per hour, a rate that rises with inflation each year and is more than $2 more than the federal minimum. Meanwhile, cities across the country have instituted their own standards; take San Francisco, where wage rates are set to rise to $15 per hour by 2018.

However, neither the presence of workplace protection laws nor, indeed, active efforts to improve and strengthen them ensures that they are respected or that abusers will be held accountable. Moreover, these laws only regulate a narrow set of workplace behaviors, and there are many employer practices that, while perfectly legal, workers may nonetheless find unfair, exploitative, or otherwise harmful. Even within the realm of legal workplace violations, labor standards enforcement agencies face a wide range of challenges, from insufficient resources to short-staffed investigative units and, in some cases, lack of political will (Bernhardt et al. 2008; Government Accountability Office 2009; Kerwin and McCabe 2011). Furthermore, the claims-based system requires that workers know their rights and be willing to exercise them. In an increasingly de-unionized labor market where employers need little or no reason to fire a worker, filing a claim is a gamble most deem not worth taking. Even when workers do successfully pursue charges against an employer, their victories can ring hollow, as often they must then fight the employer to comply with a judge's order (Cho, Koonse, and Mischel 2013).

This book goes beyond the simple story of employers seeking to maximize profit on the backs of their workers. Rather, it emphasizes the inequities that persist throughout the system of workplace justice and details workers' experiences with a wide array of institutional gatekeepers. I home in on the cracks in these bureaucratic systems. Where does the system fall apart for aggrieved workers, and why, even in the best of circumstances, do workers often remain unprotected? The answer lies partly in the claims process. Beyond confronting their employers, workers must also learn to navigate complex management hierarchies, multifaceted government agencies, insurance companies, doctors, and language interpreters. Legal brokers, while essential to this process, encounter their own challenges, including a limited capacity to take on complex cases, fluctuating budgets, and staff turnover.

Employers have recently taken steps to make the claims-making process even more daunting. Despite the protections ensconced in federal and state law, firms have increasingly established a range of internal mechanisms to manage conflict between workers and management, often to the former's disadvantage. Labor scholars and advocates have been critical of these internal processes, which are executed by sophisticated, some might say cunning, human resources departments. Discussing civil rights legislation, Lauren B. Edelman (1992) demonstrates how the ambiguity of antidiscrimination laws grants organizations "wide latitude" to comply in a way that gives the impression of earnest compliance while also meeting management's interests. In the sexual harassment arena, Anna-Maria Marshall (2005) argues that company grievance procedures create obstacles to women's efforts to assert their rights while shielding firms from legal liabilities. My findings highlight how logics of compliance and mediation can reduce the opportunities for restitution under the guise of procedural justice.[3]

Though we like to imagine it as such, the law is not a neutral institution; similarly, the process of claims-making is fraught with bias. Kitty Calavita and Valerie Jenness's (2014) expert analysis of the prison grievance system reveals how the cards are stacked against many claimants from the beginning. Though they focus on a "total" institution that represents the full force of the state, the experiences of incarcerated individuals provide an important lens through which to observe how claims-making bureaucracies unfold. To begin, the grievance process, which the authors describe as "byzantine," is designed for a closed environment where prisoners have few rights and fewer resources to exercise them. Despite the landmark creation of the Prison Litigation Reform Act (1996) and the inmate grievance system it created, these new rights have not ensured an easily accessible and efficient system. In fact, as the authors show through interviews with prison staff, the grievance system serves almost as a pressure valve for prisoner discontent—that is, to release pent-up frustrations without really addressing injustices. In a similar fashion, the creation of the individualized system of workers' rights was, according to labor historians, an attempt to quell the discord prompted by the now-dying breed of social movement unionism (Fantasia and Voss 2004; Lichtenstein 2002). Again, such reforms are ultimately more concerned with avoiding conflict than establishing solid workplace protections.

Calavita and Jenness's description of how the prisoner rights system was originally perceived sounds eerily familiar to the common critical perspective of labor rights activism. While most of the state agents they spoke to believed prisoners should have the rights outlined in the act, many also felt that the system had "gone too far" by being excessively generous toward the prisoners (Calavita and Jenness 2014, 110). Similarly, turn on a mainstream news channel today and you will hear voices warning against the dangers of granting a higher minimum wage, expanding overtime benefits, or adding discrimination protections and health and safety standards: decreased business innovation, trampled consumer rights, and curtailed corporate free speech. Like the prisoner grievance system, which is steeped in the logic of individual rights *and* carceral control, the labor standards enforcement bureaucracy must be understood within the logic of capitalism, which naturally limits workers' rights even as it forms well-meaning, rational bureaucracies intended to enforce them.

These logics, the one exploitative and the other protective, often clash, and as such it should not be assumed that the predominant model of legal protection can ultimately eliminate economic and social inequality (Calavita and Jenness 2014, 3). Workers may create their own logics for defining harm that differ from those standards laid out under formal law. Marshall (2003), for example, highlights the deeply personal or extrajudicial agency that women invoke when deciding whether to pursue a legal claim against sexual harassment; these claimants may draw not on formal law but rather on notions of labor market productivity and feminist interpretations of power at the workplace. Similarly variable interpretations of workplace injustice can emerge in other violations, ranging from wage theft to workers' compensation. This variability hinges in part on how workers learn about, interpret, and decide to mobilize the law as they develop their distinct legal consciousness.

LEGAL CONSCIOUSNESS AND DEPORTABILITY

My previous work examined how workers develop a legal consciousness about their rights and identified what factors keep them from coming forward with a claim (Gleeson 2010). The concept of legal consciousness has become somewhat shopworn in the field of law and society, but it is still useful for understanding how laws sustain their institutional power and how individuals understand their rights under the law and make decisions as to whether and how to exercise them (Silbey 2005, 2008). One's position in the social and economic order can influence legal consciousness; for instance, poorer individuals (including nonwhites, who tend to be less affluent) engage lawyers and the courts less often. The negative effects of this imbalance are compounded because those with past experience in the system do better than first-timers (Galanter 1974; Curran 1977).[4]

In the arena of immigration, undocumented individuals (who are overwhelmingly Latino) are by definition excluded from full citizenship and actively pursued for expulsion by an ever-growing immigration enforcement apparatus. And yet undocumented workers have formed the core of many worker struggles (Milkman 2006) and will be crucial to any revitalization of labor unions. Therefore my claim is not that undocumented workers do not mobilize their rights, or that those who do cannot be successful. A quick scan of the press releases proudly disseminated by enforcement agencies and worker advocates reveals many high-profile, as well as more modest, victories. For example, Olivia Tamayo, an undocumented farm worker who was awarded more than $1 million after being repeatedly sexually assaulted by her employer, became an icon in the struggle against the impunity with which growers often operate in California's Central Valley and across the nation (US Equal Employment Opportunity Commission 2008). More recently, five female farmworkers in Florida were awarded more than $17 million after a federal jury found supervisors guilty of having forced them into "coerced sex, groping and verbal abuse, then fired them for objecting" (US Equal Employment Opportunity Commission 2015h). Beyond the discrimination arena, the Department of Labor Wage and Hour Division's EMPLEO program targets outreach to immigrant workers in the western region, many of whom are undocumented, and has helped ten thousand workers recover more than $15 million in back wages over the last ten years (Wage and Hour Division 2014b). Even the National Labor Relations Board, which is constrained by a Supreme Court ruling that prevents the reinstatement of undocumented workers, has certified union representation for many of those engaged in organizing (Jobs with Justice 2014).

It has been demonstrated across various institutional contexts, however, that despite certain protections and occasional victories, an immigrant's relationship to the law is determined in large part by legal status, especially in the current uncertain policy environment. Migrant illegality represents a form of "legal violence" (Menjívar and Abrego 2012) against undocumented workers, even if the specific impacts may vary across age and institutional setting (Gleeson and Gonzales 2012; Abrego and Gonzales 2010), generation and family formation (Abrego 2014; Dreby 2010; Menjívar and Abrego 2009; Zatz and Rodriguez 2015), and the specifics of national origin and homeland politics (Coutin 2000; Golash-Boza 2015).[5] The immigration enforcement apparatus, working in conjunction with a broad network of law enforcement at the state and local levels, implements a racialized dragnet of detention and removal that targets Latinos disproportionately (Golash-Boza and Hondagneu-Sotelo 2013; Armenta 2015). Within the workplace context, the deportability of undocumented workers, despite expansive worker protection reforms at the federal, state, and local levels, is a looming reality for those engaged in claims-making.

Moreover, undocumented workers are not randomly distributed across the labor market; they are concentrated in certain areas whose risk factors can complicate their ability to seek and gain restitution. For example, undocumented workers are overrepresented in industries (e.g., certain agricultural fields, domestic labor) that are not covered by key government protections. Furthermore, undocumented workers are more likely to be misclassified as independent contractors (Carré 2015). Employers who classify them as such not only avoid paying taxes and other worker benefits but can also avoid adhering to many of the workplace standards afforded to employees. Undocumented workers are also generally more likely to work in dangerous occupations and don't receive the concomitant wage differential to account for this risk (Hall and Greenman 2015). In addition to this labor force distribution, undocumented workers are more likely to have low levels of human capital and face English language limitations that pose instrumental barriers to filing a claim. Finally, as they are predominantly Latino, undocumented workers also face social discrimination that reflects and reinforces their racialized exclusion (De Genova 2005).

These structural barriers do not negate the strong efforts of worker advocates. Immigrant rights organizations, unions and worker centers, and both the pro bono and private bars have played an important role in improving the rights of low-wage workers by pushing for new laws and protections (such as raising the minimum wage and legislating rights for LGBT workers). These intermediaries are also crucial in helping these workers access these rights (Gordon 2007; Cummings 2009; Fine 2006; Zlolniski 2006). Existing research confirms that engaging with legal advocates can have a transformative impact on how marginalized individuals perceive, experience, and interact with the law (Hernández 2010). Yet, as this book reveals, the heroic efforts of these advocates are hampered by the shoestring budgets with which they operate, the limited remedies under the law, and the practical challenges posed by the behemoth bureaucracies that enforce the law and the quotidian struggles of low-wage workers' lives.

DEFYING THE ODDS AND MAKING WORKERS' RIGHTS REAL

There is a deep disjuncture between rights in theory and rights in practice, and the process of "making rights real" is fraught with challenges (Epp 2010). Consider one of the most common workplace violations: nonpayment, or underpayment, of wages. Let's assume the violation occurred in California. In this case, California workers are covered at the federal level by the Fair Labor Standards Act, at the state level by the California Labor Code, and at the local level by an increasing number of municipalities that have enacted minimum wage ordinances of their own. Finding that their employer has not paid them what they are owed, and that their attempt to recoup their missing wages falls on deaf ears (or garners retaliation), workers may turn to the law to demand restitution. The first step in this process requires knowing enough about the law to know that they have been wronged. Next, workers must determine what to do with this knowledge. Perhaps they have learned where to go for help and which agency has jurisdiction—through a workers' rights poster, conversations with coworkers, or a local organization's outreach. Workers may then decide to visit a local labor organization, or some may even go to the government agency directly if they feel comfortable doing so. There, they will be asked to provide evidence that they worked the hours they claimed to have worked and any other documentation for the pay they received. If the employer did not keep records and paid in cash, and the workers cannot recall the specifics, they will be asked to provide their best estimate. Their legal advocate may also help them gather this information and attempt to contact the employer first to remedy the situation without having to file a formal claim. In some cases, a call from an attorney does the trick. In others, indignant (and occasionally cash-strapped) employers continue to evade and avoid.

Generally, an aggrieved worker will next decide if they have the energy and resources to file a formal claim at the labor commission, to which they would send the paperwork and await a settlement conference, which could take another six months. At that conference, the employer will ideally show up—they often do not—and with a neutral agent of the state present, sort out the facts of the claim. The employer may make an offer to make the issue go away, and the worker may counter (or the other way around). Either party may walk away. If nothing is settled, the parties are calendared for a formal hearing, which could be scheduled for up to a year later, and where, assuming all goes as planned, both parties and their advocates would again be present. At this point, the presiding officer or administrative law judge hears the evidence and renders a verdict. If at any point in the process either party requires translation, it will be provided. If the losing party disagrees with the decision, they may choose to appeal at superior court. If not, the decision is binding. If the worker wins the claim, the employer is expected to pay up. Lawyers, while not required, can give parties a crucial advantage at navigating the ins and outs of this process.

The details of a claims scenario certainly differ from statute to statute and agency to agency, but generally claims share the following qualities: 1) there are several places along the way where workers could ostensibly resolve their issue without ultimately pursuing a formal claim, even after initiating said claim; 2) workers may choose to proceed with or without the help of a legal advocate, a decision that hinges on social networks and resources available to the worker and could prove enormously consequential, especially for those who lack linguistic skills and experience with the legal process; 3) initiating a formal claim by no means precludes workers from dropping their claim at any point along the process and moving on with their lives.

We have limited data on when and how often workers initiate and complete a workplace claim. One difficulty is that the labor standards enforcement system is really a series of splintered bureaucracies that span federal, state, and (increasingly) local jurisdictions. Agencies enforce different statutes, rely on different data tracking systems, and sometimes don't even define claims in the same way. To further complicate matters, these public agencies fiercely guard the confidentiality of their claimants, and rightly so. But as a result, it is nearly impossible to comprehensively measure *all* workplace violation claims at once, much less connect multiple claims that a worker may have, by relying on administrative data alone. Beyond these government agencies, the rise in internal dispute resolution systems and mandatory arbitration, even for nonunion workers, means that many claims may never get past a company's human resources department.

However, some revealing data do exist that, at a minimum, help illustrate the challenges workers face in filing a claim. Several researchers have done the impressive work of tracking these claims through the "dispute pyramid," and what they have found is alarming, though perhaps not surprising. Gary Blasi and Joseph W. Doherty (2010), for example, focused on administrative data from the Department of Fair Employment and Housing. To begin, they state a basic fact: for every one million employees in California, about 1,000 employment discrimination complaints are filed every year. Of these, 250 are filed with the federal Equal Employment Opportunity Commission; the other 750 go to the California Department of Fair Employment and Housing (DFEH). Of these latter claims, 375 are granted a Notice of Right to Sue letter, where the claimant then has to rely on a private attorney. Continuing on, 165 of these cases will end up in court, but only 2 will receive a verdict. Another 375 (of the 750 DFEH cases) are pursued administratively by the agency.

The fates of these cases vary tremendously, but it is most important to note that of the 375 cases pursued by the agency, approximately 73 will be outright rejected for investigation, 33 will be dismissed for reasons unrelated to the merits of the case, 34 will request a Notice of Right to Sue letter to pursue claims outside the agency process, 20 will be dismissed due to insufficient evidence, 165 will be dismissed due to insufficient probable cause, and only 46 will be settled or resolved during the administrative process. In other words, claims can take many different paths and end in very different outcomes. In fact, according to Blasi and Doherty's research, the odds of a complainant receiving a monetary award are one in fourteen, with a median award in the range of $3,000 to $4,000 when working through the administrative system. Those who proceed to the courts garner a median payout of $205,000 (with significant variation according to the basis of the claim, with race claims only garnering a median of $105,000) (Blasi and Doherty 2010).

These dynamics can be explained in part by what we already know from Max Weber about the function of bureaucracies, which can quickly harden into inflexible iron cages even as they purport to operate with objectivity, rationality, and fairness (Weber 2009, 1978). These hierarchical structures execute well-oiled systems governed by set rules meant to combat the biased and subjective approaches of an older, more nepotistic tradition. Yet despite this seemingly transparent system, and as the stories in this book reveal, not all workers are equally equipped to navigate these bureaucracies, even with help from advocates and state workers.[6]

Given the factors that keep workers from standing up for their rights, the workers in this study have already defied the odds and won a victory of sorts by coming forward in the first place. However, to expect the average worker to be "successful" in her claim proves fanciful given the reality revealed by these data. Of the 89 workers who completed a follow-up interview, only 43 reported filing a claim directly with a labor standards enforcement agency. Among those who chose not to, some happily reported that they were able to resolve the issue without a formal claim, but others cited reasons such as lacking the money to pay an attorney, the perception that the claim would lead to a "dead end," the desire to get back to work and their normal lives, or simply the fact that they did not have a case that their legal advocate felt was worth pursuing. One respondent explained her rationale for dropping a claim despite feeling strongly about it: "I became discouraged, even though I know it was unjust." Overall, when asked whether they had ultimately received what they wanted from their claim, only 16 of the 89 follow-up survey interviews provided an affirmative "yes."

In part, such dissatisfaction motivates my study. The central goal of this book is to provide an account, from the ground up, of the context of worker precarity that leads to workplace violations, how workers weigh the costs and benefits of pursuing a claim, what resources they draw on to navigate the complex workers' rights bureaucracies, and what impact these acts of legal mobilization ultimately have on their everyday lives.

THE COSTS OF PURSUING WORKERS' JUSTICE

A unifying theme of this study is that engaging the law comes with costs, such that those with more capital (economic, social, cultural) have an easier time navigating and are more successful when they do. In this book I examine what actually happens once workers come forward. What propels a worker to file a claim given all the evidence we have about the barriers to claims-making? And once a worker has filed a formal claim, what challenges lie ahead? In short, filing a claim is a psychologically taxing process. Workers exercise agency to decide which violations to prioritize or disregard, how far to carry the fight, and when to settle and for what amount. To be sure, these decisions are structured by economic forces (attorney fees, financial situation, et cetera), but as life continues past the initial excitement of courageously coming forward to file a claim, everyday pressures continue to mount. Rent comes due, cars break down, children need care. The time commitment and opportunity costs of persisting in a claim can become just as burdensome as the financial costs. The truth is that it takes tenacity to pursue a claim to the end.

During the claims process, workers may also change their purpose and their goals for achieving justice. They may originally initiate a claim out of an affective stance rooted in general convictions of right and wrong, even if they do not *really* understand how the law protects them. Over time, they may turn to a more rational approach that weighs the costs and benefits of continuing to fight. Their engagement in the administrative process can lead claimants to "reformulate and reinterpret these problems, meanings, and consequences" (Merry 1990, 3). In my research, I found that one to three years after their initial claims were filed, workers had generally lost their initial reverence for the law, and along with it the hope of success via the formal system. Not every claimant persisted, and many sought alternative routes for justice (Ewick and Silbey 1998). Others came to reinterpret what they had previously understood to be a just outcome. Ellen Berrey, Steve G. Hoffman, and Laura Beth Nielsen (2012) refer to this contextual effect as "situated justice," which depends a great deal on claimants' economic circumstances and social context (legal status, job, age, and other factors).

This study asked workers to reflect on their claims-making experience on the heels of its conclusion, seeking to discover what claimants felt was gained and lost in the process. Many of the low-wage workers I spoke with had no desire to return to their original job, to which they generally had no allegiance. Yet many were also frustrated by their inability to find new employment in a recessionary (and even post-recessionary) environment. Those employed in industries with strong social networks were especially cognizant of the power their previous employer had to refuse a positive reference and essentially blacklist them. Workers had to engage with government bureaucrats and the many ancillary players in the system, including insurers, doctors, and interpreters. Finally, as I focused on claimants who had sought legal help in this process, I also investigated the role that attorneys play in shaping their experience. Complaints of perceived attorney incompetence, problems communicating with legal staff, prohibitive fees, and the challenges of *pro se* (unrepresented) litigation abounded. Just as important, workers repeatedly emphasized their expectations of respect from the system, their frustration in how the "objective" expertise of technocrats was elevated above their own experience, and ultimately the toll the claims process took on their personal lives.

METHODOLOGICAL APPROACH

This research draws on the experiences of workers in the San Francisco Bay Area and Silicon Valley, one of the most affluent regions in the country. That region is also home to millions of low-wage workers who serve the needs of the postindustrial information economy. Northern California has a long history of immigrant labor, a vibrant civil society for immigrant and low-wage workers, and some of the most progressive policy environments in the country. Of the 8.4 million residents in the San Jose–San Francisco–Oakland CSA (combined statistical area), 44 percent do not identify as white, 26 percent identify as Hispanic or Latino, and 29 percent are foreign born.[7] These immigrant workers are often concentrated in nonunion, low-pay, no-benefit jobs. Temporary and seasonal work is increasingly common, both in service work and in agriculture. An hour south of Silicon Valley along the Central Coast, the laborers in the fields of Watsonville and Salinas are almost entirely Latino immigrant workers, many of them undocumented. Whereas 5 percent of US workers are estimated to be undocumented, 7.8 percent of California workers have no authorization (Passel and Cohn 2009). These figures for undocumented workers vary widely throughout the state: only 3.7 percent in dense and expensive San Francisco, 8.4 percent in the East Bay (Alameda County), and 10.2 percent in Silicon Valley (Santa Clara County) (Hill and Johnson 2011).

My findings are based on three primary sources of data. In the first, I surveyed workers attending one of six workers' rights clinics in the San Francisco Bay Area and Central Coast region. My team attended 93 separate clinic events and collected 469 surveys from June 2010 through April 2012. Of these, 385 workers agreed to a follow-up interview. Ultimately, we were able to contact 89 of them, who then participated in an in-depth interview 12 to 36 months after their initial survey. I supplement these data with a second sample: interviews with injured workers engaged in the process of filing a workers' compensation claim. I recruited these claimants by attending 29 workshops (14 in English and 15 in Spanish) provided by the California Division of Workers' Compensation in Oakland, Salinas, and San Jose between December 2008 and December 2013. In sum, I conducted formal interviews with 24 of these attendees. Lastly, my conclusions are based on my observations as a volunteer for a small legal aid clinic in a rural farmworker community on the Central Coast. From November 2010 to June 2014 I attended 40 clinics in total (25 dedicated to workers' compensation, 14 dedicated to wage claims) where I interviewed workers (mostly in Spanish), consulted with attorneys, and offered advice to clients. Furthermore, I draw on formal interviews with agency staff, attorneys, and clinic volunteers across the San Francisco Bay Area, as well as my occasional visits with clients to their settlement conferences and hearings.

The nonprofit legal aid organizations I worked with were run mostly by law students and volunteers and staff attorneys. The organizations relied on support from local universities, foundations, and a wide variety of grants.[8] They ran workers' rights clinics on a regular basis, typically on weekday evenings. While the particular focus and capacity of each legal clinic varied, each saw cases involving wage theft, discrimination, sexual harassment, and workers' compensation. The clinics also frequently helped workers who were appealing an unemployment claim denial or who had problems with their pensions. These clinics lasted several hours, and depending on capacity, anywhere from 5 to 20 workers would be scheduled to meet with a staff member (often a law student or other volunteer), who conducted an initial intake consultation. They then consulted with a supervising attorney who supplied advice, determined whether the clinic was in a position to provide follow-up assistance, and, if necessary, provided an outside referral.

Each clinic lasted between two and three hours. Our team approached workers while they waited for their initial consultation, in between their initial meeting and their follow-up advice session, or as they left their appointment. Workers were assured that they were free to opt out of our study and that their participation would in no way positively or negatively impact their ability to receive services

TABLE 1A: Key Survey Characteristics (Means)

	All Survey (N = 453)	Survey Follow-up Interview (N = 89)
Survey Conducted in Spanish	.58	.67
US Born	.27	.26
Age	43.3	44.2
Male	.52	.48
Married	.53	.47
Has Children in School	.52	.49
Did Not Complete High School	.27	.28
Does Not Speak English	.12	.16
Currently Employed	.36	.38
Union Member	.14	.21
Industry		
Construction	.07	.09
Restaurant	.15	.09
Janitorial	.08	.08
Still Employed at Claim Firm	.21	.25
Has Filed Claim Before	.17	.24
Claim Type		
Wage	.39	.43
Discrimination	.24	.27
Sexual Harassment	.04	.06
Unemployment	.07	.06
Workers' Compensation	.04	.03
Other	.26	.22

from the center. The survey lasted approximately twenty to thirty minutes and included questions regarding workers' employment history, the conditions that gave rise to their claim, and the resources and referrals they relied on prior to coming to the legal aid clinic. Each survey was conducted on site, and each respondent received a $15 gift card for their time. All but four interviews took place in person, and they lasted on average one hour. Interviewees were again incentivized with a $15 gift card, and, when appropriate, provided a beverage or meal (depending on the meeting place). Sixty interviews were conducted in Spanish, and one in Mandarin.[9] During these interviews, respondents were asked to elaborate on the circumstances that led them to file a formal claim, what challenges they encountered, and whether they were satisfied with the final outcome. Pseudonyms are used for all references to respondent data.

Survey respondents represent the diverse communities that these legal aid organizations assist. Seventy-three percent of respondents are foreign born, two-thirds are Latino, and a small minority of workers identify as African American (9 percent), Asian/Pacific Islander (11 percent), and white (10 percent). I estimate

TABLE 1B: Distribution of Interviews and Follow-up Interviews by Nativity and Legal Status

	Survey	Follow-up Interviews
All	**453**	**89**
Native Born	122 (.27)	23 (.26)
Foreign Born	331 (.73)	66 (.74)
Foreign Born, Citizens	89 (.27)	15 (.23)
Foreign Born, Noncitizens, Legal Permanent Residents	72 (.22)	16 (.24)
Foreign Born, Noncitizens, Non–Legal Permanent Residents	170 (.51)	35 (.53)

TABLE 1C: Distribution of Claimant Characteristics Across Clinics (%)

		N	Wage/ Hour	Discrimination	Sexual Harassment	Unemployment	Workers' Comp	OTHER
San Jose	SU	237	96	77	10	12	7	54
	IN	54	23	18	3	2	2	10
Oakland	SU	61	37	7	0	0	2	18
	IN	10	6	2	0	0	0	2
San Francisco	SU	97	24	15	6	13	3	30
	IN	15	6	4	1	2	0	4
Berkeley	SU	58	19	8	1	8	2	20
	IN	9	2	0	1	1	1	4
TOTAL	SU	453	176	107	17	33	14	122
	IN	88	37	24	5	5	3	20

	Latino	Black	Asian or Pacific Islander	White	Native Born	Undocumented Immigrant
San Jose	.81	.02	.08	.05	.18	.45
Oakland	1.00	.00	.00	.00	.05	.69
San Francisco	.31	.21	.22	.21	.47	.09
Berkeley	.34	.28	.12	.21	.52	.21

NOTES:
· Race categories are not mutually exclusive.
· Claim categories are also not mutually exclusive. Percentages do not sum to 100; the residual category is "other" and includes allegations of wrongful termination.
· These claim categories reflect a worker's initial declaration of their issue, but not necessarily what their claim evolved into, which could include, or be replaced by, other claim categories.
· SU = initial survey, IN = follow-up interview
· Totals do not include additional interviews with injured workers (workers' compensation claim) who did not participate in the original survey, nor one follow-up interview with a survey respondent from a smaller clinic who participated in the pilot phase of the project.

that 37 percent of respondents are undocumented;[10] of these, all but one identify as Latino. Nonetheless, the interviewed workers constitute an established immigrant population, with the average time in the United States being 17.6 years for documented and 12.3 years for undocumented respondents. Surveys were conducted mostly in English (186) and Spanish (262), but also in some cases in Mandarin (5).

The respondents are low-wage workers with generally low levels of education—60 percent reporting a high school degree or less—and only half speak English. They are concentrated in the retail, day labor, and food service sectors, though some respondents were unemployed throughout the recession years. The distribution of these interviews is consistent with the original sample of survey respondents.

This research was designed to examine the challenges that workers who have already ventured into the labor standards enforcement process continue to face. Therefore, the sample is not representative of the general low-wage worker population. By design, this survey sample represents those workers who are generally aware of their rights and who have begun the process of filing a formal claim. These are workers who, relative to their counterparts who have not come forward, likely possess more information and resources to make their claim successful. By returning to examine the experiences of workers beyond the initial stage of claims-making, my findings highlight the important but limited role of the labor standards enforcement bureaucracy for improving the conditions of low-wage workers.

Lastly, it is crucial to note that throughout the process I relied on the kindness and generosity of those willing to tell their stories. There were some challenges. I simply could not get hold of some claimants. One to three years is a long time in the life of a low-wage worker. People move, cell phone bills go unpaid, numbers change. Sometimes family members would agree to pass my message along, but rarely did I receive a call back. This is understandable, given that the prospect of sharing one's story of struggle with a stranger defies logic. I am conscious that the time I took from workers—meeting in local coffee shops or in their homes—took away from time they could otherwise be spending with their families, sleeping, or tending to the demands of everyday life. To say that the opportunity to speak with me represented a welcome cathartic valve would be presumptuous and likely untrue for many of the workers. Moreover, I doubt that the modest honorarium I offered was a major incitement to come forward.

Several of the workers I was initially able to get on the phone explained the reasons why they could not speak with me. A few feared that the settlements they had negotiated would be at risk, despite all my assurances of confidentiality. Others, especially injured workers, were so traumatized by the long series of depositions, medical appointments, and bullying calls by insurers that they simply were wary of me and reluctant to engage further. Typically I attempted to reach individuals at least twice, erring on the side of respect for those not interested even though I realized that by doing so I would likely miss a few who needed some persistence. After two tries, I would mark the record closed and move on.

Usually people were firm but friendly, though on occasion my follow-up calls would be met with hostility and distrust. Not every worker I surveyed at the legal aid clinic was actually able to get help, depending on the merits of their case or the clinic's inability to take on complex cases that really required private counsel. Facing a situation where help was unavailable, workers were sometimes resentful and declined to say more to me. A few workers were still in the thick of their cases, in a holding pattern with little to report. In some of those instances, I was able to follow up later on down the road.

The most common responses I received from workers who declined a follow-up interview, despite having originally consented, were that they were tired and ready to move on or had no time. In some cases, workers were too busy with their jobs or families to speak with me. Some immigrants had returned to their countries of origin, either for an extended stay or for good. In a handful of cases, I would show up for an interview and the respondent would never arrive. Oftentimes a sick family member, a last-minute work schedule change, or unreliable transportation was the culprit.

In sum, it is important to understand that the workers I ultimately was able to speak with were those who had the time, ability, and willingness to share their stories. Though I cannot be sure, my impression is that these cases were positively selected from the claims I did not get to explore. Our conversations focused primarily on the claim at hand, but often veered into broader discussions about the challenges associated with being a low-wage worker in one of the most expensive housing markets in the country. Because my data are based on retrospective discussions with workers, it is very possible, indeed probable, that the nonexpert claimants I spoke with had a poor understanding of the legal minutiae associated with their cases. In fact, the answer to even the simplest question—With which agency did you file your claim?—was not always apparent to the respondent. Was it with the federal or the state government? Did you go to superior court or just a settlement conference at the agency? In many cases, workers did not know. To the extent possible, I triangulated these data with interviews with attorneys and other advocates who deal with these types of cases on a regular basis. However, due to confidentiality concerns, I never discussed a specific case with an attorney at the clinic where the worker sought assistance, nor did I disclose enough information to reveal the identity of the claimant.

The strengths of these interviews are twofold: what they reveal about the claimants' lay understanding of a complex system, and what they reveal about the impact that pursuing their case had on their everyday lives. While 60 percent of respondents had a high school degree or less, they were well-versed in the systems that governed their workplaces and gained a keen understanding of the biases inherent in the legal bureaucracies in which they had put their trust. It is their perspectives that I lean on the heaviest, with the hope that their insights will help illuminate the limits of formal labor law and how we must do better to address inequalities.

CHAPTER OVERVIEW

The remainder of the book proceeds as follows. Chapter 2 begins by discussing the state of worker precarity today, and highlights the key differences from eras past. I then provide a brief overview of the current system of workers' rights in the United States, as it also interacts with the immigration enforcement regime. Labor standards enforcement provides a useful case study for understanding how rights are implemented, the factors that shape legal consciousness, and the conditions required for workers to realize their rights. Successful claims are few and far between, and I preview how the long-term impacts of pursuing them can weigh heavily on a low-wage worker and his or her family. I end with a description of the data for this study, which includes survey data, interviews, and ethnographic observations.

Chapter 2 opens with the story of five workers engaged in the labor standards enforcement process whose experiences illuminate the range of challenges low-wage workers face, such as accessing benefits, negotiating autonomy on the shop floor, fomenting collective power, addressing harassment and abuse, and avoiding deportation. At-will employment also fuels worker precarity, as do nonstandard worker arrangements such as subcontracted and temporary positions. I describe how employers discipline workers via explicit and implicit threats, and a variety of administrative tools such as performance standards, periodic evaluations, and warnings that can quickly lead to dismissal. Social relationships, which may involve complicated management hierarchies, coworkers, and well-meaning but sometimes powerless unions, also shape workers' experiences on the job.

Chapter 3 reviews the legal framework for enforcing the rights of low-wage workers in the United States. I critically examine the logics and the fissures plaguing the bureaucratic apparatus. I focus especially on employment law, including wage and hour standards, discrimination protections, workers' compensation, and unemployment and state disability. I also briefly review the system of collective bargaining and the union grievance process. I emphasize the limits of statutory protections, as much of the exploitative practices that workers endure fall outside their purview. As such, the line blurs between legally prohibited employer abuses and accepted or overlooked coercive practices. I end with a brief overview of the negative impact of employer sanctions and immigration enforcement efforts on undocumented workers.

Chapter 4 follows the experiences of workers as they make their way through the bureaucracy. I begin by examining the logics that create a successful claim and how workers learn about the rights they do and do not have. I discuss the factors that ultimately shape a worker's decision to come forward, and challenge the limited focus typically placed on rights education. I next unpack the various gatekeepers and brokers who manage the labor standards enforcement system, including government agents, private insurers and medical experts, language brokers, and attorneys. As workers navigate the bureaucracy, they must weigh the financial considerations, time and opportunity costs, and stress of the process in deciding whether to continue fighting and when to stop.

Chapter 5 focuses on the aftermath of workplace exploitation and legal mobilization, which can amplify existing precarity. I highlight three sets of consequences workers must cope with, including reinventing their professional identity and managing financial devastation, the impact on their physical and mental health, and the burden on their families here and abroad. I reflect too on those undocumented workers who grow tired of enduring abuse with no hope for immigration reform, and eventually return to their home countries. The chapter concludes by considering how workers take stock of their experiences as precarious workers navigating the claims bureaucracy. Some walk away enlightened and empowered, whereas many more find themselves resigned to the injustice and regretful for what they have lost in the process.

The book concludes by reflecting on how the current system of workers' rights institutionalizes workplace precarity, and the deep divide between laws on the books and laws in practice. I highlight the importance of institutional intermediaries and increasing access to justice, and the limits of claims-driven enforcement approaches. As we march toward expanding the legal rights of individual workers, I call on us to consider also the many challenges workers face in realizing these protections. Immigration reform, while absolutely necessary, I caution is also insufficient to address worker precarity alone, as both undocumented and documented workers have much in common. I end by considering what this bottom-up perspective on rights mobilization reveals about precarity, agency, and the pursuit of justice.

2

Inequality and Power at Work

LOW-WAGE WORK IN THE SAN FRANCISCO BAY AREA

The San Francisco Bay Area is known for its stunning landscapes, hipster neighborhoods, and status as a hotbed of innovation. Yet there is another side to the affluent region that is largely invisible behind its public image of tech start-ups, world-class universities, and tourist attractions. Toiling among the software developers (who make an estimated $60 per hour) are thousands of low-wage workers such as landscapers ($13.82), janitors ($11.39), and security guards ($14.17) earning far less than what it takes to survive and thrive here (Working Partnerships USA 2015). These wages pale in comparison to the increasingly untenable cost of Bay Area living. Five of the six most expensive counties in the country are in the greater San Francisco Bay Area (Bolton et al. 2015, 10).[1] In 2014 monthly rent costs averaged $2,042. Rents were much higher in San Francisco ($3,057) but still unbearably high in San Jose ($2,066) and Oakland ($2,187) (Avalos and Carey 2014). Home ownership is even further beyond reach, with home sales in 2014 averaging $575,000 in Alameda County (Oakland), $800,000 in Santa Clara County (San Jose), and more than $1 million in San Francisco (Carey 2014; Pender 2014). Higher minimum wages in San Francisco ($12.25 per hour as of May 2015) and San Jose ($10.15 per hour as of January 2015) do little to make these astronomical living costs affordable. According to the National Low Income Housing Coalition, a full-time (forty hours per week) worker would have to make $31.44 per hour to afford to rent a one-bedroom apartment in San Francisco, and $27.29 per hour for one in San Jose.

Beyond low pay, workers who mow, clean, and guard offices labor in an environment characterized by extreme precarity and frequent rights violations (Burnham and Theodore 2012; Valenzuela et al. 2006; Restaurant Opportunities Center of New York 2009; Bernhardt, Spiller, and Polson 2013). Among the workers surveyed for this project, three out of every four had experienced wage theft at some point in their working lives. Forty-three percent felt that they had worked in unsafe or unhealthy work conditions, and 55 percent had become ill or injured due to unsafe workplace conditions. Only 41 percent of all workers reported ever receiving safety training at the job site related to their claim. Eighteen percent said they had been injured on the job at least once and subsequently denied workers' compensation. A third reported having been forced to work overtime against their will, and similar percentages had been denied time off for illness or other personal issues. Nineteen percent had been sexually harassed or been the recipient of other unwelcome sexual advances at work, while 64 percent had experienced verbal abuse or degrading treatment from an employer or coworker. In other words, worker exploitation is ubiquitous in this bastion of global innovation.

THE LIVES OF LOW-WAGE WORKERS

In the pages that follow, I tell the stories of five workers who face various challenges at work and navigate distinct social identities and power dynamics with their respective employers. Each of these workers has sought help from a pro bono legal service provider, although there is nothing uniform about their struggles. Each faces unique challenges in his or her fight to contest workplace inequalities. Their stories make clear the importance of understanding the context-specific dynamics of legal mobilization.

First we meet Jordon, a fifty-year-old African American man who was fired from his job as an attendant for a national parking company when he attempted to take his accrued sick days after contracting a nasty flu—from another sick employee who had been compelled by the company to come to work sick. Then there is Nick, a unionized casino server and committee leader in his seventies; he was fired for alleged theft only days after he delivered a petition to management to contest persistent break violations, reductions in health care benefits, and a promised raise that never materialized. Maritza is a Mexican immigrant in a fast-paced health care field who experienced a series of accidents and struggled to access workplace compensation benefits to recover from her injuries. She was ultimately unable to return to work. Next we encounter Yael, a young, undocumented landscaper who suffered years of wage theft before demanding his due, only to go back into a job market rife with similar violations. We end with Gloria, an undocumented woman working as a unionized grounds maintenance worker. Her story of sexual orientation discrimination and sexual assault puts into stark relief the vulnerability of subcontracted work arrangements, the narrow options for deportation relief, and the severe consequences of economic and legal precarity for workers and their families.

Too Sick to Work? Too Bad

Jordon is a fifty-year-old African American man who had worked for years as a professional driver, then suddenly found himself out of work.[2] On the recommendation of a friend, he applied for an opening at a major parking company in downtown Oakland. He alternated between running valet, processing cars, and providing security detail on the lot. He had been at this job for four years when one day he caught the flu from a coworker. Catching it was an inevitable scenario, he explained. Although all attendants have paid sick days, management frowns on workers actually using them. As a result, the sick coworker showed up to work before he was well: "They [management] told him if he didn't come back he would get fired. He only missed like one day, so he came back, and then he got me sick with the flu, and I was older than him . . . so it hit me harder, and I was down like three days." Jordon brought a doctor's note to his manager, showing that he had not only caught the flu but also had pneumonia: "I showed it to them, and told them I was still not well [enough] to go back to work, so I took some more days off because he [the doctor] told me to. . . . And then they fired me."

Jordon was not alone. Many of his coworkers had experienced similar treatment but kept quiet out of fear of losing their jobs, and they had encouraged Jordon to do the same. Though the company had "floaters" on call to step in precisely in the event that an employee had to take time off, management used them only selectively:

> He [the manager] just wanted people to come to work sick. He could use these floaters for the other important people's vacation time, you know people they look at [as] more bigger [sic] than you. . . . Like when other managers take vacation, he would have the floaters take their spot, so that way they can all be covered, but if we tried to do anything or if were sick or anything, he would fire us. So they would just cover themselves . . . they would use them to take their place, but as far as us, if we got sick, he said we got to come to work sick.

The lot manager was often aggressive and would frequently stress the importance of having a full staff every day when discouraging workers from taking vacation or sick days: "Every time my vacation time would come, he would call me and say, 'Why don't you take that in cash, we don't need you to take your vacation time.' I said I worked for my vacation time." When workers did take a day off, they would subsequently be taken off the schedule and deprived of shifts. This managerial style led to employee infighting; Jordon's coworkers were hardly allies in this hypercompetitive environment.

The lot's head manager was aware of, and appreciated, this supervisor's strict approach. Jordon's supervisor was especially known for hiring ex-felons, which he did for a very specific reason: "They're more desperate for jobs, and would hold on to [a job] more because they're used to making a penny a day or whatever. . . . They started going toward hiring people out of the prison system because they were more desperate. . . . They would say, 'Well, I'm gonna keep my job. . . . I just got out of prison, and I was treated worse in there, so I might as well take this punishment right now and save up money, then go to another job.'" Jordon likened his workplace to a plantation: "If I rebelled everyone would look at you like, he's rebelling, and they didn't want to take that chance." Given the uncertain futures of many of his coworkers, some of whom were homeless despite being employed, their hesitation was understandable.

When he returned to work, Jordon's supervisor sent him away but assured him that he would be called in two days. Two days turned into two weeks, and then two months. He was never called: "I said that's illegal. I said I was sick, and I have sick days, and I'm utilizing them. He said no, we're laying you off anyway. So that's when I knew I had to take action and fight back. I knew it was an illegal practice." When he started at the lot, Jordon had received a company manual, which he hoped would help him make his case. There was one problem: "I lost the book that had the rules and regulations, and when I asked for another one, they wouldn't give me one."

Jordon went to three different lawyers, to no avail: "I didn't really get any help because they wanted bigger cases because that's how they eat." Jordon proceeded with a claim anyway, telling me that he had "nothing to lose." Many of the people he reached out to encouraged him to go to the community law center, where he sought help immediately. He first filed a discrimination claim with the Department of Fair Employment and Housing for unjust termination, which he laments never went anywhere. He ultimately filed and settled a separate claim with the California Labor Commissioner, which included a penalty for the delay in receiving his final paycheck, which was due seventy-two hours after he was fired but wasn't delivered for two weeks. Jordon was pleased with his outcome, though regrets that he couldn't garner sufficient support to file a collective claim. Unfortunately his coworkers, while subjected to the very same violations of the company's own rules, were uninterested in a collective claim. Due to their criminal records, many had few options on the job market, making them perfect recruits for this company.

When I last spoke to Jordan, there was a silver lining for him; he was happy to have finally moved on to a higher-paying and easier job.

How can we understand the huge gap between his company's comparatively progressive sick day policy and the reality Jordon and his other sick coworkers experienced? Jordon recovered some meager wages, but how is it that this national company fired him with impunity and continues to exploit its workers and disregard its own policies? As his story illustrates, Jordon's case is indicative of larger structural injustices that go far beyond his meager wage remedy.

Organize All You Want. But Find Another Job

I met Nick in a coffee shop in a suburban strip mall.[3] He walked in with his wife, carrying a neatly organized folder of forms gathered from his ordeal. A soft-spoken man in his seventies, Nick had migrated from Hong Kong forty years ago and built a career in the hospitality industry. He had worked at a casino for more than fifteen years, and before being fired, had become a committee leader for his union. Nick had worked in many different positions at the casino, including as a dealer, a post he eventually left due to the stress of appeasing disgruntled customers and the constant pressure from management to monitor money exchanges. Most of his career at the casino was spent as a server.

Nick liked his job and felt that with enough tips, he could support himself and his family. His main complaint, however, was about the "house": "The company doesn't treat their workers fairly." Nick cited a long list of conditions that he and his coworkers constantly protested, including being forced to skip breaks, sometimes going as long as seven hours without a chance to step away. He believes that his role in these discussions contributed to his eventual firing.

Nick was scheduled to work New Year's Eve, one of the busiest nights for the casino. Whereas three individuals might normally work a service area of the size to which he was assigned, Nick was ordered to cover the floor by himself that night: "It was a lot of work. They just want to try to get a customer complaint, so they can fire you, you know?" During his shift, Nick found a $100 bill on the floor. Staff would often find money on the casino floor, and strict protocols mandated that workers return the funds immediately to security. Nick explains what happened next: "I picked it up from the floor. I wanted to return it, but I was very busy. It was only myself and over a hundred customers on the floor where I was serving coffee, drinks, everything. I was running like a dog." Pulled in a million directions during the last call for drinks, and unable to take a break to leave his post, Nick resolved to turn the bill in after his shift. That night, he was called into his manager's office and asked about the money he found, whose recovery had apparently been caught on surveillance video. He was reprimanded and told not to tell anyone about the incident, and *definitely* not the union. Nick went home scared, with instructions to call in Monday to speak with his direct manager.

In the weeks leading up to this incident, Nick had been at the forefront of a campaign to hold the casino accountable for implementing a raise management had promised during contract negotiations. Citing a lull in profits, the company failed to hold true to its promise. The union was also organizing to change the company's policy on consistently denying workers their breaks. Nick had led a group of workers in a march upstairs to the office of the casino's CEO to deliver a petition on breaks that had garnered support from 98 percent of the staff. Nick was convinced that because of these organizing actions, he had become a target, and that the $100 was a planned farce. After all, on the day of the worker march, security had locked Nick up alone in a room to warn him that there would be consequences for his advocacy. "It was only me and [the security officer]. . . . He could have done anything, and nobody would know. I was really scared that time," Nick recounted.

The Monday after New Year's Eve, Nick called his manager, who asked him to come in. When Nick arrived, a human resources representative gave him his last check and told him that the company had accused him of stealing, and that he no longer had a job. She handed him a form to sign, which Nick felt compelled to do. Nick's direct manager, with whom he had a great relationship, told him that he should speak with his union; she was later fired as well. Without hesitation and with the help of the union, Nick went on to file a claim with the National Labor Relations Board (NLRB) against the company for wrongful termination. Nick felt confident in his decision to file with the NLRB: "I wasn't scared because I'm no liar. . . . There's nothing to be scared of if you tell the truth."

Nick may have been confident, but his immediate concern was his lost income and how he would support his family with minimal savings. Two weeks after Nick was fired, he filed for unemployment benefits with the California Employment Development Department. Three months after that, he finally learned his application was denied due to his employer's allegations of theft. With help from the legal aid center, Nick appealed the court's decision. After a nerve-racking hearing, Nick won his unemployment benefits and finally received an unemployment check six months after his initial firing.

However, Nick has lost hope for his NLRB case and has grown somewhat disillusioned with his union: "After a few years, they said they won the case, but still they do nothing. Win what? I don't know." In the time since his ordeal, Nick's old union lost ground during contract negotiations, and four of his other colleagues and union leaders were fired. He now works part-time for a temp agency earning $12 per hour, with no benefits and an unpredictable schedule. At the casino, Nick earned $8 an hour but collected $60 to $80 a night in tips; he also had health insurance and a retirement plan. He now pays $550 a month for health insurance for himself and his wife. He is constantly on call and has to take whatever job comes up, even if it means driving hours in Bay Area traffic on his own dime.

The prospects for a permanent position, Nick admits, are grim. Despite his decades of experience, and despite holding many industry certifications, he knows prospective employers find him too old: "Some people say they are not allowed to ask, but, you know, [they do]. One time I applied, I filled out the form, and they were very interested. . . . They called me, and said, 'We like you. By the way, how old are you? . . . Okay, I will call you.'" They never called back, he says.

What happened in Nick's case is perplexing, if all too predictable. In an industry with some of the lowest union densities, Nick was among the choice few to have union representation. Nonetheless, basic workplace protections were routinely ignored, and the collective power of the union to negotiate for better pay and benefits proved insufficient. When Nick exercised his right to make employee complaints known, he was at worst framed, and at least very clearly fired without recourse, and the union had no power to help. As a result, after forty years in the industry, a seasoned professional found himself working as a subcontracted temp.

Work Faster, Get Injured, Good Luck

Maritza is a naturalized Mexican immigrant and licensed health care professional.[4] She had worked for more than twelve years in a large health care setting, preparing patients and processing orders into an electronic records system, and generally enjoyed her job. But Maritza had been injured several times at work. Once, as part of a hospital service team, she got into a car accident on the way to a convalescent home to make a delivery. A few years later, she developed carpal tunnel syndrome. Initially she chose not to submit a claim for either workplace injury because she didn't understand how the system worked, feared that she would have to pay, and had seen others fail in their attempts to be compensated. She remembers trying to justify her silence to herself, thinking, "You tell yourself, *no te pasó* [it didn't happen], you deny it happened, you exaggerate, you blame yourself."

The carpal tunnel eventually proved too bothersome to ignore. After months of dropping things and enduring pain, Maritza went to her personal doctor for help. She was sent to a specialist, who recommended surgery. However, given that this was a workplace injury, Maritza was eventually sent back to speak with human resources and warned that this was her only chance to file a formal claim. When Maritza summoned up the courage to speak with HR, she was discouraged from filing: "Sure, fill out the form, but they [the insurer] will deny it."

When Maritza's workers' compensation claim was in fact denied, she had no other choice but to pursue surgery through her private insurance and incur the related co-payments and deductibles. By the time I talked to Maritza, she had taken disability time to recover and wasn't working because her employer had denied her request to perform modified job duties, which didn't surprise her given the way other injured coworkers had been treated. Maritza's doctor had authorized nine months of disability for her, but after seven months, she received a letter from her employer stating that her insurance had been cancelled. She was forced to switch to an expensive COBRA plan to keep her medical benefits. By this time, Maritza was desperate. She begged her doctor to send her back to work, despite his insistence that she was not ready. When she eventually returned to her employer with clearance to work, she was told that she had been "removed from the schedule."

Outraged, she first went to the Division of Labor Standards Enforcement, who offered empathy but little else. After two months she finally got an appointment at the Department of Fair Employment and Housing (DFEH), who assured her that she had an unfair termination case. She was instructed to return to work and ask human resources to provide a reason for her dismissal.

Maritza was placed back on the schedule, but on the condition that her doctor, for the company's liability purposes, write a note indicating that she was not injured at work. The human resources staff, meanwhile, was furious, reprimanding Maritza for contacting the DFEH. The original copy of the modified work order from her doctor had conveniently gone missing from their files, and she was unable to procure another copy. Maritza now found herself stuck in between her doctor, human resources, and DFEH. When her doctor only allowed her to return with some limitations, the human resources staff responded that this was proof that she was unable to work, emphasizing further that, since this was not a workers' compensation claim, which they of course had initially denied, they had no further obligation to her.

Maritza was called back to work on a Thursday at 4 p.m. and ordered to work at 5 a.m. the next day, a significant change from her previous schedule. "They knew I had a sixteen-year-old and no bus to get her to school," Maritza surmised. She had for years dropped her daughter off at 7 a.m. in order to be at work by 8 a.m., and relied on her asthmatic mother to take care of her younger daughter. When she went to plead her case to her supervisor, Maritza was curtly told, "Well, that was the only opening."

With no other option available, Maritza returned to work and did her best. She even asked for a 7 a.m. lunch, which many others had done to deal with child care. This request was promptly denied, and she was chided for "wanting so many luxuries." The early lunch option was shortly thereafter taken away for everyone, which did not generate goodwill with her coworkers. So, Maritza summoned her resources as best as possible: "Don't ask me how I did it, but I showed up at 5 a.m." She spent $500 on driving lessons for her daughter; illegally, her daughter then started driving herself and her younger sister to school on a provisional permit.

Once back at work, Maritza had to adjust to her new early shift with a much faster rhythm than she was used to. She felt under constant pressure, and was called into her supervisor's office and reprimanded almost daily: "They wanted to fire me based on my inability to work that fast." She still was dealing with carpal tunnel pain, made increasingly unbearable by a supervisor who exerted enormous pressure on her and was especially harsh with his female subordinates. Already feeling the cold shoulder from her coworkers, Maritza didn't want to complain again, lest they think that she "spends all day filing claims." In any case, the DFEH has refused additional assistance, explaining that "we're not going to take a case we can't win." Her union never got involved at all.

One morning after her return, Maritza fell when tending to a patient in a room with a broken light sensor, which had been reported long before but never fixed. When she reached to turn on the light manually, Maritza fell, seriously injuring her shoulder. She was immediately taken to the emergency room for treatment, and her supervisor wrote up a report. Maritza was promptly given three days off, then sent to the occupational health clinic, where x-rays revealed that her hand, though swollen, was not broken. She was next sent to therapy and given pain medication.

Still in immense back and shoulder pain after her three allotted days of recovery, Maritza sensibly took vacation days to rest and recover.

Eventually, an MRI revealed a pinched nerve. Cortisone shots have not helped, and Maritza's workers' compensation doctor (a "qualified medical examiner") has referred her for surgery. A full accounting of her injuries includes scar tissue in her shoulder (damaged further because of lack of sustained physical therapy, which was cut off after three weeks), two slipped discs, loss of sensation in her legs, and constant lower back pain. Maritza's condition has now been deemed "permanent and stationary," that is, she has met the maximum stage of medical improvement. Her previous doctor, who seemed sympathetic and understanding, has been dismissed. Her new doctor has refused the surgery referral and threatened to send her to a psychologist because "each time you show up, you're crying." She has returned to her primary care physician for help, who has sent her back to a specialist.

When Maritza returned to work once again after her fall, she was offered a one-year contract. She refused, and now feels stuck. The human resources staff glare at her "like they want [her] dead." Yet she knows she cannot get another job in her injured condition.

What explains the complete failure of the workers' compensation system, a no-fault benefit afforded to *all* workers in the event of a workplace injury? Why do workers regularly keep quiet about injuries sustained on the job? What does it say about the system that Maritza, a health care professional with years of experience and a well-trained human resources department and union at her disposal, found herself with multiple well-documented injuries, an unworkable schedule, and a terminated contract?

You Don't Like It? Go Ahead. I'll Have You Deported

I met Yael, a young, single Salvadoran immigrant, in an apartment he shared with several other men in a dense suburban neighborhood in the South Bay.[5] His "room" consisted of bedsheets pinned to the ceiling to cordon off a private space in the living room. Yael had worked as part of a landscaping crew for a boss he described as "racist" and "exploitative." Workers were constantly complaining about the oppressive conditions, which enraged his employer, who was prone to spewing threat-filled tirades: "He would say that he would fire anyone who didn't like it, and would threaten to fire anyone for any little thing." Yael had found the job through a friend and, apart from his hotheaded boss, he acknowledged that it was a job he enjoyed.

The problem that drove Yael over the edge occurred on a Thursday. His coworker had been fired for drinking on the job, and he was left to pick up the slack by himself, as his boss refused to hire another crew member. Yael voiced his concern, after which his boss immediately abandoned him on the side of the road. Yael had to call a friend for a ride. The next week, when it became clear that his boss would not pay him what he was owed, Yael, after consulting with friends and doing some online research, began the process of filing a claim with the California Office of the Labor Commissioner.

Yael had endured ongoing abuse on the job. The Korean owner of the company, also an immigrant, would frequently remind Yael that he himself was a citizen (while Yael was not) and thus could not be touched: "We always had problems. He was always aggressive with me. I would get in at 7 a.m. and couldn't leave until eight or nine at night." For working a twelve- to fourteen-hour day, Yael was always paid the same amount, $75, far below the minimum wage. There was no talk of overtime. When Yael had complained in the past about his wages, his boss simply replied: "Do you want to work or not? Tomorrow I can find someone new, no problem." He would also physically assault some workers and threaten to call immigration on them if they rebelled. So Yael continued working, explaining his resigned attitude as a matter of necessity: "Sometimes when you just really need to work, you make do."

Upon filing his claim, Yael received notice of a hearing, and though he arrived ready to argue his case, his employer never showed up. Next, Yael learned that his claim had stalled because his former employer had declared bankruptcy. Desperate, Yael sought help from a local law center, which identified a two-month work period in which the employer's bankruptcy protection did not apply. Not counting the many Sundays Yael worked without pay and couldn't prove it, as well as the missed breaks and lunch periods, Yael was owed at least $15,000 in unpaid wages and penalties. But with little proof of his cash payments and work schedule, and unwilling to wait the years that a claim could go on, Yael agreed to a settlement of $3,800.

The two parties reached an agreement at the settlement conference. Yael received $850 up front, with the promise of $200 to be paid on the first of each month for twenty-five months. However, checks came sporadically, sometimes not until the third week of the month. By the time Yael and I spoke, twenty-one months after the settlement, he hadn't received a check in three months.

After Yael was fired, he went six months without a steady job, relying on help from friends. He cycled through a series of gigs, which always ended with the revelation that he was involved in a claim against his former employer: "They always fired me for the same reason. . . . The [old] boss would go and tell them not to give me a job. . . . He would see me [out working], then go directly to the employers to tell them. . . . I would see him. . . . They all know each other."

Ultimately Yael went to work in a restaurant, pulling the night shift from 6 p.m. to 1 a.m., admired by his coworkers for lasting nearly two years in a place where others would often quit after one day. By the time we met again, he was back on another landscaping crew, whose leader he told up front about his claim. He generally gets along with his boss, who pays him $100 per day. His hours are not too different than before. He goes in at 7:30 a.m. for regular ten- to eleven-hour shifts, six to seven days a week. Missed breaks and meal periods are par for the course: "It's hard, but sometimes one just gets used to it because you want to work, not because you want to [put up with the conditions], but to support oneself in a stable place. All the employers are the same. . . . The truth is, for now I feel good. . . . I'm here alone, I'm single, no one depends on me, and I've bought some land in El Salvador."

Yael had arrived in the United States eight years earlier at age eighteen, fleeing the violence in his home country, having seen many of his friends perish. Despite his problems with his boss, he is happy with his life. His greater fear, he explains, is that he will lose his job, not so much that he will be deported: "I've always said, what is going to happen, will happen. I've never really feared that they would call immigration on me. . . . I'm not afraid of the police. . . . Go ahead, I'm not from here, but you're not going to do whatever you want with me." He knows that all workers have rights in this country and feels confident enough to exercise them. But in the end, all he wants is to work and for his boss to be fair with him.

What made Yael speak up when he did, despite the many workplace violations he had experienced over the years? What was the tipping point for him, and what set him apart from his coworkers who *se conformaron* ("just conformed") to the abusive system? How did his unauthorized immigrant status shape his decision to come forward? More broadly, how can we understand the inextricable connection between unauthorized work and disposability in a competitive, at-will work environment? Finally, what might the future hold for Yael, and how will that shape his legal consciousness moving forward?

Harassed, Sexually Assaulted, Fired

I met Gloria one sunny afternoon in her modest South Bay apartment.[6] To get there I drove past throngs of Silicon Valley start-ups and sprawling, overpriced housing developments. Eventually I parked at the end of a street of apartment complexes and stepped into Gloria's clean and orderly home. She invited me inside, cleared a space for me at the kitchen table, her son's whimsical SpongeBob SquarePants–themed bed in the living room nearby, and offered me something to eat and drink. Her roommate excused himself, nodding as he departed, as if he knew the weight of the conversation to follow.

It had been nearly two years since Gloria and my research team had been in contact. Now, in this small apartment, I would hear her full story. Before our team met Gloria, she had lost her job following the death of her mother. Undocumented and unable to return to Mexico City to attend her mother's funeral, she missed three days of work to mourn. She was promptly fired, though she miraculously found a new and relatively well-paid union position on a maintenance crew. By the time we surveyed her, she had lost that job and was fighting to keep her family afloat.

As a maintenance worker, Gloria often worked alone in isolated areas under a specific supervisor in the unit that had contracted her unionized company. This man exhibited a pattern of manipulation and abuse toward Gloria that eventually culminated in repeated sexual assaults. Gloria believes that because she was an out lesbian, her homophobic manager felt particularly violent and vindictive toward her. When she tried to push back, he would remind her that he knew she had no papers. Gloria eventually mustered the courage to report the months of abuse she had suffered, but management deflected her complaints. Appalled, she followed the advice of her therapist (whom she had met through the help of a local advocacy group) and went to the police, who quickly identified her aggressor as a convicted offender. Meanwhile, Gloria sought help from her union, but her complaint was ignored. With few other options for recourse, she eventually filed a workers' compensation claim for her psychological trauma and was put on disability pay, which was far less than the $15 per hour she had been earning.

During this time, she was required to see another therapist appointed by the workers' compensation insurer, who forbade her from continuing to see her current provider. This therapist spoke no Spanish and immediately prescribed her medication to calm her anxiety. In fact, few of the many doctors she visited for her trauma spoke Spanish, and no one honored her requests for interpreters. She found herself at an impasse: her employer refused to take her back (citing the inability to provide modified work), and her doctor refused to release her from disability and the meager pay it offered. Undocumented and having no other benefits or support to rely on, Gloria eventually lost her apartment. She had to uproot her family to an unfamiliar and unsafe (but more affordable) location.

Desperate, she started working for another janitorial company to supplement her disability income, as well as cleaning the office of a community leader who, she lamented, did little to help with her case. Increasingly frustrated and feeling as if she had nowhere to turn, Gloria succumbed to temptation and stole a few hundred dollars' worth of grocery vouchers from an office safe. She was promptly caught, charged, and convicted, and as a result nearly lost her chance of obtaining a U visa, a form of deportation relief meant for victims of crime like Gloria. Currently awaiting word on her likely deportation, she is certain that despite the courage she displayed in reporting her manager's abuse, her actions were ultimately in vain. She explained, sobbing, "My aggressor went to jail and is now out. But I am left here with nothing." She now relies mostly on food stamps, a modest amount of child support, and odd jobs.

When I asked Gloria to reflect on the benefits the workers' compensation system afforded her in the wake of her assault, she emphasized that she had lost far more than she gained. Yes, she had received a $15,000 settlement, but it didn't come close to covering her basic costs in one of the most expensive housing markets in the country. Moreover, she was required to attend endless meetings and appointments to keep her benefits, obligations that prevented her from returning to the full-time work she desperately needed. All told, she had driven hundreds of miles across the Bay Area and was never properly reimbursed. To make matters worse, her older son, also undocumented, had decided to leave college to help keep the family afloat.

I asked Gloria to consider what she would have done differently, and she replied without hesitation: "If I had to go back, I wouldn't have spoken up. Wouldn't have said anything. I spoke up, and this is what happened to me. And I am left with nothing." Why, in two years, had everything gone so wrong for Gloria? Here was clearly a case where the workers' compensation system failed someone when she most needed support. The overlapping forces of misogyny, homophobia, and immigration enforcement stripped the workers' rights apparatus of its main function: to help people like her. Despite the fact that the law explicitly prohibited the abuses Gloria faced, she felt like she was left without a meaningful remedy.

CONDITIONS OF PRECARITY

The conditions of precarity for workers like Jordon, Nick, Maritza, Yael, and Gloria are widespread and all too common. While the details of each case differ (industry, tenure on the job, and other worker attributes), some common characteristics bear mentioning.

At-Will Employment and Weak Unions

Over the last century of labor and employment law, a complicated patchwork of protections has evolved. Concurrent with this increase in individual workplace rights has been a rapid decrease in work unionization. In 2014, 11.1 percent of US workers were union members, compared to 20.1 percent in 1983, representing a drop from 17.7 million to 14.6 million union members (Bureau of Labor Statistics 2015d).

The specifics of union protection will be laid out in detail in the next chapter, but for now we should note that nearly nine out of ten US workers are at-will employees who are not covered by a union contract. At-will employee relationships have divergent implications for workers depending on their social position. Most important, at-will employees lack collective representation and have diminished job security, and are left to the limiting, individualized systems of employment law to demand their rights. For example, to be fired on the spot and abandoned on the side of the road, as Yael was, is an egregious and damning violation of human dignity, but in practice it does not run afoul of any law. Many others were fired in less dramatic, more protracted ways. Jordon was simply never placed back on the schedule, and Maritza was given a contract with a finite end date following her injury. Workers who are covered by a union often find that their union is limited in its power to contest workplace abuse. Nick, an active member of the union, nonetheless found he was alone in contesting his termination. Gloria was told by her employer, as was his right, that there was no modified work option available to accommodate the disability resulting from her assault.

In the best of circumstances, collective bargaining contracts attempt to provide stability to workers, and a support system to address workplace abuse and demand better working conditions. In contrast, at-will employees are in effect free agents—free to leave, and with no support if they stay. For example, Melita, a day care worker, had clashed repeatedly with new management when the small child care provider she worked for changed ownership.[7] The new administration made blatant attempts to replace long-standing staff with newer teachers who could be paid less. When Melita requested a day off to attend her daughter's college graduation in Southern California, her request (made long in advance) was rejected for having been made using the wrong form. After Melita missed work anyway to attend this special day, she was fired.

Exacting protocols are not uncommon in complex organizations. They are the tools that keep order, facilitate equity, and avoid nepotism. However, rules that, say, prevent phone use, institute "theft prevention" measures, and establish precise clock-in/clock-out procedures serve two purposes. They impose discipline *and* facilitate punishment. Workers I spoke to were constantly surveilled through progressively severe warning systems about rule breaking. These sometimes culminated in performance evaluations that became the basis for dismissal. Infractions such as using a phone on the shop floor, borrowing an umbrella, or arriving late because of public transportation delays can prove disastrous for an at-will worker, few of whom have the autonomy that professionals such as I, and likely you, take for granted. Without a collective bargaining contract in place, at-will workers subject to these circumstances are left with little recourse.

Workers are monitored by complicated management hierarchies, and competition between workers generates a collective self-discipline that erodes trust and at times even negates the need for supervision. But management plays a heavy hand. In one instance, Magnolia explained how her manager at the country club where she washed dishes was a constant presence:[8] "He didn't even let me talk with my friends, who would often pass by and say hi. The chef [manager] would watch over me. He would even hide. I even had to ask permission to go to the bathroom." If she was ever gone too long, or did not first ask permission before using the restroom, Magnolia was issued a warning for violating company policy. Magnolia eventually was taken away by ambulance for an emergency gallbladder removal, a condition that had quickly worsened due to her inconsistent bathroom access. She was unable to return to work.

At-will employees have little power to push back against such practices. They operate on a take-it-or-leave-it basis. For example, I met Octavio, a trucker who regularly puts in long hauls: "I worked on average about sixty, more like sixty-three, hours a week, six days a week, . . . sometimes twelve to thirteen hours a day."[9] His schedule was predetermined by management, and he never had a say in the route he was given. Worse, driving was inherently unpredictable: "There are many factors—traffic, accidents, sometimes the highway was shut down, it might even snow . . . so it was never what I planned." As a result, Octavio could rarely plan for much else in his life: "I dedicated myself exclusively to work. That is, I never missed work. Maybe I arrived late once a year, but never because I wanted to, but because I was sick with a fever perhaps. But I would show up, then go back home. I grew accustomed to never missing work." At-will workers must show this exhausting dedication if they are to stay employed.

Subcontracted, On Call, and Flexible

In addition to at-will employment, low-wage workers also frequently occupy subcontracted, temporary, or seasonal positions. Subcontracting is an attractive arrangement for employers hoping to specialize their resources and maximize their flexibility for a client. Rather than maintaining equipment and a crew with in-house expertise and capabilities, a talent pool that needs to be maintained year-round, companies often choose instead to bid that part of the production or service process to a specialist. According to a 2010 study by the UC Berkeley Labor Center, 2 percent (282,000) of California's workforce was either in the temporary help services industry or worked for employee leasing firms (Dietz 2012). Though their ubiquity may not be obvious to consumers, temporary workers can be found in a range of industries such as hospitality, retail, and day labor.

Subcontracting can create conditions that are ripe for workplace violations. When contractors underbid each other to win business, that leaves labor costs as the primary savings and profit-generating mechanism. Subcontracted work also obfuscates the chain of command for workers seeking to contest poor conditions, leaving clients able to brush off responsibility for any wrongdoing. This system of plausible deniability has been a key concern of organizing in the janitorial industry (where, in a victory, large property owners are forced to be accountable to the nighttime cleaners who care for their buildings), construction (where both large companies and the prime contractors they hire often subcontract out to small crews that use day labor to cut costs), and even the hospitality industry. For example, Nick worked as a crew leader for a Bay Area caterer, for whom he was on call for events all over the region.[10] While he was paid $12 per hour with no benefits, the client paid $35 per person hour, generating a huge profit for the temporary labor agency that employed Nick.

Bad Jobs: Beyond Low Pay

Low-wage workers have limited opportunities for social mobility, often even in unionized contexts. Many workers surveyed for this book had lingered for years in low-pay positions without a wage increase. Only 53 percent of all workers (and 47 percent of undocumented workers) had ever received a raise. But, perhaps more consequentially, only 38 percent of claimants reported that their jobs provided sick leave (17 percent of undocumented), and 46 percent had paid vacation (23 percent of undocumented). And employer-provided health insurance in this pre–Affordable Care Act era was far from the norm. Only 39 percent of all claimants (and 15 percent of undocumented) had health benefits, levels that are far below state and national means, both of which were more than 50 percent during the period in question (Fronstin 2011).

Rogelio had worked at a print shop for almost seventeen years and fantasized about finally leaving.[11] He regularly worked from the shop's 8 a.m. opening until 6 p.m., ten hours a day, seven days a week. He was paid in cash $9 per hour, never earning overtime. Despite these terms, he explained that he was not really looking for a new job: "I know times are hard, plus my problem is that I have diabetes. My feet hurt so much that sometimes I struggle to walk . . . yet even so I do my work, what needs to get done. But that's why I feel like I can't just get another job. I know that if I stay here, nothing is going to change. I am going to keep hauling ass and working, and that's just it." At one point, the shop's owner provided health insurance, but then eventually stopped offering it and cut everyone's pay by 10 percent to boot. She promised to reinstate the benefit but never did, and ever since, Rogelio has had to rely on county services to get occasional treatment. Still, he is forced by circumstances to stay at this job.

For other workers with whom I spoke, benefits were technically available, but they were so cost prohibitive that the option was practically meaningless. Many of the workers either could not gather the hours necessary to qualify for benefits or had no way of covering the high deductibles. Particularly for some of the young men, who saw themselves as invincible, health insurance seemed like an unnecessary, and unaffordable, scam. Whatever the case, the broader point is that at-will employers often cannot or will not devote resources to providing their workers with a safety net.

MECHANISMS OF EMPLOYER RETALIATION

How is it then that workers navigate these challenging conditions to make demands on their employer? For example, one undocumented landscaper regularly worked mandatory and unpaid overtime.[12] He and his other undocumented coworkers systematically earned less than those with a "valid social." He had on several occasions pressured his employer to pay everyone equally, and each time the response he received was blunt and unequivocal: "[He told me], 'I'm not going to pay you anything. Do what you want.' When he threatens us, of course people are scared. His exact words were, 'There's the door . . . clock out.'"

TABLE 2A: Previous Work Experiences

Have you ever, either at this job or at a previous one here in the United States, experienced **any** of the following? (N=453)	N	%	SD*
Paid less than you were initially promised	143	.316	.465
Paid less than the minimum wage	89	.196	.398
Denied a rest break, or had it shortened	231	.510	.500
Denied a meal break, or had it shortened	189	.417	.494
Had problems getting paid, or been paid late	226	.499	.501
Forced to work overtime against your will	149	.329	.470
Denied time off for illness	167	.369	.483
Denied time off for vacation/personal issues	165	.364	.482
Had to work in unsafe or unhealthy working conditions	198	.437	.497
Became injured on the job, or became ill because of your job	248	.547	.498
Denied workers' compensation (if you were hurt)	82	.181	.385
Received retaliation or threats for complaining about work conditions	183	.404	.491
Received retaliation or threats for organizing a union	44	.097	.296
Received sexual harassment or unwelcome sexual advances from an employer or coworker	87	.192	.394
Received verbal abuse or degrading treatment from an employer or coworker	290	.640	.480

*SD = Standard Deviation.

Despite these challenging conditions that put low-wage workers at an extreme disadvantage, workers do cope, and sometimes even manage to make effective demands on their hostile employers. But the threat of retaliation remains very real. Based on our survey of workers, no clear patterns emerged among those who said they "received threats for complaining about workplace conditions" or who "received retaliation or threats for organizing" (see table 2a). However, one of the key factors shaping whether workers decided to come forward was the fear that their employer might retaliate. In some cases, retaliation was transparent, especially so for undocumented workers.

Overall, only one in five—21 percent—of survey respondents were still working for the employer against whom they were filing a claim. When examined in a multivariate context, the sole significant driver of whether workers were still working for the target employer was whether they were union members. About 40 percent of workers reported that they "received threats for complaining about workplace conditions." All else being equal, restaurant workers and those with limited English proficiency were significantly more likely to report that their employer "threatened to fire me, or cut my hours, if I complained." Perhaps not surprisingly, these same two categories of workers were more likely to cite "I was afraid it would affect my job" as a driving force for not coming forward when controlling for other factors (see table 2b and Gleeson 2015a).

TABLE 2B: Claimant Talked Directly to Employer

	All Claimants—Talked to Employer			Wage and Hour Claimants— Talked to Employer		
	Log Odds	**SE**	**P value**	**Log Odds**	**SE**	**P value**
Male	−.015	.220	.944	−.051	.418	.903
Age	−.042	.053	.434	−.039	.099	.696
Age squared	.000	.001	.663	.000	.001	.798
Education: less than HS	−.273	.263	.298	−.864	.436	.047
English: do not speak at all	−.119	.368	.747	.129	.533	.808
Industry: restaurant	−.149	.307	.628	.250	.499	.616
Industry: construction	.536	.466	.250	.610	.643	.343
Cash payment	.085	.379	.822	−.325	.459	.479
Union	.194	.318	.541	.099	1.143	.931
Undocumented	.352	.276	.202	.022	.493	.964
White	.543	.390	.165	.228	.853	.789
Constant	2.077	1.209	.086	2.656	2.070	.199
N	450			175		

	Talked to Employer— Threatened			Did Not Talk to Employer—Afraid		
	Log Odds	**SE**	**P value**	**Log Odds**	**SE**	**P value**
Male	−.198	.442	.654	−.600	.591	.310
Age	−.138	.088	.119	−.069	.127	.588
Age squared	.001	.001	.152	.001	.001	.487
Education: less than HS	.067	.527	.899	.624	.598	.297
English: do not speak at all	1.430	.585	.015	1.548	.739	.036
Industry: restaurant	1.161	.499	.020	1.647	.714	.021
Industry: construction	−.818	1.117	.464	(omitted)	.	.
Cash payment	.485	.609	.425	−.733	.938	.435
Union	−.010	.701	.989	−.958	1.144	.403
Undocumented	−.597	.569	.294	.320	.664	.629
White	−.041	.809	.959	.865	.931	.353
Constant	.458	1.930	.813	−1.056	2.930	.718
N	320			123		

Firing a worker for complaining constitutes a form of illegal retaliation in most cases. However, at-will employment provisions allow an employer to fire a noncontract worker for largely any reason, thus rendering a claim of retaliation extremely difficult to prove. Perhaps because of this difficulty, most workers sought first to settle their dispute without the aid of lawyers. In fact, 71 percent of survey respondents reported confronting their employer before visiting the legal aid clinic. For most workers who came forward, their employer's response was not reassuring.

TABLE 2C: Examples of Multifaceted Mechanisms of Employer Retaliation

Target (Implicit or Explicit)	Threat of Deportation	Making Life Hard	Threat of Firing
Individual Examples	Will call immigration	Cut hours	Dismissal
	Misrepresentation of SSN No-Match Letter	Lower scheduling priority	Won't renew contract
		Refuse pay raise	Refuse to promote from temporary to permanent
	Demand to check papers for E-Verify requirements	Disregard for safety	
		Pressure for production	
Collective Examples	Rumors of raids	Mass punishment for organizing	Blacklist entire family
	Declarations of looming audit		

Thirty-eight percent reported that their complaint was ignored, another 8.1 percent that they were threatened, and 14 percent that the problem was initially resolved but then resumed. Among those who chose to avoid a confrontation with their employer altogether, 17 percent were afraid it would affect their job, and 19 percent said they just "didn't think it would do any good" (see also Gleeson 2015a).

Retaliation manifested itself in subtle ways that often didn't overtly violate the workers' legal rights (see table 2c). Beyond being fired, workers feared that their contract would not be renewed, that they would be passed over for promotion, or that they would be left lingering in a temporary position. Workers also discussed many ways in which management could make their lives harder and disrupt the delicate balance between unpredictable scheduling and child care needs.

Employer retaliation also operated by exploiting the immigration enforcement apparatus, complicated management hierarchies, labor standards enforcement agencies and their ancillaries, and the victimized employee's coworkers. Although complex retaliation schemes allowed employers to play workers off each other through a classic "divide and conquer" strategy (Bonacich 1972), often little effort was required in this direction because the competitive environment of low-wage work already fuels worker anxiety and a reluctance to legally mobilize. The experiences workers relayed made clear that worker solidarity is far from a given.

CONFRONTING POWER AT WORK

Workers must negotiate various power struggles on the job: with their direct employer but also with a complicated management hierarchy, which can include temp agencies and subcontractors. In many organizations, sophisticated human resources bureaucracies also coordinate increasingly popular in-house "conflict resolution" mechanisms, such as forced arbitration, and are responsible for processing warnings and eventual termination. Coworkers can support one another during these processes but often find themselves in competition, which weakens solidarity. Furthermore, labor unions represent those members covered under a collective bargaining contract and coordinate their own internal grievance procedures. These actors, each of whom has different motivations and constraints, complicate simplistic understandings of how employer power actually functions in the work environment.

Who's the Boss? Managers, Subcontractors, and HR

In conceptualizing corporate power struggles, we tend to think of dyadic workplace relationships existing between a subordinate worker and a superior employer. In a small workplace environment, the "boss" may indeed simply be the owner of a landscape company or the head of a construction crew. He or she may be responsible for hiring, firing, and processing worker complaints. However, in more complex workplace environments, the supervisory chain of command may not be so clear. Take, for instance, a dishwasher working in a kitchen. Though that dishwasher takes directions from a head chef, assistant and general managers may have ultimate authority. These supervising individuals may or may not work alongside the affected workers. Therefore, when it comes time to file a formal claim against an employer, it can be difficult for workers to track down the person to whom they should voice their concern.

Subcontracted workers have an even more difficult time. For example, in agricultural work, the *mayordomo* (foreman) may be responsible for assembling and dispersing the team each morning. Multiple *mayordomos* may manage a grower's laborers, each of whom may technically be employed by an outside temp agency. As a result, a grower may have no direct interaction with, or even responsibility for, the maintenance and well-being of his or her labor force.[13] Though some workers may be well aware of these separate command structures, many of the claimants I spoke with were completely in the dark. Seasonal field workers could often recall only the name of the *mayordomo* and the location of the field, but not necessarily the name of the grower. Others believed they worked for a particular farm, only to find out later, after scrutinizing pay stubs, that they were in fact paid by a temp agency. This confusion impacts the claims process: identifying the culpable party is crucial when deciding where to send a demand letter or whom to summon to a hearing.

Candelaria's subcontracted janitor position forced her to engage with a complicated chain of command when she contested her pay irregularities.[14] While she struggled with her direct supervisor, she actually got along well with the facility director: "I went to him [the facility director] once hoping he could help me with her [the supervisor], so that she would give me my [overdue] check. And when I did, he just told me, 'Candelaria, I'm sorry, but I give her the check on time. If she doesn't pay you like she should, it's not my responsibility. So that's it. I pay her, that's the only thing I can do.' Candelaria was left with no recourse other than to file a formal claim against her uncommunicative supervisor, who would eventually fire her in response.

In large companies, claimants also have to interface with human resources departments whose job it is to carry out company policy and to comply with federal and state law. These staff have direct access to employment records and a great deal of discretion when deciding how to process complaints. In a world of internal dispute resolution mechanisms (for instance binding arbitration), human resources representatives also work to deflect potential legal challenges. And while human resources representatives are obliged to enforce company policies and other statutory protections, they may do so unevenly depending on workers' abilities to advocate for themselves. Immigrant workers in particular may struggle to communicate with staff or effectively argue their claims.

Consider the case of Octavio, an injured truck driver.[15] After alerting his employer about an injurious fall, he was promptly approached by the human resources staff at the beginning of his next shift. "They were waiting for me, with all the paperwork and questions about what had occurred," he told me. He had in fact fallen several times but never filed a formal claim until now. This time, he was immediately told that the accident was due to his negligence in failing to alert them of a missing no-slip mat, which should have protected workers from a metal loading grate that became hazardous in wet conditions. He countered that in fact this was the job of the maintenance department. The human resources staff personally took Octavio directly to the occupational health clinic that day, for which he was grateful. He felt frustrated, however, that as his claim wore on, he was unable to secure assistance in dealing with the insurance company that controlled his payments and medical authorizations. When I spoke to him three years later, he was still severely injured and unable to return to work, running out of disability pay, still battling medical authorizations, and seriously considering returning to his native Peru. Here we see the good and the bad of HR, which purports to protect workers, but only up to a point.

Workers expressed a certain lack of confidence in their human resources staff, who were purportedly there to assist them with any concerns they might have. Adán, a low-level manager for a discount retailer, routinely worked through illness and took on extra shifts when needed.[16] He almost never was granted meal or rest breaks. But when he refused to cover for another manager who was suffering from a particularly severe bout of flu, Adán was fired. With the help of his wife, who also worked at a government agency, Adán filed for unemployment and was denied. When he appealed his case, human resources staff were sent to represent not him but the employer at his Labor Commissioner settlement conference. "They were surprised that I had proof [of hours worked] and so they asked for a copy; they couldn't say anything," he recounted in an anecdote that reveals the adversarial relationship that can develop between an employee and human resources once a claim is set in motion.

Undocumented workers have a knottier relationship with human resources. Jose, an undocumented cook on a large campus, complained about his head chef's abusive treatment and the breakneck pace in the kitchen.[17] He confronted the employer directly, explaining, "We need to work out this problem. . . . I do what you ask, but nothing I do pleases you!" The chef would pull Jose out of breaks early, assign him to lengthy jobs at the end of a shift, and prohibit coworkers from assisting him. Jose felt that the chef targeted him uniquely, clearly in an effort to push him out. He eventually turned to the human resources department for help in dealing with the harassment, but was disappointed by the result: "They never paid attention to me. . . . I didn't appreciate the way they talked to me. Instead of helping me, they criticized me." When he voiced his concern to the head director, who was higher up on the management hierarchy, the chef found out and quickly fired Jose in retaliation.

Several undocumented workers told me of human resources staff who either looked the other way or actively helped workers in submitting false documents during the hiring process, but then pushed back when those same employees needed help regarding a work issue. For example, Susana and her sister worked for a small manufacturing business that readily hired the pair despite their undocumented status.[18] The human resources manager explained that, in the event of an audit, they would simply claim there was a "communication lapse" with the women. However, when the company eventually won a federal contract that required each employee to be screened for employment authorization, the same staff member told Susana and her sister to find another job or they would be reported to immigration authorities.

Nor had human resources proved supportive before the deportation threat. During their six years with the company, the women sustained months of blatant sexual harassment from their manager: "He would expose himself, stand in the scaffolding above where we worked and drop his pants, or just walk by and fondle his genitals in front of us. Once he slapped me in the ass, in fact when I was in the middle of reading over my workers' compensation report."

Another case shows just how calculating human resources can be. Mariana worked for an ethnic grocer and estimates that the vast majority of her coworkers were also unauthorized.[19] She landed the job while undocumented, but as a domestic violence survivor, she was eventually able to obtain work authorization through a U visa for victims of violent crime. But when she presented her new, legitimate Social Security number to the human resources staff, she was unequivocally denied the opportunity to make any changes. This meant that the Social Security and re-tirement benefits she accrued over nine years would simply disappear. She recalls being told, "Oh, look at you, coming here all content with your little paper, but if you only knew what will happen to you when you turn it in. . . . Think about it *chaparrita* [short one], it's either you or thousands of other employees, because when you turned it [your number] in, you either said it was real or not." The impli-cation was that they would fire her for having submitted a fake card, even though they had known perfectly well it was fake. Meanwhile, by not allowing her to submit her new documentation, they would not have to pay out the savings and benefits.

Mariana's trips to the legal aid clinic proved futile: "They said they can't do much to help me unless they fire me, or stop paying me." Mariana was effectively stuck in limbo, at the mercy of her savvy human resources staff, who also refused to grant her vacation pay while she attempted to sort out her new legal and finan-cial status. It took two months without work for Mariana to resolve her dispute with human resources, but she ultimately prevailed.

Each of these cases demonstrates the potentially obstructive role human re-sources departments play, and yet workers must interact with them if they have any hope of winning restitution.

Coworkers: Friends and Foes

In addition to management and HR, coworkers are also a crucial part of the claims-making process, often acting as witnesses providing needed testimony on behalf of either the worker or management. Many workers discussed the challenges they faced in finding a coworker willing to come forward and testify on their behalf, even if these coworkers had themselves suffered similar mistreatment. The obvi-ous factor preventing witnesses from coming forward was fear of retaliation. For example, Maya, a low-end retail worker, was told that she was not allowed to speak Spanish at work unless it was to paying customers.[20] This was a discriminatory policy enforced by her store manager, the district manager, and even the human resources department. But when she attempted to get her coworkers to vouch for her complaint, they refused: "It's because they are afraid to lose their job. . . . Maybe not directly, but slowly and surely they would push them out." Though she was able to find one supervisor to support her, management eventually transferred that em-ployee to another store and they lost contact. When she demanded answers from her district manager, she was referred back to human resources, who ultimately blamed her for causing workplace discord. The store eventually reversed its lan-guage policy, but not before putting Maya through a draining ordeal.

A similar case involved Reynoldo, who worked for a catering company and had persistent problems with wage theft and being denied breaks.[21] His employer con-trolled the time card records and would only pay workers sporadically and in cash.

Reynoldo bristled at this arrangement because, apart from needing the income, he wanted to be able to file accurate taxes at the end of the year. He sought help from the legal aid clinic, which was concerned that in the absence of formal records, it would be his word against his employer's. Thus he turned to his coworkers, all of whom had to deal with the same abusive practices. One agreed to testify on his behalf, but because his tenure at the company was brief, his testimony was rejected as irrelevant to the time period in question. The employer, on the other hand, had plenty of support at the hearing: "Various employees testified for him, I am told, for a dollar wage raise. Others were promised a promotion." Reynoldo went on to explain eloquently what motivated him to persist despite the fears he and other undocumented workers had about coming forward: "Well, it's fear, mixed with a sense that you can't do it. But ultimately it's a fear I overcame, because the truth is, one can't live all the time in fear—you'd never get anything done. You'd never even leave your house."

Solidarity among low-paid workers is neither automatic nor expected. Workers described many instances of tensions among coworkers, amplified by competition for hours and scheduling. For instance, Milo worked at a bakery and described his job as follows: "The pay is super low, they don't pay you what you are owed, they mistreat you, no one speaks up or complains, [and] they won't say anything for fear of losing their job."[22] The nonstop work was fast-paced, unbearable, and dangerous. As a result, workers were interested only in self-preservation and quick to call out each other's mistakes: "They [my coworkers] were always on top of me. 'Hey, look, he did this, he did that.'" Milo was fired after a piece of equipment broke on his watch, yet was still asked to train his replacement before leaving. Ultimately he feels that he was fired because he refused to submit to the constant harassment and pressure to work longer and harder "just because I didn't have a social." In his case, his unsupportive coworkers—wary of troublemakers—were happy to see him go.

In some cases employers actively stir up discord among workers, especially when combating a claim. Some claimants described enjoying positive relationships with their coworkers before filing their grievances. Felipe, an undocumented forklift driver for a shipping company, regularly worked (unpaid) overtime and suffered a severe foot injury after falling from a broken loading ladder.[23] Wage theft and health and safety concerns were rampant at the company, and he and another injured coworker were both fired after complaining. At first Felipe described his relationship with his coworkers as "agreeable," noting that they "would share lunch . . . [and] got along very well." After the accident, however, those relationships changed drastically: "They told me that they were being threatened, too, and they didn't want to talk to me, and so they stopped talking to me." Although his coworkers had initially agreed to testify on Felipe's behalf regarding the workplace conditions, their employer's threats kept them from helping him in the end. Ulti-mately Felipe realized that even though he has never had a problem finding a job with false papers, his status reduced his leverage during the settlement process: "It all came out [during the process], so they took advantage of me, and gave me less." He has since commenced the process to apply for a U visa, though I was unable to learn the ultimate outcome of his claim.

In the cases where a claimant *is* able to convince coworkers to support his or her cause, it usually involves significant effort and prodding. For example, JJ worked in construction for a small contractor who regularly postponed payment to his crew, sometimes for up to a month.[24] When JJ finally filed a claim with the Labor Commissioner, he knew it would be an uphill battle. His undocumented status did not stop him, though, as JJ, young and brash, had at this point little to lose. When he approached his coworkers, however, they demurred. Although they had expe-rienced the same problems, they did not want to fight, and frankly they needed the work: "They figured they wouldn't win the case, that it was a lost cause," he explained. JJ's sole ally was his (also undocumented) coworker, Manolo, "a ner-vous type who didn't like to get embroiled in legal things" but who finally agreed. Manolo had gone eight weeks without being paid but chose not to file a claim himself. Instead, he simply stopped working for this contractor and found another job. However, he opted to help JJ because he felt badly for having referred JJ to the abusive contractor. Manolo thus reluctantly joined his friend at his hearing, where the Labor Commissioner ultimately ruled in JJ's favor.

I pressed Manolo in a separate interview about his reluctance to file his own claim even as he was helping JJ.[25] Apart from feeling partially responsible, he ex-plained that JJ's level of desperation was higher than his. During the recession, they all suffered, but Manolo could rely on his employed wife to make ends meet. In good times, Manolo made $30 per hour and was relatively skilled compared to most other workers; he owned his own tools and his own truck. His friend, on the other hand, was destitute when his boss stopped paying: "Really, he had nothing, not even a dime to eat." Seeing this injustice spurred Manolo to act, even though he was adamantly determined to "avoid problems" about his own case given that he had kids to support. He even recalls saying to the negligent employer seated across from them in the hearing room: "Look, you know you owe me X, but I don't care. I just want you to pay him." Manolo's selfless behavior was all the more admi-rable given his own past workplace struggles. Apart from the unpaid wage issues, Manolo had racked up an impressive list of workplace injuries, including a major back problem, which he jokingly told me had miraculously resolved itself the last time he fell. During our discussion, Manolo at one point showed me his finger, a third of which was missing: he had lost it in an industrial accident in Virginia. "There," he said dryly, "things were way worse."

Union Representation: Possibilities and Limits

Few of the workers with whom I spoke had a union contract (14 percent of the survey sample, and 21 percent of the follow-up interviews). And of those who did, their options for legal assistance were often still limited. Union-represented workers are covered under a collective bargaining contract that provides a union grievance system. Workers are obliged to present their concerns to their shop steward, whose job it is to initiate the grievance process. When a worker exhausts this process, or is unsatisfied with its result, they may seek out assistance from a legal aid clinic to further examine their options. In these cases, the legal aid centers evaluate whether there is any possibility for further action to help union workers who feel neglected or frustrated.

Such was the case with Mario, a Salvadoran construction worker with Temporary Protected Status (TPS) who had a litany of complaints about his union's mishandling of its salary and pension commitments.[26] For months he pleaded with his union to help him until his assigned representative was eventually fired for fund mismanagement. Nothing was subsequently done to pursue his case, which prompted Mario and his coworkers to finally seek help from the community law center. Although the center concurred with the basic facts of the case, it was unable to help: "The clinic told us that we had let too much time pass for our demand. Between the time when we were owed our wage and when we filed the claim, too much time had gone by, and they said they couldn't help." Thereafter the crew gave up on pursuing their claim: "We didn't do anything else. We didn't try to mobilize more." Eventually, work slowed down, and they all moved on to another employer, where their jobs were nonunion and lower paying. Mario's frustrated attempt at justice demonstrates the shortcomings of the union system and the limits of legal aid.

Although Mario's case is one of extreme negligence, more often workers were constrained by the practical inability of unions to force employers into compliance. Yadira, an undocumented, union-represented janitor, was well aware of the terms of her collective bargaining contract, which she thought mandated a regular raise of twenty-five cents an hour every year.[27] When after three years she had received nothing, Yadira went to her union for help. They explained that because she was in a "special zone," the raise did not apply to her: "I read the little union book describing my rights . . . but they said that supposedly it doesn't matter, that because I was in Zone 5, my salary was lower. . . . I never understood what Zone 5 was." When she was later fired after receiving only one warning, she once again complained, noting that the rules required three warnings prior to dismissal. Weeks went by before her union representative was able to arrange a meeting with management. When Yadira visited the legal aid clinic for help, the attorney explained that her boss was within his rights to fire her. What to do next? "I wanted to file a claim against the union, because that is why we have a union, so that they can help us with our problems, our injustices, right?" She filed a claim with the National Labor Relations Board, and union staff were summoned to account for their investigation. Yadira didn't hear back for nearly six months, at which time she was told that there was no further remedy available. By that time, she had moved onto another, lower-paying job working for her husband's cousin, which she nonetheless prefers: "I've been there two years now, with no raise, but I feel so much more comfortable. Before I had to ask for time off a month in advance if I had an appointment or something; otherwise, I'd be fired. Here [it's more flexible]. I just have to ask if I can come in a little late so I can take my kid to the doctor, or whatever."

Even though Yadira has landed on her feet, she is still frustrated and confused about just what services her union actually provided: "What are they worth? Every two weeks they take money [out of your check] to protect and help you, but they never do anything." It is impossible to know with certainty what specific challenges were keeping unions from obtaining further assistance for Yadira or the other workers. However, Yadira's case exemplifies the limited role that even powerful unions have in advocating for low-wage workers. This limited power is partly explained by the fact that union influence fluctuates; it can win certain cases, but it can just as easily be decertified or forced to bend during negotiations. While it struggles to assist its members, the union itself must fight to maintain its position in industries seeking to purge their workforces of sympathizers. This instability can affect workers seeking union support during a claim.

Unions are particularly constrained in their ability to reinstate members who have been fired, and who have a documented track record of warnings and poor job performance from management. Take for example Juana, a naturalized citizen and hospital housekeeper who asked for only one day off after her father died suddenly.[28] Not long after she returned, she was told that she was being terminated for failure to fill out the appropriate paperwork, even though she had spoken directly with the office secretary, who approved her absence. Juana had received two warnings in the past and was now being told that the hospital was not happy with her work. She was replaced with a US-born coworker who spoke perfect English and was a close friend of her immediate manager, who often voiced her disdain for Mexican workers. This manager would often say, "Mexicans are always coming here to work, and they don't even have papers." Although her union attempted to hold a meeting with management, it ultimately had no power to change the situation. Immediately prior to Juana's firing, the union was embroiled in contract negotiations. The union decided that pressing too much harder would only further damage future attempts at contract negotiations. After a year of looking for work, Juana was eventually only able to pick up two part-time jobs at half her former pay of $23 per hour.

In the following chapter, I contextualize the experiences described here in the legal framework for enforcing the rights of low-wage workers in the United States. I discuss a well-intended and hard-won set of laws and bureaucracies meant to hold employers accountable, but that are ultimately limited in their scope and ability to protect many of the most marginalized workers.

3

The Landscape and Logics of Worker Protections

So much of what we know about workers' rights focuses on what makes them enter into the legal system in the first place, or, conversely, what factors bar their entry. What happens when workers decide to engage the law to demand their rights? And then what comes next? In this chapter, I begin to answer by examining the structure and logic underlying the labor standards enforcement system in the United States through the lens of the San Francisco Bay Area and California state systems. While not meant as a comprehensive overview, the following pages help frame our understanding of how the state regulates employer behavior and what are the narrow protections that exist for workers.

Two general trends have affected workers' rights in the United States over the past several decades: a slow decline of union strength and a growing focus on individual protections as opposed to broader collective bargaining tactics (Lichtenstein 2002). These individual rights have reconfigured the balance of power between employer and worker, with the latter bearing the enormous burden of pursuing justice despite having considerably fewer resources and less influence. This shift has paralleled the broader trend of redefining deeper structural inequalities as individual grievances that require individual, rather than system-wide, redress.

Alexander J. S. Colvin (forthcoming) outlines two distinct mechanisms in the US labor standards enforcement system: *inspection-based* and *adjudicatory-based* processes. In the former, the state has the authority to investigate labor practices, as does the Occupational Safety and Health Administration when it goes out to inspect businesses for safety protocols and hazardous exposures. Resource and personnel limitations restrict the reach of this enforcement method, which also depends on the political will of an agency's directorate (Government Accountability Office 2007; Bobo 2008; Gleeson 2012a). Adjudicatory, or claims-based, approaches allow workers to bring complaints through the courts, administrative hearings, and other bureaucratic processes. With each of these mechanisms, an individual claimant's success hinges largely on her private resources, unless she is among the few to have agency litigators representing her case. As Colvin argues, "individual employment rights will only have limited impact on employment relations unless they can alter the facts on the ground of the workplace by affecting the pattern of practices engaged in by employers."

Thus, merely establishing formal protections is inadequate for at least two reasons. First, the bureaucratic implementation of rights, even those that represent vast improvements, requires that claimants and employers alike invest enormous amounts of time and energy. Charles R. Epp (2010) calls this painstaking process "making rights real," as it requires not only familiarizing oneself with bureaucratic minutiae but also conducting staff training and community outreach. Furthermore, it also assumes that workers themselves are equipped to come forward and denounce those who have wronged them.

Second, as Ruben J. Garcia (2012a) highlights, formal protections leave marginal workers unprotected. These are workers who "are technically covered by labor and employment laws, but because of competing policy concerns or laws, they end up losing full protection. This is especially true of those workers who are more institutionally vulnerable, such as noncitizens, people of color, and women. Despite the additional protections that these workers enjoy on paper, they are often unable to fully enforce their rights" (3). These most vulnerable workers face the biggest challenges in ensuring that they enjoy the same formal protections as their coworkers. Sometimes this difficulty arises from shortcomings in the construction of the given law, but at other times, the complexity of workers' lives affects their ability, or desire, to see their claims through to the end.

Employers often count on the economic calculus of lax or nonenforcement. According to Noah D. Zatz (2008), two mechanisms shape enforcement failures. Employers may evade detection through the "manipulation or suppression of record-keeping," or instead they may choose to defy the law outright by "simply integrating noncompliance into ordinary business operations" (43). For example, common business practices such as subcontracting (relying on temporary workers) allow employers to reduce the coverage of employment law, thus reducing their labor costs.

However, beyond the problem of "judicial misconstruction," which Garcia (2012a) defines as the ways weak labor laws fail to protect the most vulnerable, a further problem is that the labor standards enforcement regime does little to address either the long-standing logics of capital production or the system of white, male, and heterosexual domination. This is a broader structural discussion that goes far beyond the limits of this chapter, though it is important to understand that legislating against inequality is not the same as undoing the foundations of such inequality. Indeed, previous laws have led to decades of compounding disadvantage for vulnerable workers, and current expanding protections are hard-pressed to address these structural disadvantages.

For example, the prohibitions against racial discrimination passed under Title VII of the Civil Rights Act have not ushered in a color-blind society. However, the mistaken belief that we do actually live in a color-blind society has determined how legal institutions function and how we address the racial implications of their edicts (Haney López 2000). These legal institutions function as if structural prejudice doesn't exist (Bonilla-Silva 2006), and oftentimes even social scientists themselves give insufficient weight to the societal factors driving certain policies (Bonilla-Silva and Baiocchi 2001). For instance the vulnerabilities of undocumented workers, despite the formal protections offered to them under labor and employment law, must also be understood in the context of immigration laws that almost exclusively impact Latino workers (Gleeson 2014b; Gomberg-Muñoz 2011; Armenta 2016). Moreover, deep-seated disadvantages can lead to institutional inequality across socio-legal realms, such as the ways in which patriarchy shapes sexual harassment (Marshall 2003) and family leave (Albiston 2010) policies. As I demonstrate in the ensuing chapters, this context of social inequality shapes not only how problems are legitimized and framed, but also how the rights established to combat these problems are exercised.

In the remainder of this chapter, I walk readers through the legal foundations of labor and employment law, including the rules governing wage and hour protections, workplace injury, employment discrimination, collective bargaining, and unemployment insurance. While by no means exhaustive, these summaries provide a scaffolding for understanding the bureaucratic environment that the workers involved in this study attempted to traverse. For the most part, workers had very basic, often inaccurate, understandings of the scope of their protections. But in order to understand the constraints that their advocates, as well as often well-meaning bureaucrats, were up against, we must start here by outlining the complex labor standards enforcement system. I end by discussing what happens when employment laws collide with federal immigration enforcement laws, which impact 5.1 percent of the US labor force, 9 percent of California workers, and a third of the respondents in this study (Krogstad and Passel 2015).

THE STATUTORY SILOS OF WORKERS' RIGHTS

Two features stand out about the labor standards enforcement system. First, it is a patchwork of agencies and bureaucracies, each with a distinct history of struggle to improve different aspects of the worker experience. Second, as with other legal arenas, labor and employment law exists within a federalist system of laws. The idea is that federal law sets a minimum floor, leaving states and localities to act as "laboratories of innovation" (Freeman and Rogers 2007; Bernhardt 2012). In restrictionist places, governments have enacted punitive policies aimed to limit workplace rights and to deter employers from hiring undocumented workers. In progressive places, state and local laws have created an added layer of enforcement to regulate employer behavior. In practice this creates a series of agencies and processes that, while they may communicate with one another on occasion, are focused on jurisdictional silos that workers on the ground may struggle to navigate.

Wage and Hour Protections

Perhaps the most fundamental aspect of the employment relationship, wage and hour standards, was first codified in 1938 by the Fair Labor Standards Act (FLSA) in the midst of an economic depression. At the time, the act covered only a fifth of all workers, set a forty-hour work week, established the national minimum wage at twenty-five cents per hour, and put in place provisions prohibiting child labor. The FLSA was the product of years of wrangling in the courts and in congressional debates (J. Grossman 2009), and the 1938 minimum wage it established, though a milestone, was comparatively low. It was a compromise with Southern business interests who raised loud objections, issuing dire warnings about massive potential job losses that would sound familiar in congressional debates on the issue today. Were the wage to be adjusted for inflation, it would be the 2015 equivalent of $4.06 (Elwell 2014).

As of June 2015, the federal minimum wage is $7.25 and currently covers approximately 84 percent of workers, or 130 million total (Bradley 2015, 1). There are two tracks of FLSA coverage, enterprise and individual, but exceptions exist within the law. To fall under enterprise coverage, workers must be employed by a company with at least two employees and annual sales of $500,000; if they don't, they aren't covered, unless their employer engages in interstate commerce. Many workers are also exempted from the federal minimum wage, most notably "executive, administrative, and professional employees," seasonal workers, and certain agricultural and domestic service workers (Bradley 2015).

Wage and hour protections vary considerably from state to state, though despite the patchwork of laws—and in some cases states have no wage laws at all—workers must be paid at least the federal minimum. Twenty-nine states have instituted a minimum wage that is higher than the federal one (Wage and Hour Division 2015). In California the minimum wage is currently $9 per hour (as it is in Massachusetts and Rhode Island). As of this writing, states with higher rates include Washington ($9.47), Oregon ($9.25), Connecticut ($9.15), and Vermont ($9.15) (National Conference of State Legislatures 2015). Failure to pay this minimum wage, or the contractually agreed upon rate if it is higher, is considered a wage and hour violation, regardless of employer intent. Failure to follow overtime rules or forcing workers to labor during uncompensated time are also wage and hour violations (Interfaith Worker Justice 2015).

Wage and hour violations have been the focus of several labor campaigns across the country. Kim Bobo (2008), whose book *Wage Theft in America* has become an indispensable work on the topic, defines wage theft simply as "people not getting paid for their work" (xii), and has described the United States as experiencing an epidemic of wage theft.[1] Advocates such as Bobo argue that in addition to stripping workers of their livelihoods, wage theft also encourages unfair business competition by inducing a race to the bottom in contract bidding wars, thus undercutting the true cost of "high road" employment (Restaurant Opportunities Centers United and Batt 2012). That is, even employers who aspire to be honest feel pressured by dishonest ones to compete by lowering their payroll and acting unscrupulously. Unpaid wages also translate into unpaid taxes, which robs local communities of resources. In their study of low-wage workers in Chicago, Los Angeles, and New York City, Bernhardt et al. (2009) found that minimum-wage violations were one of the most commonly reported worker complaints. Among that study's respondents, 26 percent of workers surveyed were paid less than the legally required minimum wage, and 60 percent reported underpayment of at least $1.

Nationally, the federal Department of Labor has the primary responsibility for addressing wage and hour violations. But in jurisdictions where state or local laws are stronger than federal ones, state and local enforcement agencies may play a much bigger role. For example, in California, the Division of Labor Standards Enforcement (DLSE), or the California Labor Commissioner, as the agency is often known, offers a higher minimum wage and more generous overtime provisions than the federal government. As such, it is incumbent on them to enforce their standards.

The new frontier of wage protection is by all accounts happening at the local level in the form of living wage policies, municipal minimum wages, and wage theft ordinances. As of June 2015, twenty-three pioneering cities and counties have also enacted minimum wage policies for *all* workers employed within their jurisdiction. The San Francisco Bay Area in particular has been a vital region in this progressive march. Oakland and San Francisco have set their minimum wage at $12.25 (the latter set to raise to $15 by 2018), Berkeley at $12.53, Mountain View, San Jose, and Sunnyvale all at $10.30, and Emeryville set to rise to $16 by 2019 (National Employment Law Project 2015). By comparison, federal and state governments are far behind the curve.

Establishing living wage policies has also been a key goal for many local labor movements. In localities where a living wage policy has been enacted, qualifying employers (most often those working under a public contract) must pay their employees at least as much as the policy demands. In some places, such as

Los Angeles, a two-tier rate has been established to incentivize employers to offer health insurance benefits to their employees (Luce 2004, 2007). Though living wage policies cover only a small percentage of workers, they can send a powerful message to employers and taxpayers about the wide disconnect between the arbitrary wage floor set by federal and state legislatures and the true cost of living in most American cities (Glasmeier 2015). For example, the current living/prevailing wage in San Jose, California, is $19.06 without health benefits; this local rate is more than 50 percent higher than the state-mandated rate (City of San Jose 2015).

Often overlooked in the struggle for fairer wages is underpaid overtime, a commonly underreported violation. The federal standard is time-and-a-half an employee's regular rate for any hour worked over forty hours in a week. Some states, such as California, provide more stringent policies, such as time-and-a-half of the regular pay rate after eight hours in a workday, and double time after twelve (State of California Department of Industrial Relations 2015d). However, not all workers qualify for overtime. As of June 2015, federal wage and hour law exempted "bona fide executive, administrative, professional and outside sales employees" who met certain requirements, including being paid at least $455 per week on a salary basis (Wage and Hour Division 2008). Advocates have argued that these exemptions should be reconsidered, pointing out that assuming one works fifty-two weeks a year earning that minimum qualifying rate, the annual salary of $23,660 is far below the poverty line for a family of four (Conti 2014). Furthermore, not only office workers but also farmworkers and some domestic workers are exempted from overtime under federal law.

Beyond compensation, rest and meal breaks are also regulated by wage and hour legislation. In California these are often industry specific, but generally workers are entitled to a thirty-minute lunch break after five hours, and a ten-minute break for every four-hour period (State of California Department of Industrial Relations 2011). The Labor Code assesses penalties for each of these violations. While regular rest breaks are seen by critics as a luxury demanded by entitled workers, evidence has shown that they "can be an effective means of maintaining performance, managing fatigue and controlling the accumulation of risk over prolonged task performance" (Tucker 2003, 123). Other studies reveal that rest breaks have no significant impact on productivity and can help alleviate worker discomfort (Dababneh, Swanson, and Shell 2001) and promote worker dignity (Linder 1998). However, despite their benefits, employers frequently deny workers their breaks, and this can be very difficult to prove in the absence of clear records (Ballon et al. 2009). Unless there is consistent evidence, legal advocates often opt to focus their cases on unpaid wages.

Once a federal, state, or local violation has been committed, the practical process of filing a wage and hour claim differs from jurisdiction to jurisdiction. The basic requirement is that workers must be able to establish that they are an eligible employee. In the context of the Fair Labor Standards Act, the Department of Labor offers the following guidance: "The FLSA defines 'employ' as including to 'suffer or permit to work,' representing the broadest definition of employment under the law because it covers work that the employer directs or allows to take place. Applying the FLSA's definition, workers who are economically dependent on the business of the employer, regardless of skill level, are considered to be employees, and most workers are employees." Various "economic realities" can be assessed for this test, including "the extent to which the work performed is an integral part of the employer's business"; "whether the worker's managerial skills affect his or her opportunity for profit and loss"; "the relative investments in facilities and equipment by the worker and the employer"; "the worker's skill and initiative"; "the permanency of the worker's relationship with the employer"; and "the nature and degree of control by the employer" (Wage and Hour Division 2014a). Time or mode of pay alone is not a qualifying factor, but nonetheless misclassifications (for instance identifying an employee as an independent contractor) run rampant and can impact a worker's eligibility for protections.

After establishing their eligibility, employees must then show the hours they worked and the amount they were paid through credible testimony and/or documentation. As a result of this requirement, one of the main outreach tools worker advocates have used in communities with high rates of nonstandard pay arrangements is to pass out calendars where workers can keep track of their schedules and payments even if their employer does not. This record keeping is vital because it is not uncommon for nonexempt workers to report a "salary" or periodic lump sum payments (sometimes in cash), for which they worked variable and often unpredictable hours, with no regard to overtime pay. In the absence of records (which the employer should have been keeping), testimony sometimes suffices.[2]

Once the eligibility and records are verified, the claim can proceed. At the Division of Labor Standards Enforcement (DLSE), the process requires that workers file their form (available online) either via mail or at one of the several state agencies located throughout the region, along with supporting evidence (State of California Department of Industrial Relations 2015c). The claimant and defendant, or employer, are then asked to appear at a settlement conference at the agency office with a deputy commissioner present. The goal is to resolve the claim without proceeding to a hearing. The employer may offer a settlement amount, and the worker will be encouraged to consider taking it based on the strength of her evidence. If an agreement cannot be reached, a formal complaint form initiates the hearing process. At this hearing, each party may bring witnesses and present evidence, which is reviewed by a hearing officer.[3] Lawyers are not required in this process, and workers can bring a non-attorney representative. If requested, the DLSE will provide an interpreter for the worker.

The statute of limitations for filing a wage and hour claim at the DLSE is generally between two to three years from when the violation occurred, depending on the specific issue and whether the worker entered into a verbal or oral contract (Legal Aid Society—Employment Law Center 2004). As a result, victims of long-running violations may only be able to recover a portion of their full restitution. Further exacerbating the statute of limitations issue is the often lengthy claims process. According to the DLSE's own official reports, a Berman claim (that is, one resulting in a hearing) takes on average 179 days from initial filing to conclusion (Su 2013).

In the best-case scenario, workers win their cases and receive some monetary restitution. However, a positive judgment does not necessarily guarantee that a worker will receive payment. Employer compliance can be the biggest challenge for workers who, even after mustering the courage to file a claim, and even after a judge rules in their favor, often never see their fair pay (Cho, Koonse, and Mischel 2013; Gleeson, Silver Taube, and Noss 2014). For example, in 2012–13 the DLSE granted $84,512,152 in hearing awards (that is, judgments actually issued by the DLSE), but collected only $11,285,085 to be returned to the claimants.[4] To remedy this, the agency has partnered with nonprofit organizations such as the Wage Justice Center to make advances in enforcing judgments, building on a partnership with the California Franchise Tax Board (Department of Industrial Relations 2013, 38). Local wage theft ordinances are also attempting to tie nonpayment to business license revocation and instituting criminal penalties for noncompliant employers (National Employment Law Project 2011).

Workplace Injury

Two sets of policies shape worker safety and health. The first, via the Occupational Safety and Health Act, is focused on enforcement and holding employers accountable for hazardous work environments. The second, via the state-run workers' compensation system, is meant to provide workers with temporary pay and medical treatment in the event of a workplace accident. I discuss each in turn.

OCCUPATIONAL SAFETY AND HEALTH

Since 1970, workers in the United States have been protected under the federal Occupational Safety and Health Act, which requires employers to provide a "safe and healthful" work environment (US Department of Labor 2015b). Since safety requirements and conditions can vary widely from industry to industry, an exceedingly detailed list of requirements is published and updated in the federal register (Occupational Safety and Health Administration 2015b). Updates aside, the agency is commonly criticized for its inability to keep up with the rapidly changing, postindustrial workforce. For example, while construction regulations for scaffolding and trench shoring have been implemented for decades, basic protections in more modern industries have often gone overlooked or are still poorly understood.[5]

A network of regional occupational safety and health advocates (Committees on Occupational Safety and Health, or COSH groups) have worked to hold OSHA accountable and highlight the health and safety needs of underrepresented workers. Some of their recent campaigns include improving training for temporary workers, making a contractor's safety record a key factor in the bidding process, addressing the vulnerabilities facing immigrant workers, and strengthening protections against retaliation (National Council for Occupational Safety and Health 2015).[6] The National Institute for Occupational Safety and Health (NIOSH), housed at the Center for Disease Control, also conducts research on how to prevent illness and workplace injury.

The data on the rate of workplace injury is limited by a variety of factors: lack of workers' knowledge of their rights, fear of retaliation, competition among workers, and limits on workers' willingness to report injuries (Gleeson 2012b; Cox and Lippel 2008). With few exceptions, employers only have to report severe injuries and fatalities to OSHA (Occupational Safety and Health Administration 2014). Consequently the "official" data provides an incomplete picture of workplace safety (Occupational Safety and Health Administration 2015a). For certain industries, existing Bureau of Labor Statistics categories do not adequately represent groups of workers. For example, no clear category exists for those doing forestry replanting work on federal land, an industry that employs high numbers of subcontracted undocumented immigrants (Sarathy 2012).

Bureau of Labor Statistics data we do have reveal that in 2013, 845 foreign-born workers died on the job (accounting for 19 percent of the 4,405 fatal work injuries that year). Of these deceased immigrant workers, 352 were from Mexico. Overall, 797 deaths were of Hispanic/Latino workers (18 percent of the total), an increase from the year prior (Bureau of Labor Statistics 2014). Research confirms that immigrant workers are at higher risk for dangerous work (Orrenius and Zavodny 2009), and undocumented workers face an especially heightened risk (Hall and Greenman 2015), though there is no evidence that they receive additional wage returns for this increased risk.[7]

The Occupational Safety and Health Administration aims to prevent these injuries or fatalities before they occur; its mandate is to monitor employer compliance, and in some cases train workers on how to prevent injury (Occupational Safety and Health Administration 2015c). It may do this in response to confidential requests for an inspection. The agency may also identify certain enforcement priorities, allotting its resources to deal with particularly dangerous workplace conditions. In addition to the federal Occupational Safety and Health Administration, twenty-two states, including California, run programs that have the primary enforcement responsibility. These states have additional protections and draw on state resources. However, there is no private right of action under the Occupational Safety and Health Act (OSHA); that is, individuals cannot file claims for restitution under OSHA.[8]

WORKERS' COMPENSATION

Once a worker is injured, she must turn to the workers' compensation system for help. Workers' compensation was established between 1910 and 1920 as a state-sponsored program that employers must comply with by purchasing insurance that covers both the medical costs of any injury that occurs "out of and in the course of employment" and temporary disability pay (Fishback and Kantor 2006). In every state except Texas, employers are required to carry insurance for their employees.[9] The contemporary workers' compensation apparatus is a "no-fault" system that largely exempts employers from civil liability; barring gross negligence, workers are taken care of and the employers are protected from being sued. As a result, assigning personal responsibility and culpability—a lengthy and costly process— is not the primary focus of claims-making in the workers' compensation system (Schmidtz and Goodin 1998). However, despite the streamlining benefits of the no-fault principle, it has given rise to a culture that systemically allows employers to shirk their obligation to maintain a healthy and safe workplace (Spieler 1994; Stone 1984).

Grant Duncan (2003) argues that, viewed in the context of industrial development, the workers' compensation system was designed to "minimize industrial conflict and maximize capital accumulation, while simultaneously managing the conduct of the injured worker" (454). Not to be confused with a universal health insurance scheme meant to maintain the overall health of beneficiaries, the goal of the workers' compensation system is to return *employees* to their "bodily, vocational, and social *status quo ante*" as determined by a team of administrative, legal, and medical experts (455). The workers' compensation system was hailed by reformers as an "economically efficient bargain" for business (McCluskey 2003, 849)—"efficient" because it stopped far short of providing workers an income that would give them a feasible alternative to the labor market (Wright 2004). Today, workers' compensation benefits provide injured workers approximately two-thirds of their wages, up to a maximum of roughly $1,075 per week (State of California Department of Industrial Relations 2014b), thus encouraging them in theory to return to work.

As with many of the other concessions workers have gained from management, workers' compensation was won out of a conflict between labor and capital. Janet Schmidt (1980) describes the program as a result "of a massive and violent struggle between labor and capital in the late nineteenth century, and an ensuing effort by the business class to co-opt, institutionalize, and bureaucratize this militancy" (46). This struggle was not as spectacular as past labor battles; indeed, the whole point was to bury conflict within a growing bureaucracy. Employers wanted to avoid the massive strikes protesting dangerous working conditions that characterized early twentieth-century labor organizing (for example the protests in the wake of the 1911 Triangle Shirtwaist Factory fire that claimed the lives of eighty-seven mostly immigrant women). Volatile strikes, protests, and unanticipated lawsuits are bad for business. Therefore, along with progressive intellectuals and middle-class reformers, the business community lobbied in favor of this new, predictable insurance scheme (Hacker 2002, 290), a workers' compensation system based on a rationalized view of individual rights.

In this system, workers' individual claims are adjudicated with bureaucratic, rational precision. Over time, Grant Duncan (2003) contends, the workers' compensation system has shifted the focus from civil liability (and the right to sue one's employer) to an arbitrary quantification based on medical observation. Industry doctors provide their expertise to corroborate the existence of a worker's injury and to evaluate the extent of the resulting impairment. Crucially, these doctors must certify the existence of a "medically verifiable injury" that occurred "out of and in the course of employment (456).[10] To verify the conditions and extent of employee injuries, insurers may even subject claimants to the video recording and monitoring of their daily activities.

Worker disabilities are quantified and ultimately assigned a monetary value. This approach, while seemingly objective and rational, can also lead to "systematic disrespect and humiliation of work-injured claimants" (Parrish and Schofield 2005, 33). Pain and suffering alone, per se, are not compensable, and palliative care and treatment geared toward long-term rehabilitation (such as chiropractic sessions or mental health services) can be challenging to obtain.

Though workers' compensation systems can vary from state to state and from plan to plan, a claim usually begins with a formal report following the incident that resulted in injury. Ideally workers would report incidents immediately to their employer, who would then assist them in filing a formal report. While data on reporting behavior is limited, one study of a sample of Washington state workers revealed that of the 13 percent who reported an occupational injury or illness, only 52 percent filed a workers' compensation claim (Fan et al. 2006). Industry-specific studies reveal even higher rates of injury and lower rates of claiming. Take a survey of unionized hotel room cleaners in Las Vegas, which found that 75 percent of respondents experienced work-related pain, while only 31 percent reported it to management (Scherzer, Rugulies, and Krause 2005).

One reason for this unwillingness to file is that the process of reporting a claim can be confusing and intimidating for workers. A number of factors may deter full disclosure of injury, as in other arenas of worker protections, including fear, lack of information about workers' rights, and the time and hassle that navigating the bureaucracy requires. Workers may also be concerned with leveraging their "health capital" in highly competitive environments where admitting pain and injury is stigmatized and can result in job loss, being passed over for advancement, or receiving less preferential scheduling (Gleeson 2012b; Bloor 2011).

Coverage can also vary by industry, even though in most states all employers are required to carry the workers' compensation benefit. "Independent contractors," who are not classified as employees, do not qualify for coverage (State of California Department of Industrial Relations 2015c). Workers in the informal economy, and who are often misclassified as independent contractors themselves, can find themselves unprotected (Quinlan and Mayhew 1999; Quinlan 2004; Nicholson, Bunn, and Costich 2008). These workers can retain their rights to coverage, however, if they are able to show that they were truly misclassified. To do so relies on appealing to the insurer and/or the workers' compensation board, a lengthy process that often requires the help of an attorney.

While workers are not required to hire an attorney to file an injury claim, attorney-involved claims generally garner higher claim awards, even if a longer claim duration, according to one Louisiana study (Bernacki and Tao 2008). Attorneys can be especially important for non–English proficient and immigrant workers (Rudolph et al. 2002). In California, workers' compensation attorneys are entitled to a fixed amount of any final settlement (15 to 25 percent), and over time, state reforms have reduced the profitability of claims, leading to a higher caseload and attorneys taking on cases more selectively.

Domestic workers, the vast majority of whom are women, have generally been excluded from workers' compensation benefits. Remedying this is a major demand of recent Domestic Worker Bill of Rights movements. Recent attempts at reform on this issue failed to gain support from the governor in California, and at present those who work fewer than fifty-two hours or earn less than $100 over a ninety-day work period are excluded (Kazan, McClain, Satterley, Lyons, Greenwood, and Oberman: A Professional Law Corporation 2015). A survey of 631 domestic workers in Los Angeles, San Diego, San Francisco, and San Jose found that only 1 percent worked for employers who paid into workers' compensation (Theodore, Gutelius, and Burnham 2013).

In large companies, centralized human resources departments often have a standardized protocol for filing workers' compensation reports. However, in subcontracted arrangements, small business workers can struggle to identify the appropriate person to whom they should report. Like all insurance programs, repeated claims can lead to an increase in premiums. These payments depend on the size of the company, the level of risk employees are subject to, and the employer's history of claims (Harrington and Danzon 2000). In addition to wanting to avoid having their dangerous work conditions exposed, then, employers also

have this other incentive to minimize claims. As for the insurers, they understandably do not want to assume more liability than they are mandated to take on,
and therefore take extreme care to verify that the employee's injury resulted from
working at the covered company. Verification can complicate matters for workers who have previous medical conditions, multiple jobs, and/or a long history of
backbreaking work. For instance, of the Central Coast day laborers and field workers with chronic pain to whom I spoke, many commonly switched among several
contractors from season to season and were sometimes working under the table.
While mechanisms exist to share liability among employers, this can be difficult to
establish, especially when workers have little information about the employer they
believed hired them.

Depending on the severity of the accident, once an injury is reported to management, the worker is either taken to the hospital for emergency treatment or
referred to a designated occupational clinic. While workers can pre-designate a
physician from a list of in-network providers, they commonly overlook this option
and are subsequently left with a narrow set of choices within a medical provider
network. Workers with language barriers and limited experience in the health care
system face additional challenges in navigating the occupational health care bureaucracy (Shor 2006). Insurance companies vary tremendously in how proactive
they are in providing workers with language-appropriate information and follow-
ups. When workers unfamiliar with the process interact with an overworked insurance staff person whose job it is to save the company money, tense relationships
often emerge between claimants and adjusters, even if the employer is supportive
of the claim (Strunin and Boden 2004).

Once the recovery process has begun, the workers' compensation system encourages employers to provide modified work (if available) to returning injured
workers. However, employers are not required to provide this benefit if they can
show that it is not economically or practically feasible for them to do so. In terms
of retaliation, state and federal laws prohibit employers from firing workers for
reporting an injury,[11] and disabled workers receive certain protections under the
Americans with Disabilities Act (Farrell 2008). But in practice it can be difficult
for at-will workers to prove that they were retaliated against specifically for filing a
workers' compensation report. And if the resulting injury leaves a worker unable
to do her job, and an alternative position is unavailable, then the worker is left to
rely on disability payments. Insurers are vigilant in ensuring that injured workers
are genuinely disabled, requiring extensive medical reporting; at times, insurers
even employ private investigators to surveil beneficiaries at home, at work, and in
their communities. Katherine Lippel (2007) describes this apparatus in dystopian
terms as a series of "big machines that seek to control the injured worker, control
his future, control costs, control his body, control his appeal, control the return to
work process, control his behavior at work, or at occupational therapy, or at the

doctor's office, and, in the case of clandestine surveillance, control his personal life and that of his family" (435).

Finally, injured workers whose employers violate the law by not carrying workers' compensation insurance may be eligible for benefits from a public fund (if it is solvent). In fiscal year 2009–10, the California Uninsured Employers Benefit Trust Fund (UEBTF) paid out more than $38.6 million in primary uninsured claims and another $20 million in subsequent injury claims (Division of Workers' Compensation 2012a, 2012b). Here, too, access to an attorney can be crucial, but workers in these circumstances often face difficulty securing one (Worksafe! 2010)

Employment Discrimination

The legal concept of discrimination is buttressed by a range of federal and state statutes. The legal landscape is constantly evolving, as litigation over what constitutes discrimination and the legality of the steps taken to combat it is ongoing across the country. At the federal level, the Equal Employment Opportunity Commission (EEOC) is the agency with the primary task of enforcing laws related to employment discrimination on the basis of race, color, religion, sex, age, disability, pregnancy, and, most recently, genetic information. The EEOC is the result of decades of civil rights struggles, and was created in 1965 with the primary purposes of enforcing Title VII of the 1964 Civil Rights Act (US Equal Employment Opportunity Commission 2015a). It has since taken on enforcement responsibility for a variety of other statutes, including the Age Discrimination in Employment Act of 1967, the Pregnancy Discrimination Act of 1978, the Americans with Disabilities Act of 1990, and more recently the Genetic Information Nondiscrimination Act of 2008, the Lilly Ledbetter Fair Pay Act of 2009, and a variety of executive orders, including a 2010 prohibition against discrimination on the basis of sexual orientation or gender identity for federal contractors.

There were fifty-three EEOC offices throughout the country as of June 2015. More than ninety state and local Fair Employment Practices Agencies (FEPAs) work with the federal government to ensure comprehensive enforcement capacity; this means that the federal agency will also enforce state laws where applicable. The complaint processes at the EEOC (US Equal Employment Opportunity Commission 2015e) and the California Department of Fair Employment and Housing (California Department of Fair Employment and Housing 2015) are fairly similar, except that workers have 180 days to file a charge under federal law but 300 if a state law also applies. In the private sector, a worker may choose to file a complaint with the EEOC either in person or by mail, and can get help online and over the phone.[12] Usually the EEOC will investigate the case within six months, subpoena evidence, and then render a decision. If the agency finds a violation, it will encourage the parties to settle. If this mediation is unsuccessful, the agency then decides whether to pursue a lawsuit on the worker's behalf. If the agency neither finds a violation nor chooses to file a lawsuit on the claimant's behalf, the worker is given a Notice of Right to Sue, which then allows the worker to file the case in court.[13] The EEOC still encourages an alternative dispute resolution, or mediation, process even after it has granted such a notice (US Equal Employment Opportunity Commission 2000).

The socio-legal scholarship on discrimination is extensive, with narrow legal decisions differing starkly from social science understandings of inequality, which tend to be wider (Lucas 2008). Many factors impact the success of discrimination court cases, such as the social characteristics of the claimants, whether they have retained legal counsel, and whether they are working within a class action suit and/or a broader social movement (Nielsen, Nelson, and Lancaster 2008; Galanter 1974; Miller and Sarat 1980; Burstein 1991; McCann 1994). In fiscal year 2014, a mere 167 suits were filed in federal district court, 144 of which reached some sort of resolution (US Equal Employment Opportunity Commission 2015c). These small numbers represent narrow definitions of discrimination under the law and the high bars to pursuing a litigation strategy.

In 2014 employment discrimination cases were classified by complaint as follows: race (35 percent), sex (29.3 percent), national origin (10.8 percent), religion (4.0 percent), and color (3.1 percent). Other bases included age (23.2 percent), disability (28.6 percent), equal pay (1.1 percent), and genetic information (0.4 percent). In 42.8 percent of cases, claimants alleged employer retaliation (US Equal Employment Opportunity Commission 2015b). As these data suggest, workers may file a claim of discrimination on the basis of multiple protected categories. However, work by Rachel Kahn Best et al. (2011) suggests that individuals with intersectional identities (such as black women) and/or intersectional claims (such as those based on religion and national origin) are less likely to win. The very specific statutory protections of discrimination law also mean that what a worker perceives as unfair treatment is not necessarily covered under the discrimination statutes. Currently, for example, there are no protections against dismissal on the basis of gender identity (National Center for Transgender Equality 2015) or sexual orientation (Human Rights Campaign 2015) in the civilian workforce.

Oftentimes the real reason behind a worker's termination may be at odds with what that worker believes is the reason. For example, Gilda, a longtime, union-represented nurse, was suspended multiple times, then ultimately fired, after aggressively advocating for improved patient care.[14] She perceived her supervisor's behavior as racially motivated, since she was a Filipina immigrant and her superior was black. Unfortunately for her there was no clear evidence to label her termination as racially motivated, and patient advocacy is not a protected status. Her experience is one of many illustrating the complicated intersections between sanctioned and unsanctioned discriminatory practices, as well as the complicated dynamics of race, immigrant status, and power at work.

Employment discrimination is difficult to prove. Critical race and feminist scholars have examined the wide gulf that exists between the legal test of discrimination and the lived experience of marginalized individuals (Saucedo 2009; Crenshaw 2011; J. Grossman 2003). The standard concepts of differential treatment and disparate impact tend to ignore "individuals' complex and entangled experiences with inequality at work" (Hirsh 2014, 256), not to mention long-standing inequalities entrenched in the broader society (Fischer et al. 1996). Compounding this limitation is what Samuel R. Lucas (2008) argues is a legal preoccupation with individual intent rather than cultural or institutional injustices. (One exception would be the notion of hostile work environments in sexual harassment cases.) According to Lucas, unless a specific individual with prejudicial views and intentional behaviors can be assigned blame, there is no mechanism for assessing a remedy. Consequently, structural inequalities can be buried under seemingly equitable practices, and the bar for actually proving discrimination is exceedingly high.[15]

Mediation has also become an increasingly important element of the discrimination claims process, a trend that is evident in other statutory arenas as well. While the EEOC itself has a long history and well-developed system for referring cases to mediation (US Equal Employment Opportunity Commission 2015d), workers alleging discrimination are also likely to be urged by their companies to enter mediation. At the same time, companies have responded to increased discrimination laws, Lauren B. Edelman (1992) argues, by instituting elaborate formal structures that create visible signs of compliance.[16]

Underpinning many of the cases classified as discrimination suits in this study was a misunderstanding of the bounds of discrimination protections and the nature of at-will employment. Many workers believed that they were the victims of unjust discrimination when actually other, no less unfair economic factors were at play. For example, in the last chapter we saw how Melita was fired for having made a minor error on her vacation request form, a misunderstanding with her supervisor.[17] She and many of her coworkers were gradually let go and replaced under such pretexts when new management took over the child care facility where they worked. She described her disillusionment with how she was treated with a keen understanding of the motives behind her dismissal: "Look, I feel very frustrated, deceived, and I attribute a lot of it to the economic situation going on in this country, but I feel a lot of discrimination. . . I think especially toward Hispanics, because there almost always has to be a scapegoat during an economic recession who they will target to take their jobs away." Though Melita had years of experience and had completed more than four times the required professional development hours, she was more expensive than the young, US-born women who replaced her. As with many other such cases, it is difficult to determine whether Melita's firing was a case of outright, prosecutable discrimination or the sadly inevitable outcome of her precarity as a low-wage, at-will worker.

All too often, the evidence available is simply not strong enough to prove a legal basis for discrimination. For example, Wanda, another child care provider, needed to take time off from work to recover from two separate surgeries.[18] In a variation of a story I heard in many of my interviews, Wanda's director promised that she would have a job waiting for her but ultimately fired her after her unanticipated seven-month break. She had made the mistake of asking for a minor accommodation upon her return. Though Wanda felt entirely able to fulfill her duties at work, she informed her director that she would need to use the bathroom on occasion: "She told me, 'You cannot leave the children even one minute; you cannot leave the room or have someone cover you . . . at any time.'" Wanda ultimately regretted having shared information about her condition, especially after finding herself without a job after three years with this company. Unable to afford a lawyer, she submitted her claim directly to the EEOC, but was told that she had insufficient evidence to proceed.

Not only do wage and hour claimants find it difficult to find an attorney to represent a case alleging minimum wage, overtime, or meal or rest break violations, but discrimination cases like Wanda's can also be exceedingly difficult to pursue due to their high evidentiary standards and the narrow scope of protected categories. Although the EEOC/DFEH system allows workers to take their claim to court if the agency does not find cause or chooses not to pursue an investigation, the resources required are simply prohibitive for many. Most attorneys will not take a case on contingency, demanding an hourly fee that is out of reach for most low-wage workers.

Collective Bargaining

In the United States, employees have the right to collectively bargain under the National Labor Relations Act (NLRA). The NLRA was passed in 1935 to "to protect the rights of employees and employers, to encourage collective bargaining, and to curtail certain private sector labor and management practices, which can harm the general welfare of workers, businesses and the U.S. economy" (National Labor Relations Board 2015d). The Wagner Act, as it was also known, set up for the first time "a government-monitored election system" that initially favored the industry-based organizing style of the Congress of Industrial Organizations (CIO), which merged with the American Federation of Labor two decades later (Fantasia and Voss 2004). The Wagner Act, however, excluded several significant categories of workers, most notably agriculture and domestic workers, two industries made up overwhelmingly of immigrants, African Americans, and women, in a clear reflection of the lasting racist and sexist foundations of US labor law (Perea 2011). In California, by contrast, agricultural workers have been uniquely protected under the California Agricultural Labor Relations Act since 1975. This has been a salutary development, although, as research shows, "almost four decades [after the California act passed], fewer than 20,000 of the 600,000 to 800,000 workers employed for wages sometime during the year on state farms are covered by collective bargaining agreements" (Martin 2012, 5).

Nationwide, union participation has long been declining. In 2014, 7.4 percent of private sector workers were represented by a union, a nearly 16-point drop from the earliest available data in 1977 (Hirsch and Macpherson 2015). Unionization levels vary substantially from state to state, due to provisions in the 1947 Taft-Hartley Act (National Labor Relations Board 2015a). Briefly, in states with "right to work" statutes on the books, unions that attain majority status through elections or voluntary card check agreements are required to represent all employees covered by a collective bargaining agreement, regardless of whether the covered employees pay union dues. In these contexts, a union must administer nonmembers' grievances and bargain on their behalf to gain contractual rights above statutory minimums, even though the nonmembers are not paying for these services. This state of affairs severely limits the capacity of unions to mobilize and collectively bargain. In 2014, the anti-union National Right to Work Legal Defense Foundation boasted of twenty-five states in which unions were thus hamstrung.[19] Not surprisingly, the ten states with the lowest union representation in the private sector are all among these Right to Work states. Of greater concern to organized labor is that several heavily unionized states with long histories of organizing in manufacturing (most recently Wisconsin, Indiana, and Michigan) have adopted Right to Work legislation in recent years. California, which is not a Right to Work state, ranks eighth in the nation, with 10 percent of the private sector represented by unions. The San Francisco Bay Area, the focus of this study, had a union representation rate of 10.7 percent in 2014 (Hirsch and Macpherson 2015).

What is the function of a labor union? Depending on whom you ask, you will receive a different response. The NLRA sees its mission as protecting some forms of collective activity around workplace concerns from employer interference. Despite this mission, collective bargaining rights in the United States are far more limited than in other countries, such as France, where unions may act as the collective voice of broader groups of workers (Lichtenstein 2002, 37; Fantasia and Voss 2004, 25). Critics of the emergent "business unionism" era in the United States note that US unions have generally evolved toward a focus on processing individual grievances rather than organizing new workers. Rick Fantasia and Kim Voss (2004) point to the growth of automatic dues and the role of the business agent in the postwar period to exemplify this contrast from earlier militant tactics. Bureaucracy was taking root: "Much less concerned with the mobilization of workers than it was to the servicing of existing labor agreements . . . the job of the business agent is mostly absorbed by the minutiae of job specifications and the arcane language of the legal contract (84)."

We should be careful not to paint an oversimplified picture of an automated or bureaucratic union. Few could look at the tremendous mobilization carried out by immigrant labor unions over the last decade and not be impressed by their vitality. Beyond organizing new contracts in key sectors such as the janitorial and grocery industries (Jayaraman and Ness 2005; Ness 2005), unions have also ventured into supporting alt-labor groups such as the National Day Laborer Organizing Network, the National Guestworker Alliance, OUR Walmart, and the Fight for $15 (a minimum wage group). Organized labor has also played an important political role in fighting for key protections that working people in the United States often take for granted (Murolo, Chitty, and Sacco 2001).

However, the majority of unionized workers I spoke with were disillusioned with their union.[20] Given the context of our conversations (that is, in a legal aid clinic where they were seeking additional assistance that their union was unable to provide), this is not surprising. Their experiences highlight some of the limitations of union representation and reveal cracks in the current systems of protection.

It will be useful to outline the process of union organizing before proceeding. When a union is engaged in a new campaign to organize, it must typically either conduct an election or come to an agreement using the more streamlined "card-check" process. To call an election under NLRA rules, the union must get 30 percent of workers in a unit to agree. In practice, though, many unions strategically wait until they have support from at least half of their workers to call a vote. This is more time-consuming than the "card-check" method, which calls for workers merely to sign cards rather than participate in a government-supervised election.[21]

Employers are formally restricted from interfering with some forms of collective activity, though they do have the power to shape worker attitudes. For example, "captive audience" speeches—that is, assemblies that employers require their on-duty workers to attend—are permitted, as long as they do not occur within twenty-four hours before the election. Critics argue that such gatherings are in essence one-way conversations that emphasize the risks of union membership, most palpably job loss. Employers, on the other hand, have argued that they are merely exercising their free speech rights (Secunda 2009; Masson 2004).

The power imbalance is so stark between management and the union that it makes formal restrictions on management interference extremely inadequate, especially with the threat of job loss hovering in the air. Indeed, a thriving industry of union-busting consultants guides employers as they chip away at labor power (Massachusetts AFL-CIO 2016).

Once a union overcomes these challenges and is in place, one of its key functions is to negotiate a collective bargaining agreement for workers. These agreements put in place contractual benefits and procedures that the employer must agree to for a set period, as well as the specific steps to be followed in a grievance procedure. The structure of unions at the workplace varies, but in general, a work unit that is represented by a union will have a steward on the "shop floor" to whom a worker can go for help and who will meet with the supervisor, then upper management if necessary. A grievance panel may be convened, and then typically arbitration follows. This process demands time and resources from union staff, and therefore not all worker complaints turn into actual—or successful—grievances. For example, as the Service Employees International Union communicates to its members, "the decision to go to arbitration will not be made lightly. It will depend on such things as importance of the issue (problem), severity of the case, cost, and chances of winning. Your investigation, notes, and reports will become really important when such decisions have to be made" (SEIU Local 521 2015). Despite its clear limitations, arbitration provides an opportunity for recourse, and in this context allows workers to have a representative present in disciplinary proceedings.[22]

Despite the advantages of union representation, many of the workers in my study who sought help from the legal aid clinic were upset with the outcome of their union grievance and/or frustrated by their inability to communicate with their union leadership. Some of the complaints I heard from unionized workers included: an employer refusing to pay the raise that the union negotiated;[23] the union refusing to address bullying management behavior;[24] the union's inability to help a worker get their job back after an arbitrary termination;[25] an unjust firing for having led a group in concerted activity to demand better conditions;[26] and a union's complicit refusal to address a sexual assault.[27] However, just as unions have limited resources, which they distribute among efforts to launch new campaigns, negotiate collective bargaining agreements, and address individual complaints from members, so do workers' rights clinics have to pick and choose where to invest the time of their staff, volunteers, and law students.

Consequently a busy legal aid clinic will often seek to steer workers toward other resources available to them. If a union-represented worker showed up at the clinic seeking help, she was first directed either to return to the union to file a grievance or to seek help from the National Labor Relations Board to lodge a complaint against the union. As with discrimination claims, however, the requirements to successfully win a charge before the board are significant. According to the agency, the board receives 20,000 to 30,000 charges per year from employees and unions (National Labor Relations Board 2015e). In 2014, of the 20,415 unfair labor practice charges that were filed, 6,504 were settled and 1,216 turned into a formal complaint (National Labor Relations Board 2015c). The number of cases actually heard in appellate court has gone from 298 in 1974 to only 13 in 2014 (National Labor Relations Board 2015b). It is possible that fewer cases in appeals signifies a more effective initial claim. Yet evidence does not reveal that a more efficient process has emerged. While the charges that are dismissed for lack of merit (28 percent), are withdrawn (35 percent), or are settled (34 percent) are handled fairly efficiently, the contested cases are often drawn-out affairs. In 2011–13, for instance, the median time from the filing of a charge to a board decision ranged from 508 to 653 days (Harper, Estreicher, and Griffith 2015, 70).

Unemployment and State Disability Insurance

A final set of protections available to some workers, and often not discussed in concert with other workers' rights policies, is unemployment insurance, a frequent issue that brought workers to the clinic. Unemployment insurance is a national program coordinated by the Department of Labor under the Social Security Act but administered separately by each state (State of California Employment Development Department 2015). The benefit provides "partial wage replacement to workers, who are unemployed through no fault of their own, while they conduct an active search for new work" (Legal Aid Society—Employment Law Center 2009). It is funded by employer contributions, and therefore employers have an incentive to avoid liability whenever possible. Furthermore, there are several categories of workers who may find themselves ineligible for benefits if they didn't pay into the system, were an independent contractor, or were otherwise self-employed.

During the period of this study, unemployment in the United States fluctuated between an annual average of 9.6 percent in 2010 to 7.4 percent in 2013 (Bureau of Labor Statistics 2015c). In California, unemployment was at 12.2 percent in 2010 (Bureau of Labor Statistics 2015a), dropping to 8.9 percent in 2013, but still among the highest rates in the country (Bureau of Labor Statistics 2015b). Of all the workers who participated in this study, only 160 (35 percent) were employed at the time of the initial survey, as were 34 (38 percent) of 89 follow-up interviewees. Given that workers had to meet low-income requirements to receive services at this legal aid clinic, it is not surprising that they were some of the hardest hit by the recent recession.

Workers in California must work through the Employment Development Department to apply for and manage their unemployment benefits. After a one-week waiting period, payments go out based on the highest earning quarter of the base period (the prior twelve months ending four to six months before the claim began). This means that while workers should apply for benefits as soon as possible, they must also be sure to have enough past earnings to qualify. In California, benefits are generally $40 to $450 a week, paid out for up to twenty-six weeks, and can also cover bouts of underemployment. For many workers I spoke to, an unemployment claim was often the consolation prize for broader, failed attempts to win unfair termination charges.

For those workers unable to return to work, state disability insurance provides another set of benefits. Workers could turn to this in the wake of an unsuccessful workers' compensation claim, while they awaited their workers' compensation claim to come through, or if they became injured outside of work (Legal Aid Society—Employment Law Center 2015d). State disability insurance claims require careful monitoring, often with the help of an advocate, to avoid receiving dual benefits that would have to be repaid later.

WHERE AND HOW DOES IMMIGRANT
LEGAL STATUS MATTER?

A third of the workers surveyed and interviewed for this study were unauthorized. The Immigration Reform and Control Act (IRCA) of 1986 was notable for creating a legalization program for an estimated three million undocumented immigrants, including those who had been in the country since 1982 and other seasonal agricultural workers. It was the last major broad-based legalization program in this country. IRCA also placed immigration enforcement in the hands of employers by instituting employer sanctions and verification requirements. Recognizing that this could lead to employer abuse, IRCA enacted protections against some forms of immigration status–related employment discrimination, creating the Office of Special Counsel at the Department of Justice, which works in coordination with the Equal Employment Opportunity Commission (EEOC).[28]

In theory, immigration status has little to no effect in legal terms on a worker's right to *file* a claim against workplace abuse. However, as held by the 2002 US Supreme Court decision in Hoffman Plastic Compounds Inc. v. the National Labor Relations Board, undocumented status precludes these workers from accessing some key remedies.[29] Specifically, this seminal case ruled that unauthorized immigrants cannot receive payment for the hours they would have worked if they had not been illegally fired for engaging in collective concerted activity. Though specific to the NLRA context, the case has caused negative ripple effects across a range of other statutory arenas (Garcia 2012b).

At the state and local levels, there seem to be divergent trends regarding undocumented workers' rights. Some states have sought to strengthen punitive policies against undocumented workers. For example, Arizona's Legal Arizona Workers Act (2008) has mandated that all employers use the otherwise voluntary federal E-Verify system, leading to a decrease in both naturalized and noncitizen Hispanic workers (Bohn, Lofstrom, and Raphael 2013). State courts have also differed in their rulings regarding undocumented workers' access to workers' compensation benefits (Chen 2013). Meanwhile, other states have expanded rights to undocumented workers. Most notably, California has recently strengthened sanctions against employer retaliation against undocumented workers (National Employment Law Project 2013).[30]

Still, there are a range of employment-related benefits that unauthorized workers simply do not enjoy. For example undocumented/unauthorized immigrant workers do not qualify for federal benefits such as unemployment insurance, even if they have paid into the system by using false identity documents. As a practical matter, this is due to the fact that they are not legally permitted to work and are thus "unavailable and unable" to return to work (Legal Aid Society—Employment Law Center 2015b). Other benefit areas are a gray zone. For example, because workers pay directly into state disability accounts, undocumented workers could also apply. However, as with any legal proceeding, undocumented workers I observed were often advised to tread carefully for fear of revealing their status and true identity. Further, unauthorized immigrants also pay into the Social Security and Medicare systems, but upon retiring are unable to collect these federal benefits. In 2010, undocumented workers paid an estimated $12 million into the Social Security Earnings Suspense File, which currently holds approximately $1 trillion worth of tax contributions (Kugler, Lynch, and Oakford 2013).

Despite this patchwork of formal protections, most undocumented immigrants face a constant threat of deportation in the United States. The Barack Obama administration gradually moved away from the previous administration's approach of staging public-spectacle raids that would arrest hundreds of workers at a time, as in for instance the 2008 raids on a poultry processing plant in Postville, Iowa (McCarthy 2009), and an electronics factory in Laurel, Mississippi (Bacon 2008). Instead, the administration has increasingly favored "silent raids," which use methods such as Social Security No-Match Letters, IRS audits, and the voluntary federal E-Verify program (National Immigration Law Center 2012) to identify undocumented workers. Immigration advocates argue that mandatory adoption of employer-based enforcement, such as E-Verify, runs contrary to workers' rights enforcement efforts and stifles fair business competition.[31] While the Obama administration invested in advancing the workplace rights of undocumented workers by empowering the Department of Labor's more aggressive enforcement of abusive employers, IRCA's legacy continues to enhance employers' power. Critics argue that these restrictive policies and employer sanctions work in direct opposition to the goal of holding employers accountable for worker protections.

Many undocumented workers on the ground remain wary of the separation of powers between the immigration enforcement arms of the federal government (the Department of Homeland Security and Immigration Customs Enforcement) and the many federal, state, and local government agencies whose job it is to hold unscrupulous employers accountable and protect workers' rights (Griffith 2011b; Griffith and Lee 2012). Various federal labor standards enforcement agencies do have memoranda of understanding that preclude Immigration Customs Enforcement (ICE) from interfering in their investigations, and legal scholars have argued in favor of additional coordination (Griffith 2011b; S. Lee 2009). However, as a practical matter, I found that workers often were fearful of the consequences even if they had already worked up the courage to come forward with a claim. When asked about the workplace climate of fear with regard to immigration enforcement, only one out of the 170 undocumented workers said she had experienced a raid at the workplace, and only four had employers who had threatened to call immigration authorities on them. And yet, this is not to say that these workers did not grasp the vulnerability of their position. Among all immigrant workers, 60 percent affirmed that they had "been treated unjustly at work" because of their immigrant status, and 86 percent agreed that "workers who don't have papers are more targeted for workplace abuse."

Beyond the workplace, it is important to contextualize the everyday lives of immigrant workers within the broader community, where they are also at risk for deportation. In California, undocumented workers were ineligible for drivers' licenses (although this changed in California under Assembly Bill 60 on January 1, 2015) and at the time of this study were still subject to coordinated enforcement through the Secure Communities program (despite the efforts of some localities to resist coordination with federal authorities). The recent passage of the California Trust Act, which limits hold requests in local jails and was meant to foster trust and cooperation with rights enforcement authorities, has only somewhat improved the situation ("California Trust Act" 2015).[32]

In the next chapter, I walk readers through the process of navigating the labor standard enforcement bureaucracy, and identify the various gatekeepers that workers must confront and the strategies they must develop for seeking restitution.

4

Navigating Bureaucracies

In this chapter, I examine the opportunities and pitfalls workers encounter while navigating the bureaucracy of workplace rights. The claimants I interviewed for this project faced a range of scenarios.[1] Some discovered that they had no legal protections under the law. Others found that although the law technically protected them, they lacked the evidence to prove that they were wronged. Even for those workers who were eligible for protections and had the necessary proof, the cost of filing a claim often far outweighed the potential benefits, and so they understandably backed out. Among those who were ultimately victorious, some settled for less than their claim was worth, and many never saw a dime once their employer declared bankruptcy or went missing. For each of these workers, mobilizing their workplace rights required tenacity and persistence.

To begin, I revisit the central logics of the labor standards enforcement regime. As the legal overviews in the previous chapter demonstrate, workplace protections emerged owing to the dogged efforts of labor movement and civil rights leaders, but also remain shaped by and embedded in the context of capitalist production. The claims-making process tends to treat the claimant as a cog in a machine. Rational bureaucracies adjudicate claims by relying on documented evidence, eyewitness testimony, and legal and medical expertise. For a worker's claim to be successful, either an individual or corporation must be held accountable—there is little room for nuance.

I next examine the ways in which workers develop their legal consciousness regarding their workplace rights. Just as important as learning what rights are available to them, a key part of workers' rights advocacy is imparting the brutal reality regarding the limited reach of the law. Keeping these limitations, and the requirements that a viable claim demands, in mind, workers consider the range of time and opportunity costs before deciding to come forward. A particular episode

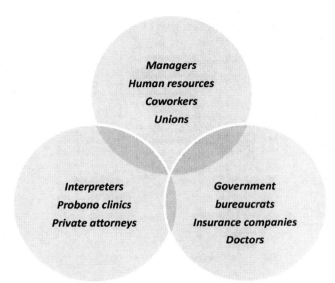

FIGURE 1: Gatekeepers and brokers in labor standards enforcement.

might mark the final straw for some, after years of enduring similar abuse. Obligations to family, and the limited options available in the broader labor market, shape whether and when workers decide to come forward.

In the final sections, I discuss the various actors whom workers encounter when they call for change. As discussed at the outset of this book, workplace actors (complicated hierarchies of managers and supervisors, human resources departments, coworkers, and in some cases unions), government enforcement bureaucrats (frontline staff, commissioners, judges), private sector ancillaries (insurers, doctors, interpreters), and especially attorneys (both pro bono and for-profit) stand guard at various stages along the bureaucratic route that claimants attempt to traverse. Here I focus on the role of institutional gatekeepers at government agencies, and the ancillary function of private companies and experts who verify and manage claims. I next discuss the importance of official brokers such as language interpreters and legal advocates, who are meant to assist workers in navigating these processes. Gatekeepers and brokers are present at every step of the claim, both steering and complicating the administrative process for the worker. I focus on the barriers workers face in each of these arenas and highlight the challenges workers themselves recount about the process.

I conclude by walking readers through the decisions workers make when deciding to end the claims process: whether and how to fight their way through the system, what to demand, and when to walk away. Some decide to cut their losses

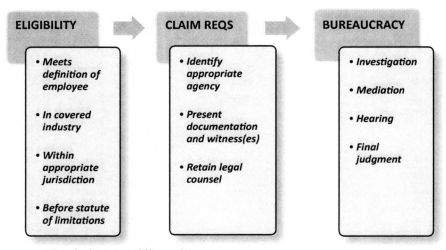

FIGURE 2: Standard process of filing a claim.

early on before a formal claim even ensues; for others, the long haul wears them down. Those who make it to the end have had multiple opportunities to avoid further wrangling with the bureaucracy and persevered nonetheless, though the time and opportunity costs involved often lead them to settle for far less than the law would otherwise technically grant them.

THE LOGIC OF CLAIMS-MAKING

The primary principle of any adjudicatory process is objectivity, that is, the assumption that the agency will evaluate all evidence equally and without prejudice. In reality, however, it is well known that various staff and administrative law judges throughout the system have particular leanings and predispositions. As proof of these idiosyncrasies, professional listservs are full of requests for information about the right strategy to use when coming before a given deputy labor commissioner or administrative law judge. Bias within the judicial system has received wide academic attention, and is at the core of the fields of critical legal studies and critical race theory.[2] Indeed, certain circuit courts are known for the political leanings of their legal opinions and precedents. Similarly, administrative law judges can develop a reputation for systematic bias. In the labor and employment law context this can shape who is allowed to bring a claim, what resources they must muster to do so, and the ultimate fate of that claim (Galanter 1974; Clermont and Schwab 2004; Kang et al. 2012; Nelson et al. 2016). As a result, workers who can afford an attorney, or whose claims have sufficient pedagogical worth to be taken on by a teaching clinic, have a significant advantage over those who choose to or must go it alone. Without legal help, most workers have no way of knowing which paths, or biased judges and bureaucrats, to avoid.[3]

Regardless, the labor standards enforcement regime is based on an assumption of rational objectivity, which is ostensibly attained through the use of documented evidence such as employer records, and in some cases even diaries and logs maintained by the worker. With this information in hand, an administrative law judge, or commissioner, should ideally be able to construct a clear timeline of events that establishes when the alleged harm occurred, for how long it persisted, and ultimately the amount of compensable damages the worker is owed. Recurring violations must be accounted for separately, and the time window of the harm suffered clearly outlined.

This process sounds fair enough, but for workers with erratic schedules, multiple jobs, and limited literacy or language proficiency, the mountain of evidence required to file a claim can be difficult to compile. Moreover, workers who have moved frequently, are not used to maintaining such documents, or simply never had them to begin with, can struggle with this process. In fact, one of the primary roles of legal aid clinics and their volunteers is taking the subjective experience of a worker and repackaging it in an evidence-based arsenal of documents that will help the client plead his or her case.

Eyewitness testimony can be crucial, especially in cases where formal documents may be unavailable (as with meal and rest period violations) or when measures are taken to hide unsafe work conditions or harassing behavior. A source on the inside is often precisely what hearing officers need to substantiate what is otherwise a he-said, she-said scenario. Convincing equally precarious workers to argue on one's behalf can be a very trying prospect. Though workers are required to swear an oath under penalty of perjury, many of the claimants I spoke to said that coworkers were easily bought off (or threatened) by their employer. Consequently, claims that require eyewitness testimony to be viable are often abandoned in favor of more cut-and-dried ones.

Another key factor in the claims process is the ability to assess culpability. In almost all cases, the employment relationship is divided neatly between plaintiff (workers) and defendant (employer). Liability and blame must be established in order to issue a remedy, a requirement that Samuel R. Lucas (2008) refers to as the "punitive imperative" (194). But in many areas of low-wage work, these roles are not clearly defined. Workers are not always considered employees, and complicated management hierarchies can obscure who is precisely responsible for the well-being of workers. A further structural problem has emerged in the US labor force due to the increased vertical disintegration of large companies, a problem David Weil, economist and current administrator of the Department of Labor Wage and Hour Division, characterizes aptly as the "fissured workplace." The increasing use of subcontractors has led to vagueness about the responsibility of joint employers (Weil 2014).[4]

Who is responsible for teaching workers about their rights and the minutiae of the law? On the one hand, labor standards enforcement agencies have developed outreach programs, with varying success. For example, the Department of Labor's We Can Help initiative was rolled out to address the rights of the most vulnerable workers, including immigrants (Department of Labor 2010). The Equal Employment Opportunity Commission has deployed various initiatives targeted at educating teens (US Equal Employment Opportunity Commission 2016b) and workers of color (US Equal Employment Opportunity Commission 2016a). However, more commonly, workers develop a legal consciousness about their rights from a more decentralized set of information sources.

DEVELOPING LEGAL CONSCIOUSNESS ABOUT WORKERS' RIGHTS

The extant literature on worker mobilization has generally focused on the ways in which workers learn about their rights, and the importance that access to this legal information and civic empowerment has for claims-making (see for example McCammon 2001; Albiston 2005a, 2005b; Gleeson 2009; Trautner, Hatton, and Smith 2013). I will focus here on the importance of social networks and past experiences of adversity and civic learning for imparting these lessons. I also highlight the importance of understanding the limits of the law, and examine the ways in which workers recalibrate the hope they may initially place in the law as an emancipatory tool.

Learning to Demand Rights

When speaking with workers, I started by asking them about how they learned where to go for help. Only 2 percent reported hearing about the workers' rights clinic from the television, radio, or newspapers. Six percent got their information from the Internet, and 8 percent from their church. Unsurprisingly, given that they had sought help, these claimants were a relatively engaged group. Thirty-five percent of respondents reported volunteering at a church (24 percent), school (10 percent), union (7 percent), or another organization (12 percent). For these workers, civic spaces were important venues for resource exchange, even if the focus of that exchange had nothing to do with worker or legal advocacy. Berta, for example, somehow managed to find time to do volunteer work at her church, a neighborhood group, and her children's school.[5] While she doubted that any of these experiences directly led her to seek legal help, she clarified the role that her network of fellow mothers played: "It's not like we go around passing out propaganda, but you know how us women are. We discuss. 'Hey, you know I had this problem,' this and that. 'Oh, why don't you go to this place, maybe they can help you, they're free.'" Indeed, a quarter of respondents credited friends and family as their major source of information.

These informal channels of information were particularly important for immigrant claimants. Whereas 16 percent of native-born respondents heard about the workers' rights clinic from a friend or family member, 31 percent of the foreign born (and 40 percent of the undocumented) received their information this way. Older immigrant workers, for example, often turned to their children for counsel. For example, when Ramón, a grounds manager for an apartment building, was fired after nearly twenty-one years of service, he asked his daughter for help.[6] Her boyfriend, a student at a local university, directed Ramón to the clinic: "He told me to go there, and what to do." For those claimants who spoke little English and had little understanding of how the system operates, the ability to tap into these wider networks was crucial.

Beyond information about available resources, some workers traced their decision to come forward directly back to the support they found in family and friends. For example Angelina, an undocumented single mother, had endured her supervisor's constant sexual harassment and was initially reluctant to speak out.[7] Then a discussion with her sister changed her mind: "My sister and I started to talk about it. . . . We decided to look for help. We didn't complain to the company, but looked for other help." After learning about the workers' rights clinic on the Internet and the radio, they made an appointment. Others, like Alonso, who developed a painful hernia while working at a popular restaurant, credited his mother's influence: "I [spoke up] because I get it from my upbringing from my mom. . . . It's essential to know that you have rights, that you can *do* things, and that you don't have to be fearful of others."[8]

Apart from a supportive social network, previous adversity can prove to be an excellent training ground for workers filing a claim. Take the case of Cristela, who had no use of her right arm due to a lifelong disability and had worked for years as an administrative assistant through a temp agency.[9] She eventually transitioned into a permanent position, where she covered the front reception area and did some office purchasing. About three years into the position, a spot in the actual purchasing department opened up, and she requested a transfer. She was told that she was not qualified because she could not "type fast enough," even though she was already performing the main functions of that position. Cristela felt that this slight was another instance of the ongoing harassment she received from her direct manager, who she felt was continually sabotaging her by overloading her with work and then writing her up for "performance issues." Her manager would also exclude her from key company functions and would regularly ignore Cristela's queries: "I would send emails; she would say she never got them." In one egregious instance, after arranging an entire room of office supplies that she was in charge of so that she could work around her physical limitations, she returned later to find they had all been moved back, many out of her reach. Moreover, she claims her order data was tampered with to make her look bad: "My data log sheet would not be accurate when I know I put it accurately on a shared drive that we would all share." She was, for example, called to account for extraneous orders she never placed: "But . . . there was no way to prove it or back it up."

Cristela also endured social isolation at work, and was told repeatedly not to interact or communicate with other coworkers, and was reprimanded unprofessionally in front of colleagues if she did. The hostile environment also meant she was shown none of the leniency others were granted in emergencies. As a single mom, Cristela would on occasion be late. Since her manager arbitrarily targeted many of her coworkers as well, they were reluctant to cover for her, and she was repeatedly written up. Ultimately, Cristela was never officially fired, but, in her view, "pushed out." She was told that a temporary worker whom she had trained to fill in for her while on leave was more efficient and would be retained instead. When Cristela complained to the president of the company, she was offered a two-week severance if she would quietly quit and not file a complaint.

Cristela attributed her determination to nevertheless file a claim to her past experiences, which, despite the suffering she endured, had one benefit: she had come into contact with a range of advocacy organizations: "I got myself out of a domestic violence marriage and went into the welfare system, and a workers' program, and then I . . . broke through those barriers and needed to get a job . . . with an income that supported me and my kids, and that wasn't happening because of my disability." Because of her long engagement with these support systems, Cristela refused to take the president's offer. She relied on the advice of a feminist disability rights advocate she had worked with in the past and decided to seek legal help. In the process of doing so, she also received training on how to present her disability to potential new employers in a proactive and empowering way.

Cristela's story is one of perseverance and resourceful advocacy. Her experience demonstrates the importance of social networks in learning about rights, but also in providing the support to carry that claim to fruition. Her intersectional experiences with women's rights and disability advocacy groups provided an added layer of support in the workplace arena.

Learning You Have No Rights

After individuals learn about workers' rights and become empowered to demand them, the next step is verifying what is available under the law. To begin, workers must come to understand the legal definition of their work arrangement and determine whether they are covered by relevant labor standards.[10] This can be a confusing process for some who may not understand the nuances of employment law. For example, as described in chapter 3, misclassification of independent contractors is rampant, which can render workers ineligible for basic rights such as minimum wage and overtime payments. Especially for workers in the informal economy, these legal categories can be muddled and leave workers without any recourse.

Take Benjamin, an undocumented Latino security guard who, in addition to his own hourly job, also ran a small security services enterprise for events such as weddings and *quinceañeras*.[11] He found himself with nowhere to turn when one of his clients issued him check payments with insufficient funds. Though he understood that he was not her direct employee, practically speaking, he felt that his workplace rights had been violated. At a minimum, the legal aid clinic was able to help him send a demand letter to the client, even though he was not technically covered under the California Labor Code. The letter went unanswered. When he returned to the clinic for help, the law students who had originally helped him were no longer there, and he was told that the clinic had no more options to offer. He subsequently gave up the claim. Though he clearly did not fit the criteria for an employee with wage and hour rights, Benjamin was out $1,000, and had to pay his crew members out of his own pocket. The requirements for filing a claim in superior court for breach of contract seemed far out of his reach.

Other workers find that they have been legitimately misclassified as independent contractors, but tend to overestimate the laws covering them as at-will employees. For example Dana, a Korean office worker in her thirties, sought legal assistance to complain about what she felt was an inappropriate level of instability in her job.[12] She had unknowingly entered into her informal production job as an independent contractor, and was paid under the table in cash. But Dana's primary complaints concerned not her pay, but the lack of a regular work schedule: "[My manager] really didn't do anything that was out of line in terms of a proper work environment, in terms of breaks, in terms of being paid. He always paid me. But I just never knew what the hours were going to be. So ultimately, I just felt very jerked around." When Dana visited the law clinic, a volunteer explained to her that her feeling of labor exploitation, however substantive it was to her, had no standing under the law. Dana persisted and sought out a private attorney who might assist. None called back. In the end she did not file a claim with a government agency because "it just seemed like a dead end." Such cases demonstrate the limits of legal labor protections. Though there was clearly little in the formal law that protected her, Dana nonetheless felt dissatisfied with her lack of control: "If [my manager] wants to give me no hours next week, there's nothing I can say because I'm an independent contractor. I'm paid under the table. . . . He didn't give me any reasonable promise to expect anything . . . so I just didn't have any power."

As bearers of bad news, such as in these cases, legal advocates nonetheless saw value in educating workers about their "phantom rights" (Eliasoph 2008). Indeed, much of what I observed during the workers' rights clinics I attended was workers coming to terms with the wide gulf between the unfair treatment they experienced and the actionable definition of a workplace violation under the law. This ranged from workers who felt they were owed a raise after years of stagnating at entry-level pay, to those who felt their loyalty to a company made their dismissal unconscionable after new management replaced their crew, and even those who sought what they felt were reasonable accommodations (such as time off to attend their child's event). One of the most common complaints involved managers' exacting and mean-spirited behavior that was nonetheless safely within the bounds of legal employer activity. Degrading comments, preferential treatment among coworkers, and exhaustingly fast-paced workflows were almost always well within the bounds of the law. In the minority of cases where a clear violation had been committed, the steep evidentiary requirements and resources needed to successfully pursue the case were far out of reach for most workers. In chapter 5, I explore the effect of these experiences on workers' sense of fairness and justice, and the lessons they took for future claims-making. In the remaining part of this chapter, I focus on the decisions workers make to move forward with a claim and the intermediaries they have to engage in the process.

Deciding to Mobilize Your Rights

Given the high stakes and difficulties of filing a claim, which are time-consuming and can cost precarious workers their jobs, why do some workers actually pursue this course of action? In this section, I focus on those workers who chose to exercise their rights. Many workers who came to the legal aid clinic had suffered a long history of poor workplace conditions, and, in some cases, outright and persistent abuse. Yet for the vast majority, this was the first time they had filed an actual legal claim. Workers often attempt multiple strategies to address the situation before finally turning to the legal aid clinic as a last resort.

Within this limited sample of respondents who sought help from a pro bono workers' rights clinic, 41 percent reported having tried to go it alone first. This percentage holds true across nativity and race/ethnicity, though immigrant workers were less experienced in the process of claims-making—15 percent having previously reported a claim, as compared to 23 percent of native-born workers. Certain workers were more likely to seek help from the start, including those who had been paid in cash (11 percent of respondents), 82 percent of whom were undocumented. Workers who had continued on at their job after initiating their claim (21 percent of respondents) were also more likely to proceed with caution by seeking legal help before attempting other strategies. Claim type also seems to matter, as the complexity of the claims process, and the barriers to entering it, can vary drastically from statute to statute. Unsurprisingly, wage and hour claimants (39 percent of respondents) were more likely to take a leap and proceed to the Labor Commissioner directly, while others with more complicated issues were more likely to seek a broker to guide them.

Whichever path they chose, a key concern for workers was the ripple effect from losing their job. Jose Luis, for example, was an undocumented restaurant worker whose wages were supporting an entire family in Oaxaca.[13] He was the youngest and only unmarried son of ten siblings, and he had a fierce devotion to his mother. After following his brother north and working in a small factory for a stint, he landed a job at a fast food restaurant: "I earned about $2,100 a month, and, well, it was enough to get by, to go out and buy things and food and have something to send home to my family." When Jose Luis lost his second job, he was left with only a few shifts at a fast food restaurant, picking up all the extra hours he could. In this economic context, persistent workplace safety concerns were a secondary matter; it was simply not worth making noise and risking getting fired.

Workers who labored alongside their own family members faced a unique set of considerations. For example, Julián worked on a line in a tortilla factory; his wife worked in the same unit.[14] For months there had been rumors of pending layoffs following an immigration audit. Even though he had previously joined other employees in demanding a long-overdue raise, he backed off when the firings started. He regularly worked unpaid overtime, had never sought medical attention for his various injuries, and chose to ignore constant verbal abuse from management because of his concern for his wife's job.

Claimants often waited for a threshold to be crossed before deciding to come forward: losing their job, needing income or medical care desperately, or reaching their breaking point after prolonged and severe harassment. That is, workers made strategic decisions regarding which abuses to push back against, which to set aside, and when to speak up. I found that workers were surprisingly informed about their rights, and even those who expressed palpable fears regarding deportation and job loss engaged in legal mobilization selectively and strategically, sometimes opting to hold employers accountable for some forms of injustice but not others. Undocumented immigration status created a contradictory and surprising dynamic. While undocumented workers feared losing their jobs or being deported, they also grew emboldened, feeling that their extreme precarity had left them with little to lose.

One such bold employee was Jeremías, an undocumented immigrant who worked for a catering company, often as the team captain.[15] He admits that despite the long and unpredictable hours, he liked his job of fifteen years: "We would always encounter different people, [which] was fun." For a long time, he felt he was neither mistreated nor unhappy at work. This all changed, however, when he caught his manager stealing tips from the workers' pool. He and two coworkers approached the manager to complain and were told brusquely: "I'm the manager and I can distribute the tips however I want."

Not long after he and his coworkers filed their complaint, Jeremías began to lose hours from his schedule, he assumes as a way to silence him from complaining to the company's owner, with whom he had a good relationship. This pattern persisted for nearly four months, until finally he was only given two days a week, about twelve hours total, down from the forty hours a week he used to work. Jeremías sought help from the California Labor Commissioner, who admitted that he had a good case but one that required additional legal assistance. He was referred to the legal aid clinic, where he received assistance in navigating the settlement conference process. Each appointment meant lost hours and lost pay from his new job, but he ultimately recovered $6,500. This was little more than half of the $12,000 his attorney calculated he was owed. However, in the interest of avoiding a lengthy hearing, and on his counsel's advice, Jeremías took the offer.

Through his years of experience in the hospitality industry, Jeremías has come to understand his basic rights as a worker: "Everyone knows [when abuses are occurring], I suppose, but many times we don't say anything to avoid losing hours, or to not harm our own bosses, because, look, I have absolutely nothing against this company's owner. He seems to be a good person. It's just that his management are the ones who acted against me, so I had to take action." When I asked Jeremías why he spoke up when he did, he explained that the writing was on the wall. His dismissal seemed imminent, and the steady loss of hours meant he was being pushed out: "I figured, well, if they are attacking me and intend to leave me without a job, then I'm going to file a legal claim so that they can pay me the overtime they owe me." Driven into a corner, he felt emboldened to act despite the risks.

GATEKEEPERS

Once workers move forward to file a claim, they must prepare for the labyrinth of bureaucracies that stand between them and the restitution they seek. After filing, claimants (and their advocates) will come face to face with a range of gatekeepers, including representatives of labor standards enforcement agencies as well as a whole host of private companies and experts enlisted to verify and manage their claim.

Government Bureaucrats

The first set of gatekeepers a worker will likely confront after initiating a formal claim is one of many frontline agency administrators who screen applicants and guide them through the initial stages of the claim. If they get that far, workers will also come face to face with hearing officers, who evaluate the facts of the claim and ultimately attempt to resolve the dispute through mediation or a hearing. Private sector ancillaries are especially common in the workers' compensation system, and while presented as customer service representatives at workers' disposal, their job is often to surveil workers and limit their monetary compensation.

At the beginning of a claim, one of the primary tasks of frontline staff is to determine whether a worker's general complaint falls under the specific protections within the agency's purview. Workers may understandably be confused by the existing matrix of labor standards enforcement jurisdictions, and they may be disappointed to find that their perceived injustice is not covered by a particular, or any, agency. Workers also frequently recounted their frustration in having to track down the right agency to cover multiple grievances, ranging from rampant wage theft (the California Labor Commissioner), to workplace harassment (the Equal Employment Opportunity Commission), to recurrent workplace injuries that required medical treatment (the Division of Workers' Compensation).

Workers must affirmatively demonstrate a violation of existing law in order to establish a claim. Given the difficulty of doing so, workers with multiple claims often take, or are advised to take, the path of least resistance during the claims process. Certain cases, such as unpaid wage claims, are far easier to make than, say, cases against unjust termination. Workers who attempt to proactively address retaliatory threats are frequently told that there is nothing to be done until they are actually fired, and even so only if it is undeniably clear that the firing is in response to their attempts to assert their rights. Claimants with no substantiating evidence are necessarily turned away, even when it is clear that the employer is cleverly averting the law. For example, Pepe was a nighttime janitor whose boss regularly put his overtime hours on the timesheet of Pepe's daughter, who also worked at the company, to avoid paying extra.[16] As Pepe explained of his efforts to rectify the situation: "When I got to the agency, they told me that the checks had to be in *my* name if *I* wanted to claim overtime. Since I had my daughter's [checks], they said that they could not do anything unless she testified on her own behalf." She was afraid do to so, and, as a result, the administrative bureaucracy was ultimately useless to him.

Discrimination claims are equally, if not more, difficult to pursue. For example, Marcia, a college-educated housekeeping supervisor, was fired for allegedly failing to call in sick according to company protocol.[17] This transpired just weeks after she had filed a complaint about ongoing sexual harassment from her manager: "It was a good relationship with my supervisor; [but] it was very complicated. He was very possessive. For example, he wanted me to call every day, or he wanted to be funny every day. He wanted to flirt every day. And I was like, oh, I'm tired of this. . . . He would stare. And he would say, 'Oh, I can't concentrate because I'm looking at [your breasts].'" Another coworker, who was also fired, filed a case with the EEOC and urged Marcia to do the same: "She won . . . but she kept documentation, wrote everything down." Marcia, on the other hand, was told that her case was not strong enough. Thus she poured her energy instead into fighting for the unemployment benefits she was initially denied. In the context of racial discrimination claims, Charlotte Alexander, Zev J. Eigen, and Camille Gear Rich (2016) refer to this as a process of "post-racial hydraulics," whereby a more complex and difficult-to-prove claim (such as discrimination) is replaced by a more straightforward one such as wage theft.

Once a claim has found its legal home, workers must come before a hearing officer or other administrative law judge, whose job it is to evaluate the veracity of the claim, mediate a solution if possible, and ultimately determine the terms of restitution. These actors are authority figures who hold the fate of a worker's claim in their hands. Unsurprisingly, workers whose claims had positive outcomes reflected positively on their administrative hearings. However, only 28 percent of workers who participated in follow-up interviews reported feeling satisfied with the outcome of their claims.

Some workers were frustrated by the formality of the courtroom setting. The semblance of civility was jarring for those who felt that they had been manipulated and discounted by their employer and the administrative process. Others felt abused by the process supposedly designed to protect them. Ronald, a cargo driver, had gone back and forth with the Workers' Compensation Appeals Board to settle a nearly two-decades-old injury claim.[18] He recalls being called "uncooperative" and "lackadaisical" by the judge. "I had to look up the word," he said, "and once I put it into English . . . [I see it means] that I'm lazy and argumentative. Well, let's see, I'm here [fighting] for my right to my benefits that I'm not being given for whatever various reasons. But so you call me argumentative? Well, how else do you people proceed here?"

Other workers were simply mystified by the process and unprepared for the disruptive inquiries into their lives. For many workers, the hearing was simply a blur. Juanes, for example, walked away stunned by the questions he encountered at his workers' compensation hearing.[19] As he recounts: "I felt confident, but then they started asking me questions that had nothing to do with my case . . . questions about my life, to see if what happened to me was actually a result of previous trauma, like if my father hit me, if he drank, things that really have nothing to do with my case." While disconcerting, his experience was a common protocol for workers seeking benefits under psychological claims.

Government agencies often *did* attempt to connect workers with additional help for their claims. Forty percent of the clinic attendees I spoke with had been referred to the law clinic by a government agency. If a worker does not speak English, is semiliterate, has difficulty filling out the relevant forms, or simply does not have the necessary evidence at hand, staff may send them to a community organization, such as the workers' rights clinic, for assistance. Such referrals reflect two constraints facing labor standards enforcement agencies. The first has to do with resources. Labor standards enforcement agencies are severely overworked and understaffed. During the economic recession, these staff were furloughed in California, and agencies experienced drastic cuts that impacted the administrative process. Aside from time, agencies also lack the linguistic resources to help all clients, translate documents, or walk them personally through the claims process. Second, the role of agency staff is not to advocate for workers but rather to objectively evaluate a worker's claim and determine if restitution is justified. Therefore, they are limited in the kind of help they can provide to workers, rendering them ultimately inadequate advocates, even if workers have nowhere else to turn.

The frontline staff of a bureaucracy are particularly important intermediaries because they set the tone for the claimant's experience. Practical resources such as language and cultural competency matter, as do a willingness to walk unfamiliar workers through the process. As part of my study, I attended state workshops for injured workers provided by the California Division of Workers' Compensation, which revealed to me the importance of outreach staff for decoding the intimidating nature of the Labor Code. Yet even these dedicated educators were limited in their ability to help workers who needed more than a fifteen-minute consultation. Given the few outside resources available and the complexity involved, institutional intermediaries such as legal aid clinics thus play an important role in fighting for the rights of workers (Gleeson 2012a). Most of these legal aid clinics, however, are themselves severely constrained in their capacity. While some offer clinics once a week, others can only offer assistance once a month, and oftentimes with volunteer attorneys who are only available via Skype. Considering that many companies have a team of attorneys on staff, even those lucky workers who secure representation are at a disadvantage.

In a perfect world, a single bureaucracy would examine the multiple injustices that low-wage workers are subject to on a daily basis. But our labor standards enforcement system is sprawling and messy, much like our work lives, which produce conflicts that do not always fall neatly into legal categories. The federal and state bureaucracies rarely coordinate with one another, and it is left to the claimant and her legal advocate to decide which route to take and where to invest limited energies. In complex cases involving multiple issues, workers must consider not only the strength of their respective claims but also their ability to take on yet another bureaucracy.

Experts and Technocrats

Beyond the government bureaucracy, injured workers especially must confront an additional set of private-sector actors to legitimate their claim. One of the oldest protections of workers' rights is workers' compensation insurance (described in chapter 3); state law mandates that employers carry this coverage to protect workers in the event of an injury. In exchange for receiving medical treatment and disability payments following an accident, workers lose the ability to sue their employer. Central to this process are private insurers (who insure the vast majority of workers not covered by the state fund) and an array of doctors who certify the extent of an injury and provide medical treatment. According to Ellen MacEachen (2000), the workers' compensation system is built on a series of mundane decision-making processes that have been at the heart of major reforms in California over the last decade. These processes, however mundane, have caused much debate, pitting workers' rights advocates against critics who decry those workers who, they argue, take advantage of the system. These critics have pushed certain reforms through that have made workers' compensation, on measure, more restrictive and cost conscious. A cornerstone of these overhauls has been perfecting the "objective" nature of claim determinations (as opposed to subjective determinations about pain and suffering, et cetera). The ultimate goal of workers' compensation is to repair the *specific* occupational injuries incurred while working in a covered position, or to compensate the worker accordingly, but no more.

Insurance adjusters and authorized medical experts are the main actors in this system. An insurance adjuster complies with workers' compensation law by evaluating an injured worker's claim for medical treatment and disability pay. These adjusters are the sole source of information for workers seeking to find out about their claim. Adjusters inform them about the timing and extent of disability payments, as well as coordinate approvals for medication, surgeries, and other therapies. One of the primary challenges facing claimants is the high rate of adjuster turnover. When a worker's claim is assigned to a new adjuster, this *can* be beneficial to a worker, especially if the replacement has skills or insight that the previous one did not. But more often than not, these changes come unannounced and feel arbitrary. For example, Dan, a firefighter with his own history of workplace injuries, recounted his efforts to help his disabled daughter with her claim following a violent armed robbery at the store where she worked.[20] At the workers' compensation appeals board hearing, Dan and his daughter learned for the first time that her adjuster had been changed: "They all showed up there and they said, 'Well, we don't know.' . . . The judge . . . called the workers' comp carrier and they said, 'Oh, well, her adjuster is no longer employed here.' Apparently . . . nobody knows what's going on with her case." Such occurrences do not inspire confidence, given the vital role that insurance adjusters play.

The bureaucratic distinction between the various types of doctors workers are required to see is also a major source of confusion. The doctor who treats the injured worker is almost never the claimant's primary care physician. A different doctor must certify the extent and compensability of the injury. These qualified medical examiners (QMEs), as they are called in California, settle the case by determining whether a worker has reached "maximum medical improvement" (MMI)—that is, "as good as it gets"—or is ready to be declared "permanent and stationary," at which point "a doctor can assess how much, if any, permanent disability resulted from your work injury" (State of California Department of Industrial Relations 2015a). QMEs, along with the "independent medical reviewers" (IMRs) who have replaced them in recent years, are intended to be objective experts who can evaluate the extent of an injured worker's disability and provide appropriate care, all while keeping insurance costs to a minimum.

These consultations with insurers and doctors often require claimants to submit to invasive and confusing lines of questioning. Moreover, workers can struggle to find an authorized doctor in their insurer's medical provider network.

Medication, therapies, and treatments all have to be authorized, which sometimes takes months. The process is slow and unpleasant.

The workers I interviewed also complained that these evaluations were done by doctors with only a passing understanding of their cases. Wendy's experience exemplifies this frustration.[21] As a public employee who had endured workplace bullying for several years, she had to undergo a grueling, eight-hour-long assessment when she filed a claim for psychological distress. The bullying, she claimed, had left her in a state of deep depression that kept her from eating for days at a time. After the QME performed the one-day evaluation, he declared that her condition was not workplace related. Seeing a copy of the report, Wendy was shocked: "When I read through his report, [there were] so many mistakes. He even mentioned someone else's name . . . he wrote the dates wrong . . . .[just] so many errors." The source of Wendy's distress, this doctor concluded, was not workplace harassment but rather her childhood in China during the Cultural Revolution, which was news to her.

Workers' compensation clients sent to occupational health clinics expressed particular frustration with the process of seeking medical treatment. Eleanor, a child care provider who had fallen and injured her thumb on the job, went to three doctors before she was told she needed a cast.[22] She recounted, "You have to wait for hours. You have an appointment, but it doesn't mean anything to them. You wait for hours to see somebody even with an appointment." Eleanor especially resented the lack of individualized treatment she received: "What I found really upsetting about this [one] specialist . . . [was that] if she spent five minutes with anybody, that was a very long time. She spent thirty seconds with you. . . . You were like cattle. You were sitting in a long row of chairs outside of her office. She would come to the door and she'd call 'Eleanor,' and she would leave the door [open], like HIPPA privacy laws didn't apply to her."

The low quality of care, questionable professionalism, and baffling medical processes are even more problematic because contingent workers who become injured at work very rarely have health insurance. More than half of low-income, noncitizen immigrants are uninsured, and those who are unauthorized are ineligible for means-tested public health insurance, with the exception of emergency room care (Ku 2006; Portes, Light, and Fernández-Kelly 2009) or Affordable Care Act subsidies.[23] As such, these workers relied exclusively on the workers' compensation system for their care, inevitably blurring the line between occupational injury and general health needs.

BROKERS

Beyond the gatekeepers meant to adjudicate and manage claims, there are several actors in the system whose intent is to help workers succeed. Some of these are meant to be funded by the government and private entities (such as insurers and hospitals), while legal advocacy for low-wage workers often relies on a fragile network of pro bono assistance.

Language Interpreters

Workers with limited English proficiency struggle to communicate in the rights enforcement bureaucracy. In California, where I conducted my research, 37.6 percent of the population is Latino, and of the 43.5 percent of residents who speak a language other than English at home, more than half speak Spanish. State legislation attempts to accommodate this diverse population as a matter of equal access to justice. Federal agencies, for instance, have adopted similar language access plans (LEP.gov 2015).[24] However, the availability of bilingual staff varies widely from jurisdiction to jurisdiction, the recent recession limited new hires, and retirees are not always replaced. Nonetheless, agency-appointed interpreters are in theory readily available, and phone bank translator services help fill the gap. Again, though, the quality of these services varies significantly.

For some workers I spoke with, accessing language resources was a seamless process. When Lucrecia, an undocumented restaurant worker who filed a claim for unpaid overtime, attended her Labor Commissioner hearing, she was pleased to find that the entire settlement conference proceedings were held in Spanish.[25] Others had more frustrating experiences with either the system or the individual interpreter. Reynoldo for one was wholly dissatisfied with his interpreter.[26] He recounts: "I asked for an interpreter . . . [and] the experience was horrible, to not be able to express with the proper words of one's own what I wanted to say. . . . To be honest, the person who went to translate, I don't know, I don't feel that they expressed everything I wanted to say." Regardless, Reynoldo had no choice but to rely on the subpar interpreter.

For those who speak neither Spanish nor English, translation services can be even less reliable. For example, many of the agricultural workers who come to the California Central Coast clinic speak indigenous languages such as Triqui and Mixtec. Court-appointed interpreters have to be certified in order to participate in official proceedings, but few indigenous-language-speaking community members meet this standard. This dearth of interpreters leads to complex, three-way translation sessions that rely on multilingual family members to convey complicated legal information. Naturally much gets lost in translation. In my experience agencies rarely had staff language capacity beyond English, and few offices had staff who spoke even languages that served dense immigrant populations (such as Chinese and Vietnamese in California).

Paperwork proves to be another obstacle. Injured workers in particular complained that they were unable to understand the documents they received in the mail. Clinic clients often arrived with stacks of paperwork, some unopened, that they needed help understanding. Moreover, they would often have to respond to insurers by writing in English. Octavio had naively assumed that since his adjuster communicated with him in Spanish, and sometimes wrote in Spanish as well, that he could respond in kind.[27] When he composed a letter and never received a response, though, he found out that "the letters have to be in English, even if they know exactly what I am asking for." This is a difficult task for a worker who is far from fluent and has many other obligations.

Legal Advocates

To pass through this gauntlet of bureaucratic, medical, and linguistic barriers, the claimants in my sample turned to clinic lawyers for help, sometimes at the beginning of a claim, but more frequently when the process had stalled. Attorneys help workers make sense of the options before them and are especially important for facilitating communication with bureaucratic gatekeepers. But finding and retaining counsel can be challenging, and workers recounted significant frustrations in communicating with and trusting the counsel they did retain. As such, attorneys, though they are a crucial asset, are yet another aspect of the rights bureaucracy that claimants must learn to manage.

Attorneys provide crucial assistance in helping workers understand what rights the law affords them. They do identify promising cases, but they frequently have to explain to claimants that they in fact have no legal basis for protection. Essentially, attorneys provide workers with the information necessary to determine whether the costs associated with pursuing their claim are worth it. They can also help workers communicate with reticent, or outright obstructionist, employers and insurers, as well as compile an evidentiary paper trail and solicit eyewitness testimony. Most important, especially for limited-English-proficient workers and those unfamiliar with the bureaucracy, attorneys act as brokers. Beyond legal advice, attorneys can alert workers to what they can expect from a particular judge, which doctors will be sympathetic to their condition, and how to deal with notoriously stingy insurers.

Ultimately, attorneys help workers determine the difference between what they are theoretically owed under the law and what is actually winnable. Berta, an undocumented restaurant worker, discussed how the legal aid clinic counseled her on which aspects of her wage claim were winnable (unpaid hours worked) and which were a stretch (break penalties): "The [law student] recommended that I fight for less [and] that I not fight for all of it, because I might lose."[28] Similarly, Adán reluctantly heeded his attorney's advice to settle, realizing he really had no other option.[29] He recalled the lawyer explaining to him: "Look, they're offering you $3,600. . . . Take it. Because if we fight for more, more time will pass, and all of a sudden they may not give you anything." Attorneys know that with these claims, sometimes discretion is the better part of valor.

At other times, no compensation at all is forthcoming, and attorneys become the bearers of bad news for workers who assume they have more protections under the law than they actually do. This is a major source of dissatisfaction for claimants, who see little difference between the flaws in the system and the perceived ambivalence of their attorneys. This was the case for Macarena, an undocumented retail worker who, en route to work early one morning, was hit by a semi-trailer truck that had swerved off the road.[30] She spent three days in a coma, was hospitalized for three months, and ultimately lost her job. Her manager, a sympathetic man who visited Macarena in the hospital, vowed to save her job until she was able to return. But when Macarena supposedly failed to submit the appropriate paperwork while on leave, she was let go and told that she would have to reapply and reverify her legal status through the E-Verify program. Another supervisor encouraged Macarena to find an attorney who could help her. After talking to various private attorneys, she found the legal aid clinic, which confirmed that her failure to submit her request for a leave of absence within the required thirty days was valid grounds for dismissal. Without work authorization, Macarena knew she would not be rehired. However, she was frustrated by the conflicting messages she received from the law clinic: "They could have said, 'You know what, there's nothing we can do for you,' . . . but they told me that they would call me later . . . that they would not abandon me." Macarena claims that she never received a call back. She ultimately gave up seeking help, deciding that there was nothing that could be done even with further legal help.

Gaps in the law are not the only factor leaving workers unprotected. Due to resource constraints, pro bono legal aid groups are generally limited in their ability to help workers beyond offering initial information and assistance. Moreover, funding requirements may limit their clientele to those who meet strict low-income guidelines. Resource constraints also may force a clinic to focus on less complex cases or on those cases where volunteer lawyers can offer their assistance. Furthermore, clinics affiliated or run by universities must balance their pedagogical goals with the needs of the clients who walk through the door. As a result of these restrictions, the vast majority of law clinic attendees will not be able to retain direct counsel to help them personally navigate their cases. In more complex cases, workers may be referred to a for-profit attorney who can provide long-term personal attention. Frequently these attorneys operate on contingency (that is, workers do not pay until and if they win a case), counting on winning their fees and other damages from the defendant (employer).[31] Attorney fees can vary from arena to arena, though they are typically limited by state law in workers' compensation cases to 15 percent of the final settlement.

Outside of the workers' compensation system, a select few attorneys will take a case on contingency. Profit considerations loom large. For those cases where they are assured a set percentage of any final settlement, attorneys must consider whether the value of any future settlement outweighs the time and costs that they will have to invest. In cases where the evidence is thin, prospects for victory are dubious, or the final payment is too insignificant, finding an attorney can be extraordinarily difficult. Workers who have had poor experiences with their initial legal counsel can find it nearly impossible to locate a replacement because the new attorney may not want to split an already meager settlement with the old one. Workers who live in remote areas, or who do not have their own transportation, are further limited by the supply of available attorneys willing to take their cases on contingency.

Though a lawyer is entirely optional in most aspects of the labor standards enforcement process, it has become nearly impossible to navigate the system without one. This makes the role pro bono legal providers play for low-wage workers who cannot afford a private attorney even more important.[32] Their work is much appreciated within the claimant community. When asked if they would go back to the law clinic offering pro bono service for help if another issue arose, sixty respondents (72 percent) said they would. Doris, a low-level administrator, was one of them.[33] She was fired by a major health care provider for taking extended lunches, a common practice she and her coworkers had long used to adjust for extra time spent on backlogged cases. What she most appreciated from the clinic was the structured way that law students walked her through what to expect at the hearing: "I don't think anything could have made it better because everything was so planned out. They told you to go to the court, pick up your packet of information. . . . Let's get together and go over the questions that the judge is going to ask you. I mean pretty much everything was laid out for me. It was like clockwork, so there were no surprises."

Doris was fortunate in receiving such help. Some workers without an attorney were unable to push their cases forward, even when they possessed glaring evidence of employer misconduct. Cesar was fired along with more than a dozen other Latino truckers, then replaced en masse by the same number of Sri Lankan drivers (recruited from the owner's networks) whom he and his coworkers had trained only days earlier.[34] While he saw his case as strong, the law clinic could not afford to take it on: "I told them that we should go to San Francisco, because the case was strong. . . . I pleaded with them, but they didn't want to. She [the attorney] explained, 'Look, if the company was 500,000 workers [I might take the case], but it's only 350.'" Cesar was told that it was best to attempt a settlement instead of pursuing a formal claim. Though he did ultimately receive a modest sum, he felt indignant that the facts of the case could not stand on their own.

Though most workers in my study sought legal advice with pro bono and legitimate private attorneys, several respondents recounted taking desperate measures with non-attorney, for-profit groups. These groups are staffed by professional helpers who purport to assist otherwise desperate workers while stopping short of giving legal advice. (In their legal slipperiness, they resemble the fraudulent *notarios* prevalent in Latino communities.) For example, Cathy was an architect who worked through a private contractor at a government facility.[35] She had had a long and varied career in the region, with previous positions as an adjunct instructor at a local college and as a screener at an airport, where she also organized as a union steward. In her architecture assignment, Cathy found herself in a typically all-male Silicon Valley environment and faced constant harassment from one of her supervisors. This supervisor one day accused her of arriving to work drunk, a claim she vehemently denied and viewed as yet another tactic to embarrass and marginalize her. A month after she complained to the parent company, she was told that her work was unsatisfactory and her contract was terminated. As an at-will and subcontracted employee, Cathy had no recourse despite her many efforts to find a lawyer willing to take her case.

Cathy eventually turned to a non-attorney "labor specialist," a futile investment she later regretted making. Cathy proactively sought out another resource once it became apparent that securing an attorney was unlikely: "I went online [and found a] labor specialist in the city. She represented one person I know, a supervisor who got terminated." Cathy tracked the labor specialist down to see if she was interested in working with her. When I asked Cathy about her experience with this woman, who charged her hourly rates lower than an attorney's, she admitted that although the specialist was helpful, she could not play a formal role in representing her: "She knows her stuff, but she's not a lawyer so they don't take her seriously. . . . She didn't have the law degree and she didn't have a license, [so] no dice, nobody cares. They [the employer] just laughed."

While this non-attorney "labor specialist" provided Cathy with admirable support, it was clear that there were some areas of misunderstanding. For example, Cathy, who had been fired for allegedly showing up to work drunk, was told that she couldn't be fired if she did have a drinking problem. The company would have to put her through alcoholic counseling. About this advice, Cathy joked: "I thought, god, maybe I should have just said yeah, I've been drinking every day because I can't stand the job." It is possible that the legal specialist was referring to EEOC guidelines on disability accommodations for employees with addictions under the American with Disabilities Act (US Equal Employment Opportunity Commission 2011). This, however, would likely be exceedingly difficult to claim without the help of an attorney. Moreover, it wasn't even true or applicable. Therefore, in effect Cathy paid for advice that didn't make much sense given her situation. Such are the pitfalls of hiring these "specialists" operating on the margins of the system.

This is not to say that the workers' relationships with actual attorneys were always flawless and free of challenges. Counterintuitively, having an attorney could delay the claims process by preventing workers from directly engaging with agency staff. Once workers retained an attorney, insurers and enforcement bureaucrats were careful not to communicate directly with workers. For this reason, some savvy workers chose to delay the process of hiring an attorney as long as possible. Vicky, a retail worker, was at her wits' end with her workers' compensation claim and unsure whether to sign the latest set of papers sent by her insurance company.[36] She contacted an attorney, who explained that once she hired him, her claim would take a different route. Attorney-represented workers go through a different system to choose qualified medical examiners and their cases often move more slowly. Therefore, because she had time while on disability to dedicate to her case, and because she had experience from previous legal proceedings, she decided to go it alone for a while longer, even though it required facing off against her adjuster and company lawyer at several appeals hearings. She made an informed decision to sacrifice representation for a speedier conclusion.

In general, the workers I interviewed reported having complex relationships with their attorneys. Clients frequently complained that they were unable to get information from their attorneys or that the attorneys seemed disengaged.[37] The profit motives built into the rights enforcement system meant that workers were fundamentally skeptical of whether they were getting a fair shake. For example, Susana, a victim of sexual harassment, eventually settled her case but confided to me that she was unsure of whether her private attorney did all he could to fight for her.[38] Confused by what actually transpired in her claim, she voiced her frustration: "Supposedly he took care of everything, but we didn't even go to court. I wasn't very satisfied with him." From her perspective, the settlement out of court was evidence that a deal was struck that was biased against her. His "cheap rate" further concerned her: "He told me, 'I'm only going to charge you $2,000.' Instead of charging me what he *should have*, I think that they [her employer] gave him something under the table. So, I don't trust it." Regardless of whether such an illegal transaction actually occurred—which is highly unlikely—Susana's dissatisfaction reveals that although monetary settlements are a practical aspect of restitution, they are only part of a worker's evaluation of justice, as I discuss in the next chapter. Ultimately, dissatisfaction with the legal service provided pointed to a broader dissatisfaction with the system itself.

CLOSING A CLAIM

Per one information and assistance officer's mantra, "All claims must come to an end."

Bringing a claim to a close is a crucial, exhilarating, and sometimes emotional and painful part of the process. Cases close when workers drop their claim, the parties reach a settlement, or a judge issues a decision. For those who are victorious, collecting restitution presents another challenge, as employers will not always pay.

Those who declare bankruptcy, for example, are able to avoid ultimate liability. In these cases, the stark contrast between the ideal and the actual outcomes leaves many workers torn over whether justice has been served and questioning what they have ultimately gained in fighting for their rights.

Because the process is so lengthy, risky, and complicated, there comes a point for all workers when they have to decide whether to keep fighting, settle, or drop the claim and move on. Above all else, workers in my study valued their time, and the opportunity costs associated with navigating the bureaucracy often proved too high. Take Milo, whom we met in chapter 2, an undocumented temp worker who was one of fifteen fired during a rash of immigration audits at a bakery.[39] Milo was furious at the way his employer publicly humiliated him, and sought to recover the years of unpaid wages he had accumulated. But a year after initiating his claim, he decided to step away: "It's just a waste of time. I decided to go back to work. . . . I had lost too much time . . . coming and going [to appointments]. What I really wanted was to just find a job."

Lino, another undocumented laborer, found that he likewise didn't have time for the long process ahead.[40] He had worked on a landscaping crew whose owners were lying about their profits (on which they based their workers' pay) and illegally deducting business costs (such as portable toilet rentals) from their checks. Ultimately most of Lino's crew pursued a formal claim through the California Labor Commissioner and won. But Lino couldn't afford to take the necessary time off from his new job and was wary about revealing his claim to his employer for fear of being branded a troublemaker. When I asked Lino if he wanted to reopen his case he said, "Sure, I want to," but then explained that to do so would not be practical, given his responsibilities to his wife and young child.

While some workers made a conscious decision to abandon their claims, other workers become overwhelmed with the other obligations. For example, Melita, the longtime preschool teacher we met in chapters 2 and 3, was harassed and ultimately fired for supposed insubordination, then quickly replaced by a lower-paid teacher with less experience.[41] She promptly visited the California Labor Commissioner in an attempt to recover her $4,000 in unpaid vacation pay: "When you know there is an injustice, when your rights have been trampled, you have to speak up." But after being directed to a series of agencies and referred to expensive lawyers, she eventually dropped her claim to focus on earning money to pay her mortgage, as her house had slipped into foreclosure.

For others, ending their claim seemed the best thing to do for their physical and emotional health. Adán, mentioned earlier in this chapter and in chapter 2, took a $3,000 settlement (less than half of what the law said he was owed) to finally bring his case to an end, citing old age, a history of heart problems, and lingering depression.[42] Merlín, an undocumented machine operator from Peru who was injured on an assembly line, described the dispiriting, and often debilitating, claims process thus: "To tell you the truth, they wore me out. . . . I saw that there was not much else that could be done."[43]

It is crucial to note, however, that for those workers who did manage to file a formal claim, a positive judgment alone did not guarantee that they received restitution. Employers use a number of tactics to avoid liability, such as closing their business, changing their name, or filing for bankruptcy (Cho, Koonse, and Mischel 2013). Alfredo was an undocumented mechanic who had been fired, along with his entire crew, after they stood up to their manager to request their unpaid wages, contest their lack of breaks, and demand an end to his egregious sexual harassment of the shop's receptionist.[44] Subsequent to their termination, the men filed claims with both the California Labor Commissioner and the Equal Employment Opportunity Commission. Alfredo's wage and hour claim was promptly scheduled for a settlement conference and resolved quickly. The employer proposed a repayment schedule, but after making only two or three quarterly payments, the employer filed for bankruptcy and the checks never resumed. Such is one example of how an unscrupulous employer and their attorneys can work the system.

Bankruptcy is a tactic that has long been used by employers to shield themselves from culpability. Making matters worse for employees, when an employer files for bankruptcy, there is little that the state agencies can do to compel compliance. Yael, whom we met in chapter 2, recalled the threats frequently lodged by the owner of the landscaping company he worked for: "He didn't like when we would talk to him about our rights. . . . He would say that he would fire you if you didn't like it. He was always threatening us."[45] As soon as Yael filed a claim, the owner filed for bankruptcy and was shielded from liability, and thus an overt abuser effectively acted with impunity.[46]

Workers often unfairly faulted legal aid clinics for their inability to compel an employer to pay out an agreed-upon sum. For example, Lucrecia was frustrated by her experience with the restaurant owner who owed her overtime: "In reality, there was no settlement. . . . Yes, the agency helped us, but they weren't able to help us reach an economic settlement, nothing. . . . [The owner] declared bankruptcy . . . [and] we got nothing. He declared bankruptcy, and the case was closed."[47] But in reality, there was little an attorney could do. Indeed, in conversations with many public interest attorneys, who themselves made far below the living wage for the region and who continued to do this work out of a pure passion for justice, they stressed the limits of their power to help. They were constrained by meager resources, by the legal system itself, and by not having enough time to deal with every worthy case. In the next chapter, I discuss the ways in which these narrow routes to victory shaped workers' well-being in the long run.

5

The Aftermath of Legal Mobilization

This chapter reflects on the nature of success, and failure, for workers engaged in the claims-making process. First I examine what happens after workers come forward to exercise (what they believe are) their workplace rights. What do workers gain and lose in this process? Do they get to keep their jobs? If so, do workplace conditions improve? If they don't, how easy is it to get another job? And are the new jobs generally a step up or a step down? For those who lose their jobs and struggle to recover, what does the social safety net have to offer, and how do workers cope in the interim period of unemployment? I also document the impacts of workplace abuse on workers' families, in the United States and abroad. I discuss how beyond their financial effects, workplace abuse and the processes of fighting for justice also affect workers' mental and emotional well-being, as well as their relationships. Finally I consider how the labor standards enforcement process either empowers or silences workers. What, in sum, are the lessons workers take away from the experience?

My central thesis here is not simply that workplace violations can have long-lasting effects on precarious workers. Rather, I argue that workers who attempt to contest their workplace abuse through the labor standards enforcement process are often embedded in a series of overlapping precarious structural positions that can unravel quickly and with devastating effects. This can include a struggle to find housing, fear of violence in low-income neighborhoods, the loneliness of social isolation, and, for some, physical and mental health challenges. Thus, labor exploitation, be it unlawful or not, is in part a symptom, and not simply a cause, of social stratification. The experiences of low-wage workers attempting to file a workplace violation claim therefore provide a window into the quotidian challenges these workers face, especially in one of the most expensive housing markets in the country.

I begin with the stories of two women, Laney and Yadira, who lost their jobs after what they believed were a series of injustices. The spiral effect this had on their personal health and family well-being reveals the weight that a particular claim can hold for a worker struggling to get by.

TWO PRECARIOUS LIVES

Laney's Story

I start with Laney, a formerly homeless woman who had struggled with addiction and was living in San Francisco when I met her.[1] After attending rehab and searching for a place to live, she landed a job as a live-in staff member at a drug treatment center. During her ten years in this position, Laney filled a number of roles, including busser, waiter, maître d', and front desk clerk. The job carried the much-needed benefit of room and board, but this meant that ongoing harassment from management and some coworkers ultimately affected both her work *and* housing situations. At one point, Laney remembers her manager, with whom she was feuding, screaming, "You're being a problem. You know what I do with problems? I get rid of them." Laney had few other options: "I had worked on and off at different outside jobs . . . but I didn't have anything consistently that would support me. You get used to not paying rent, you know? . . . So I valued the housing so much that I would just keep my mouth shut."

Laney did indeed keep quiet for months, until she learned one day that a cook with whom she worked posted her personal information on Craigslist with sexually explicit solicitations. It was here that Laney decided that this was sexual harassment that had crossed the line. Laney reported the harassment to her manager, who did nothing despite acknowledging that Laney's allegations were likely true. Laney then filed a complaint with the San Francisco Police, who also would not pursue the case. When she finally went to the owner of the treatment facility, she was soon after fired. The reason given for her dismissal depicted her as a problematic employee, citing her recent complaints about food and her public reprimanding of a coworker who forged a supervisor's signatures. She had also vocally denounced ongoing drug use among employees, demanded pay for unpaid hours, and had become an overall target for her manager, who was happy to be rid of her complaints.

All told, Laney sought help from a wide array of advocates, including a local shelter, the local police, the Department of Labor, the California Department of Fair Employment and Housing, and the federal Equal Employment Opportunity Commission. Coworkers, fearing retaliation, were of little help. Her aggressor was eventually fired after harassing another resident, but Laney was still out of a job. At this point, Laney had a diabetic episode and passed out from low blood sugar, fracturing her face. It was during her three-week stay in the hospital while recovering from two surgeries that she was evicted formally from her housing at the treatment facility where she had worked.

Looking back on the ordeal, Laney wonders what she could have done differently. For one, she laments that she knew too little too late, and wished she could have advocated for herself more effectively. She also wishes she would have "taken action more quickly," and kept more detailed records that would have allowed her to demand her full wages due at the Labor Commissioner. Despite these lessons, the price Laney has paid in the short term has been exceedingly high. She was never reinstated at her job and spent more than seven months homeless. During this time she relied on disability income, had to constantly fend off debt collectors, and had medical necessities she couldn't afford (for instance glasses and dental work). All her belongings were placed in storage, and she couldn't afford a truck to retrieve them. A year after first contacting the Equal Employment Opportunity Commission, Laney checked back in. They had just gotten around to assigning her claim to an investigator.

As Laney's story attests, the impacts of workplace abuse can be long-lasting and compounding. Yet much of what workers such as her experience exists in a gray zone of unlawful abuse and everyday, perfectly legal exploitation.

Yadira's Story

Workplace abuse and job loss can also set off a cascade of events for workers' families. This was the case for Yadira, whose case I introduced in chapter 2. I spoke with Yadira at her modest duplex behind a steel fence on an unpaved road in East Palo Alto.[2] She lived there with her disabled husband and young children, who looked on curiously while I spoke with their mother. Yadira had worked for a janitorial company for nearly five years, during most of which time she earned $8.75 per hour. By the time we met again, Yadira was tired and overwhelmed from her job and the drawn-out dispute. She cleaned four floors of a large building on her own and could barely keep up.

Yadira's central complaint was about wages. Despite a union contract that required pay of $12 per hour, her employer dismissed this obligation, and her union concurred that Yadira had misunderstood that her work zone was not covered. This "misunderstanding" frustrated her immensely: "I just never understood what it meant that I worked in the wrong zone." In response to her complaint, Yadira was given a one-time twenty-five-cent raise, which she later learned was supposed to have occurred annually.

Yadira's failed demand for a wage increase was only the start of her problems. She quickly became a target for dismissal. Indeed, soon after she filed a grievance, she was called in by her manager and accused of having used a copier without authorization: "I had been carrying a letter from my brother in the trash cart, and it fell out in one of the suites." Earlier that day, her brother had brought her a letter confirming the $500 a month he sent her, which she had to take as proof of income into the food stamps office to reapply for benefits later that week: "[When] they told me that I had used their copier, I told them, 'I don't even know how to use your copier.'" Yadira insists that she was framed: "They said they found the [letter] in the copier. That was a flat lie. . . . I know very well that they were trying to get rid of me. I was about to mark five years there, and it was time for them to give me a raise, so they got another person that they could pay $9 an hour."

The day following the incident, Yadira was called into the office, where a human resources representative gave her a form to sign acknowledging her dismissal, which she refused to do, and gave her a final check. It was all a blur for her: "At the time, I was very sad, and felt horrible. I'm the only one who works in my house. My husband is injured, and he helps me with the kids at home. So I was the only source of income. They [management] have no idea—it didn't even matter to them—the damage they were doing." Yadira was rightfully indignant that after so many years with the company, she would be fired over a single alleged error: "OK, I get it, you could have given me a warning. That I would understand. But just to fire me like that didn't seem fair. I felt so frustrated and mad and just bad." Yadira pleaded her case to an executive in the building where she cleaned. She brought her son to translate, but was told merely that she had the tenant company's regrets. When her subcontracting firm found out that she had visited the building, it threatened to call the police on her if she returned.

The union initially set up a meeting with human resources to attempt to mediate a solution and vowed to follow up with Yadira, but it never did. (Yadira told me that she wasn't the first to be fired without cause and to leave bitter and disillusioned with the union.) A claim filed with the National Labor Relations Board never went anywhere, to her knowledge. To complicate matters, because she was represented by a union, private attorneys and the legal aid clinic had little to offer her: "I was desperate. I knew I wouldn't find a job right away, and I didn't for another two and a half months. I didn't have the money to pay rent. It was a very difficult time for us." With help from her three brothers, and relying on the vacation time she was paid out, Yadira made things work, though not without a toll: "It was traumatic for me. I felt very bad, horrible." Yadira's firing came just as the economic crisis hit, increasing her already burdensome struggles. Her family had only recently moved to the relatively safer, and more expensive, East Palo Alto; they had fled San Jose after Yadira's son was shot in the head by a gang member. Their rent rose from $950 to $1,500: "I felt like there was no exit. I couldn't find a solution. I didn't know what to do."

Despite it all, Yadira seemed hopeful: "Just because all this has happened, including at work, I'm not going to let it keep me down or hold me back. . . . That's my mentality. Of course I am sad at times, and think I can't escape, but then I find courage." Yadira has no plans to return to Mexico, although all the rest of her family still lives there: "It's bad over there. The job situation is bad, it's poorly paid, and they rob you." Yadira considers one day returning to visit, but "definitely not to live, or with my kids." After two months of searching, Yadira eventually found a lower-paid, nonunion position through her husband's cousin. When I spoke with her, she had been in her new job for two years without a raise, so finances remained tight. But she appreciated the flexibility the new job allowed her.

In the remaining pages of this chapter, I examine the material, health, and familial impacts of the claims process for more workers like Laney and Yadira. I also consider the particular consequences for undocumented workers who either returned or were sent back to their countries of origin after initiating a claim. More broadly, I then explore what lessons low-paid workers learn from the claims process. While their stories reveal crucial moments of agency and self-determination, they also suggest that some workers emerge from the process more cautious and skeptical of the rights regime than ever.

FALLOUTS FROM EXPLOITATION

Judging one's past actions is a fraught exercise; one views missteps with the clarity of hindsight while speculating over the alternative paths one could have taken. When I asked workers to think back on the years they spent fighting for their workplace rights, they tended to focus first and foremost on the professional and financial costs of their protests. Whatever the job, low-wage workers valued the career they had built, and were reluctant to jeopardize the reputations they had worked to establish. For those who had lost hours, jobs, and other professional opportunities as a result of their experiences, the financial consequences were often severe, especially in the Bay Area's challenging housing market. Beyond these monetary considerations, workers also discussed the impacts on their physical and emotional health. Injuries often robbed workers of their professional identities and livelihoods; they also made them question their self-worth. Many workers described moments of despair and depression, which were often dismissed by medical professionals. Together these challenges placed enormous stress on workers' familial and social relationships, which further compromised their health and ability to start anew. For some undocumented workers who had grown tired of being exploited and had little hope for future reform, the best option was to return to their countries of origin.

Professional and Financial Consequences

Finding a new job was the primary challenge for workers who were either fired or reached their breaking point over unsatisfactory workplace conditions. Workers who were harassed and unfairly terminated often had an especially difficult time finding new work. Cristela, the disabled administrative assistant from chapter 4, spoke about the trickiness of answering a common question on application forms: "Have you ever been fired from a job?"[3] Answering "yes" would potentially bias the employer against her and raise the possibility that she would have to rehash her traumatic experience: "I didn't realize that I was scarred from [her abusive former manager], and I was emotionally distressed. I think it took almost a year to [get] that whole experience out [of me]."

When we last met, Cristela was still doggedly looking for work through a temp agency: "I bug the hell out of them." She also continues to take classes to improve her résumé and upgrade her skills. She feels stuck, however, since the classes require her to find child care and take time away from her job search. She now also sees herself as bearing two burdens: a complicated job history that leaves her having to explain why she does not have a positive reference from her former employer, and her disability (remember that she has no use of her right arm). While she feels empowered by her years of disability rights advocacy, she has little time to devote to the social justice causes about which she is passionate. Her focus, understandably, is on finding a steady income.

For professional workers who have coveted skills and are valuable company assets, losing a particular job requires redefining one's place in professional circles. For example, Cathy of chapter 4, a Silicon Valley professional who was pushed out of her job, felt that her professional identity was profoundly affected as a result of her speaking out.[4] In the immediate aftermath of complaining to management, many of her coworkers turned distant: "A lot of people didn't want to talk to me anymore. . . . People just shunned me. . . . [It was like], 'Don't talk to her, she's a pariah.' . . . If you go against [management], you are the enemy and they will treat you that way. So, yeah, you don't feel like you are part of anything after that. That was hurtful."

Once she was fired, Cathy also struggled to find, or ask for, support from friends and industry colleagues: "I . . . felt a little embarrassed about it. I didn't want to tell my friends or other professional people. I really didn't want to discuss what happened because I thought it was a bad reflection on me. . . . It seems like oftentimes when you are fired and something like that happens that there is something wrong with you, but I always felt like, no, I didn't do anything. I had nothing to do with that thing happening. Anyway, that is just the way I felt, kind of shitty and embarrassed."

Because Cathy had a very marketable skill in Silicon Valley, she was able to pick up more freelance work within weeks. But when she suffered a stroke a few months after being let go, she had to take time off again. When we last met, her goal was to start walking again, find a position that allowed her to work without her now-damaged left hand, and adapt her car so that she could once again drive (an imperative for any job search in the Bay Area).

Older workers face a particularly difficult time reintegrating into the labor market. This difficulty arises perhaps because employers may feel that the cost of investing in older workers is too high, or simply because of ageist discrimination. Research has found that unemployment later in life has negative long-term health consequences (despite some short-term benefits such as stress reduction). While those workers approaching Social Security and Medicare eligibility fare a little better, those who are somewhat younger are likely to experience a significant reduction in physical, emotional, and financial health (Leith 2014; Coile, Levine, and McKnight 2014). My study confirmed these findings.

One such older worker was Carol, a fifty-nine-year-old field organizer for a local election campaign.[5] Hers was a part-time job, only thirty hours a week, which she spent going door to door through a wide variety of neighborhoods. One afternoon, on her way up to a house, she slipped and fell, suffering a concussion, whiplash, and an injured shoulder. Her attempts to find new employment were frustrating: "They ask, 'Are you working now?' and I tell them, 'No, I'm on workers' comp.' That's the end of the conversation." Though she would legally have to be released from disability to return to work, she has found it difficult to even find viable positions for which she is not clearly overqualified. As an older worker, Carol felt that her injury, combined with her age, put her at a near-impossible disadvantage. As she was too young to draw on Medicare, she was unemployed *and* uninsured, leaving her wondering how she would cope in the event of another injury or illness. Carol lives alone and relies on a local senior center, where she receives hot meals. Once a week she also visits a local food bank. While she continues to drive (an imperative in San Jose), she is no longer able to pay her mortgage and thus foreclosure is a real possibility.

Shelly, an injured, fifty-nine-year-old fast food worker, described her own difficult journey back to the labor market as an older employee.[6] During the noontime rush one afternoon, she fell on a patch of uneven tiles, sustaining a debilitating knee injury. Her manager was not present when she fell, and the lunchtime crowd was constant, so she continued to work through the busy shift. Placing her job security above her pain, Shelly showed up to her 8 a.m. shift the next day. But she did not last long: "I realized within like half an hour that I was sick to my stomach, the pain was so bad. I started crying and said [to my manager], I am sorry I can't—I can't do anything."

Shelly eventually sought medical attention for her knee. She initially went to her personal doctor through her public county plan, with whom she had a long-standing and positive relationship, and the doctor diagnosed her injury as a meniscus tear. In order to file a workers' compensation claim, Shelly had to eventually see a doctor through the approved plan. This doctor informed her that there was evidence of age-related arthritis in her knee prior to the injury, though she maintains that she had never had any knee issues up to that point. Despite her excruciating pain, Shelly also felt that this doctor downplayed her physical limitations in evaluating her condition for the insurance company:

> He didn't listen to anything I said, he didn't care about actually how long I could sit, [and] he didn't care how long I could stand. . . . He filled [the evaluation form] out . . . using his generalities. I walk with a cane half the time to help because my knee fails and he knows that. I had a cane that day when I went into the office. He was the one who told me to use the cane, and he fills out the part that said, "Does the patient use a cane?" And he said, "No." . . . I said, "How unfair, how unfair. How could you put this?"

The doctor explained to Shelly that he was removing her work restrictions so that she could go back to work even when she wasn't ready. But how, Shelly wondered, was it fair for the doctor to fill out the form as he saw fit just so that she would be able to reenter the workforce? After all, she was filing a claim for disability. Still, the doctor wouldn't budge: "I started crying right there in the office about it. And so he told his nurse to tell me that I'm welcome to get a second opinion."

Injured and unemployed, Shelly worried about her future and felt like her professional and personal identity was forever changed: "I've always worked. I've always provided for my family, and I've always done stuff around my house . . . remodel[ing] and cleaning and all of that. I'm unable to do any of it [now], and so it's changed who I am." Shelly was left with a few bleak options: accepting a meager workers' compensation settlement, continuing a discouraging search for work, or filing for Social Security disability: "Out of having to take care of my family and stuff, I figured I had to do that. . . . I went and got the [disability] forms and filled them out."

When we last spoke, Shelly had filed the disability forms and had found an attorney in the phone book, whom she hoped to meet with soon to pursue a case against the negligent workers' compensation insurance company. Her goal, she explained, was to patch together enough income to support her husband, and to help her son and his pregnant girlfriend (neither of whom was working). She was also exploring educational voucher options, a workers' comp benefit that over the years has been reduced: "I'm not foolish enough to think that that's going to get me anywhere. But . . . I'd like to have it available to me. . . . I know that it's just a drop in the bucket—I'm fifty-nine. . . . I don't know what I need."

Other older workers described feeling an initial sense of despair when they realized they had to compete with younger, stronger, and more experienced workers. For example Adán, whom we met in chapters 2 and 4, described what life was like for him after he filed a wage claim, was fired, and was initially denied unemployment: "After I left that job, I couldn't find work. . . . I don't think it is fair. I would accept it if I had robbed [the store where I worked] and then they fired me. In that case, perfect, it's a punishment, even if they were to send me to jail."[7]

Adán felt it unjust that after working so steadily for so long, he wasn't able to find another job. He eventually found work as a landscaping assistant, starkly different from his previous job in retail. At sixty-two years old, he did not last long: "It was eight hours, going since 6:30 in the morning, picking up leaves. . . . I couldn't take it." He worked only seven days, the boss constantly telling him to "hurry" before leveling with him: "Look, unfortunately, you are starting very late [in life]." While Adán admits that he could look into a retraining program, he balks at the thought of starting all over at his age: "I just don't want to study any more."

Injured workers who had families to support felt understandably helpless when they lost their sole source of income. Undocumented workers faced especially challenging circumstances, as they had no access to the social safety net that others could at least rely on for minimal support. Macarena's case (explained in chapter 4) demonstrates these difficulties in dramatic fashion.[8] Following a car accident, her already precarious health status and financial situation further unraveled when she lost her job. She has applied elsewhere, most recently at a hotel, with no luck. She, her husband, and their three children try their best to make do. For example, she rents her living room out for $150 per month to her niece, a single mom of two who shares her food stamps with Macarena on occasion. Sometimes Macarena will also care for her oldest daughter's children for $100 per week (but often taking whatever her daughter can afford). Thankfully, her children are covered by Medi-Cal, but when I spoke with her, her oldest son was about to turn eighteen, at which point this benefit would disappear, likely leaving him uninsured.

Workers like Macarena found themselves in a cycle of precarity that could not be addressed by the workers' rights system alone. Losing one bad job seldom led to securing a good one. For example, Candelaria, a Salvadoran immigrant with legal permanent residence status, worked as a janitor for a residential care facility, as explained in chapter 2.[9] For more than a decade she was often paid late or erratically. Over time, her hours were reduced, and one day she was simply let go. Candelaria soon found another job working as a subcontracted night janitor. She liked her new supervisor, who gave her flexibility when emergencies arose with her kids, which often did because two were special-needs children. But again in this job she was regularly asked to work unpaid overtime, which she agreed to in part to curry favor with her manager so that he would continue to be flexible. One day, however, she arrived to find that she and the entire crew had been replaced. By the time we spoke, she had been looking for work for more than a year. Because neither of her employers had reported her work on the books, Candelaria also was ineligible for unemployment.

The wage theft Candelaria experienced was only the tip of the iceberg. She opened up to me about her situation: "I'm still unemployed, with no income, nothing, and no hope. I have four small children; the oldest is barely fourteen, and at the age when she needs more things than the little ones. . . . So I'm worried. I've been looking but I don't find anything. I tell [prospective employers] what hours I can work, but since I have two special-needs children . . . it's really complicated. . . . They tell me that they want me available seven days a week, twenty-four hours a day. But I can't. I have my children to care for."

It is important to note that many of the precarious workers I spoke with had experienced numerous instances of workplace abuse, and general life trauma, before even considering filing a claim. They had thus learned to weigh the comparative egregiousness of their workplace conditions. For example, when I asked Candelaria how she would characterize the last two positions she held, each of which subjected her to wage and hour violations and provided little to no stability, she described them as a step up from the decade she spent cleaning for her abusive husband's business. After a year of receiving regular pay, her husband essentially stopped paying her altogether; he would still write her checks, but they would bounce. When Candelaria discovered she could cash the checks at a nearby market that would go after him directly should there prove to be insufficient funds, her husband became even more despotic. Worse, when he left her, she unknowingly signed over all their assets to him. Her recent janitorial positions, flawed though they were, provided a way out of this desperate situation. Her experience as a domestic violence victim, as well as her past economic struggles growing up in El Salvador, shaped how she viewed her current situation: "It's better here [in the United States]. Yes, because there [in El Salvador], you kill yourself to earn only a little."

Impact on Health and Well-Being

Losing a terrible job can certainly bring about financial and professional devastation. However, some workers reported feeling liberated from exploitation. In fact, several told me that transitioning out of a physically and mentally taxing job returned them to health, despite the initial stress it created. For example Ramon, who worked as a handyman for an apartment complex for nearly twenty years, was fired after receiving a single negative performance review.[10] Pushed by his wife to "speak up and defend his rights," he sought help from the community law center, where he learned that "he didn't have much of a case." He was quickly replaced by one of his new manager's relatives, which no law prevented her from doing: "It just seemed really unjust . . . especially the way I was fired. Because I tell you, I had twenty years there . . . and the new person . . . didn't know anything." Given his at-will status, Ramon had no path to restitution. The whole process took a toll on him, but, looking back, he was ultimately grateful for the unwelcome career change: "Everything is fine now, but back then, my health was bad. Now I earn about half of what I earned then, but my health is better. Now I don't have any more problems; it was so much stress back then."

That said, more often than not, the negatives outweigh the positives in the aftermath of workplace disputes. As we saw in the previous section, injured workers in particular are often left without a livelihood, hobbled by permanent physical injuries and bearing emotional scars. Amalia, for example, worked at a periodontist's office and began experiencing persistent aching in her wrist and thumb.[11] When she alerted her employer, the periodontist sent her to her friend, an orthopedist in the same building, who suggested that Amalia seek help for a vein condition. Reluctant to burden her employer, a small business owner, she went to her primary care physician, who diagnosed Amalia with a repetitive stress injury and urged her to consider a workers' compensation claim. She approached her employer, who was beyond supportive and helped her with the paperwork. Amalia next met with an insurance adjuster, who sent her to an occupational health clinic whose parent company is infamous for the "cattle-call" conditions Eleanor described in chapter 4. She underwent surgery, after which a series of complications arose. Throughout her procedures, Amalia went through multiple insurance adjusters and doctor referrals, and suffered long delays as her doctor awaited authorization approval. Her condition ultimately was deemed "permanent and stationary," and she was granted a $9,000 permanent settlement with no further benefits. She now endures ongoing, severe pain.

When we spoke, Amalia was looking for positions that she could hold while coping with her pain. Aside from the financial necessity of working, she felt unsettled without a job: "I've been working since I was sixteen years old . . . probably much younger than that. . . . Ever since [my family] came here to the United States, it's always just been work, work, work. . . . I was always working." Though she is in constant pain, she is desperate to return to work: "To tell the truth, I don't know what to do at home. My kids are at school and I'm like, you know, I miss being there with the patients and my coworkers and everything."

She also misses being able to do the things she enjoys, like cooking, as her pain makes simple tasks such as chopping food impossible. The inability to care for her family has weighed on her heavily. Amalia has felt depressed and finds herself crying frequently. The prospect of perhaps never returning to work scares her: "I try to keep my mind busy on other things." Moreover, she tires of having to explain to her parents and other relatives why she is not working: "It has affected me a lot emotionally. . . . I don't like to go into very many details about it. I just don't like talking about it." Amalia's case powerfully reveals the full financial, but also personal, costs of precarity.

Such prolonged experiences with pain and physical incapacitation were particularly difficult for the men who worked in manual labor. The fear of not being able to continue working, along with the challenges of adapting to a disability, could prove devastating. Sometimes a worker's sense of pride suffered for having been hurt in an accident he was trained to avoid; more often, though, he was bitter at employers who refused to address his legitimate safety concerns. For example Merlín, the machinist from chapter 4, discussed the fallout from the injury he sustained when manually pulling a load off a broken assembly line.[12] At first the pain was minor, but it quickly intensified. When he approached his manager, he was curtly told that he was to blame for not following the safety rules, even though there had been many complaints about the broken equipment. Merlín received a warning for being careless, which irked him: "That bothered me a lot, because I figured I could lose my job [and] end up disabled." This indeed would be Merlín's fate.

Though Merlín's doctor sent him back to the factory after six weeks with an order to work on "light duty," when he arrived he learned that this modified option was not available to him: "[My employer] simply told me, 'Either you do the full job or go back home.'" Merlín continued to experience pain, and his prescribed medication provided little relief. While his doctors suggested surgery, Merlín was scared: "The idea that they would open me up, cut me, and move my bones terrified me. So I didn't submit. Then I think there was just nothing we could do." Meanwhile he obtained a lawyer and requested a hearing to finally close his claim. Two years later, Merlín agreed to a settlement, though it was for far less than he had hoped.

Settlement in hand, Merlín returned to work, adjusting to his tasks as well as he could despite the pain. (He has had to cut back on his medication due to damage to his stomach from long-term use.) At fifty years of age, he would like to take a less physically demanding job but has few options. He does consider himself fortunate to have received a settlement with "open medical" options, which will provide treatment in the future. However, his insurer has changed company ownership, which leaves him worried about how to claim his benefits going forward, should he need to: "I wouldn't know what to do. It's not the same company, different owners. I don't know. I have no idea."

Merlín laments the physical toll of this injury: "Even though my [lawyers] said we could fight [on] . . . to tell you the truth, all I wanted was to keep my job, regain my health—that's what I wanted the most—go on working, and stay healthy." The claims process has taken an emotional toll on him as well: "I never thought this would happen to me, that I would ever be caught up in all this, fighting with attorneys, and, well, it's affected me psychologically. I became depressed, but I'm fighting it, and adjusting." Merlín tries to remain positive, and feels that this experience has helped him become an ambassador of sorts to his coworkers, whom he implores to put their health and safety first. He admits that when his injury occurred, he could have stopped, rested, or asked for help, but he felt pressure and a "responsibility" to continue. Now he advises coworkers not to let that attitude compromise their well-being.

The stress of working in high-pressure, low-wage work environments can prove just as debilitating as workplace injuries. A case in point is Rogelio from chapter 2, the print shop employee who lost his health insurance when his employer cut his benefits.[13] Since then he has relied on county services for diabetes care and to address his chronic knee injury. The policy covers minimal care, and while his doctor has recommended him for surgery, his insurance does not cover the procedure. These health complications have slowed him down significantly at work, and the pressure is building: "It's going really bad. . . . I'm not even done with a given [print] job, and they're just sitting there watching me to see how long it's going to take me, while another job is waiting. I think this is damaging [my health] even more, you know? Because I am not afraid to work hard. I can still work [hard], but the pressure is unbearable. . . . I've already told her [my boss], and [management] just say[s], 'OK, we won't pressure you,' but then another job comes along and there they are telling me angrily to work faster, hurry up."

The very process of filing a claim also took a toll on workers' emotional well-being. After Eliana was injured, her hours (and hence her pay) were lowered.[14] After she complained, she had the sense that her bosses were trying to push her out: "I felt like they were persecuting me. . . . The stress was horrible. In the morning I had no desire to go to work, I didn't even want to get up. I did get up because I have two children to maintain, and unfortunately their father doesn't help me as he should. . . . My children are my life . . . but the stress was crushing." Often, workers, and especially parents, have no other choice but to continue on in situations made more acrimonious by their claim.

Families and Relationships Disrupted

As described above, not all workers lamented not being able to return to the job. For some, respite from an otherwise unpleasant job was a welcome break and opportunity to spend more time with their families, especially if they had alternative sources of financial support. Doris, whose termination was described in chapter 4, was one such case.[15] She characterized the aftermath of losing her job as a positive period for her family: "It brought us closer together. I'm more engaged. My relationships I think are better because I'm not distracted by work. . . . Financially it's been difficult, but the things that we have experienced now together as a family, I don't think money can buy that. . . . Like right now, I'm at home with my kids during spring break. I was never able to do that when I was working. . . . We can't buy a lot of stuff, but again, I'm more engaged, and I'm more involved with my family."

Yet these benefits were often overshadowed by the stress that accompanied the long process of filing a legal claim, which in turn adversely affected family relationships. This was especially the case for women contending with sexual harassment, which created emotionally charged dynamics at home. For example Susana from chapter 4, who filed a claim against her manager's ongoing lewd behavior, also had to manage her husband's rage: "I knew he wouldn't just stand by and let it happen. And when he found out, he was very upset with me. In fact, today we got in a fight about it again."[16] Susana's husband was angry with her for not telling him sooner, which she didn't do precisely because she feared his reaction: "Honestly, I felt stuck in the middle. Either I tell him, and he marches up to the company and 'takes care of it,' and I'm now lost, without a job and a husband who has landed in jail. Or, I stay quiet." As the details of her claim gradually emerged throughout the process, the marital tension only increased.

Other workers had their home lives negatively impacted by work troubles. Jonatán, a truck driver, described the effect his debilitating workplace injury has had on his marriage: "I've had problems with my wife. . . . I'm stressed, irritated, in a bad mood."[17] Before losing his job, Jonatán earned $27 per hour at the company where he had worked for seventeen years. But by the time I spoke with him, the years of prosperity were far behind him. After suffering a back injury, he was unable to find work, and his disability payments were running out: "I keep looking for work and sending the reports they ask for. In the month and a half to come, I will run out of money and my savings, because my costs are serious, house payments . . . four kids, . . . insurance, cars, . . . daily costs, food, electricity, water, all of that, next month. I don't know how I'm going to do it." Naturally these worries add incredible stress that makes itself felt in the home.

Other workers, such as Juvenal, faced severe depression that ultimately led to the dissolution of their marriages.[18] Juvenal began to see a psychologist, who attributed his emotional turmoil to a workplace accident. He told me: "I fell into a depression [after the accident]. Because I didn't have money, things changed. Before, we would go out to restaurants on the weekend, we took vacations . . . to Disney, to the beach. [Then] there [were] no more toys. We no longer went to Monterey, and so much changed. Everything changed." His daughter was affected as well, falling into a period of rebellion and refusing to go to school. In time Juvenal was able to return to school at a local community college, and has ambitious plans for the future. But he ultimately separated from his wife.

As these cases demonstrate all too clearly, the financial stress of a sudden job loss can roil family dynamics. Cristela, a single mother described in chapter 4, devastatingly explained to me how her oldest child started stealing in an effort to support her and his siblings through lean times.[19] He ended up in juvenile hall. Cristela's two older children are now working, and she has had to ask them to pay rent. She feels torn as she watches them try to build their own lives: "I was [the] sole supporter of my three kids. . . . I feel helpless because I used to be [a] provider [to my] kids. Now they can't even leave [because I need them to help pay rent], so I think I became more of a problem than the solution to [their] issues."

The families of injured workers faced a special challenge in that they had to learn to cope with their changed loved one. As for the workers filing claims against their employers, they often felt torn between company loyalty and their responsibility to provide for their families. Take Joaquín, a skilled welder who by severely injuring his hand lost his livelihood, his professional identity, and his role as family provider.[20] Joaquín described how before his injury, his life was dedicated almost exclusively to his demanding job. He missed many important moments in his children's lives, and as a result a rift grew between him and his wife. His son got into trouble, and he blamed himself. Nonetheless he could always support his family. After his injury, however, Joaquin's wife and children were forced to move in with family hundreds of miles away to make ends meet. His psychological health has since deteriorated, impacting the family dynamics: "Since I stopped working, everything has changed for me. . . . It's affected me. . . . There are moments when I am depressed, I get angry easily, but I'm taking medication to deal with it because I can't handle it anymore. I can't live without that pill. I have to take it every day. But I'm telling you, before [this injury], I didn't live this way."

For immigrant workers, the obligation to support families in their countries of origin can weigh heavily. The undocumented workers in my sample, 76 percent of whom sent money back to their countries of origin, especially felt this burden, compared to only 45 percent of foreign-born citizens who supported families overseas. One such worker was Octavio, the undocumented Peruvian truck driver whom I introduced in chapter 2 and who worried constantly about how to support his family back home.[21] Octavio's family obligations led him to push through his pain after he slipped and fell while loading a truck at his job delivering seafood sixty hours a week. He continued working until the pain became too severe. When he finally went to file a claim, the human resources department delayed sending Octavio to the hospital, likely in hopes that he would not file a claim. When he finally visited the assigned occupational health clinic, they dismissed his claim. A year later, he had struggled with the workers' compensation system, was running out of disability payments, and was unable to return to work. He feared that he would no longer be able to sustain the $1,000 to $1,200 he had been sending monthly to support his children's university education: "While I was working, it was no problem. . . . So for me it is very hard. . . . Even though I don't have family here, my economic obligations to my kids are strong. . . . Since I got injured, I practically don't sleep."

Financial woes, health challenges, and family stress can collide following job loss. Berta struggles to balance her obligations to her own children and to her husband's parents, who live in Mexico and to whom she feels responsible:[22] "Since we're the only ones who are over here [in the United States] . . . I send them money." This struggle almost cost her her life. As her alcoholic husband does not consistently send support, it falls on Berta to do so. Meeting these obligations has been difficult, especially after she lost her job: "Imagine, you're depressed, you get a bill [and] you think, oh god, I want to kill myself." In fact Berta did attempt suicide and spent time recuperating in a hospital after her economic obligations left her feeling isolated and hopeless.

For workers with transnational obligations, the familial and financial anxiety seemed compounded by an added responsibility to succeed; after all, they had left their loved ones behind in search of a better life. Failing to meet expectations naturally weighed heavily on workers; sometimes the stakes were life or death, and workers often blamed themselves when tragedy struck. For example Consuela regretfully recounted not being able to help her grandmother with her medical bills after she was fired: "It affected me considerably. . . . I was the one who sent her money to help her survive, and when I stopped working, her cancer advanced because I didn't send her money for the medicine. That affected me so much, and affected my pregnancy because of how depressed I became. I was so depressed that I couldn't send my grandmother money, and she died."[23]

While workers like Consuela often felt crippled by their responsibility to their families in the United States and in their countries of origin, few actually shared their anxieties with their loved ones. Gloria, the undocumented victim of sexual assault whom we met in chapter 2, had endured a long, painful, and ultimately draining process of pursuing justice against her aggressor.[24] As our emotional conversation was concluding, she received a call from her family in Mexico. She answered the phone cheerfully but quickly hung up in order to see me out the door. When I asked if she had told her family about everything she had been through, she laughed: "I don't tell them what I'm going through. They think I have it good, that I live in the United States, and that everything is great. But I can't bring myself to tell them anything." Rather than seek support, Gloria felt no choice by to shoulder the burden herself and shield her family from the truth.

Deciding to Return

Thus far, this book has focused on the experience of low-wage workers in the United States who have chosen to fight for their workplace rights. A third of the workers I surveyed were undocumented, and most were able to continue to live in the Bay Area cities where we had first met. But it is impossible to know exactly how many of those workers whom I was unable to reach ultimately left the country. The prospect of return migration, whether by choice or by force, is a fact of life for undocumented immigrants. Administrative data reveal that in the year 2013, deportations reached a record high of 438,421 unauthorized immigrants (Gonzalez-Barrera and Krogstad 2014). In 83 percent of these cases, individuals "did not have a hearing, never saw an immigration judge, and were deported through cursory administrative processes where the same presiding immigration officer acted as the prosecutor, judge, and jailor" (ACLU Foundation 2014, 2).

Among those "voluntary returnees," an unknown number of undocumented individuals leave because the strain of living a clandestine life in the United States became too much to bear. Famously advocated by conservative politicians such as Kris Kobach (Kobach 2007) and Mitt Romney (Le 2015), "self-deportation" describes this supposedly voluntary process. The idea is to "make it as difficult as possible for illegal aliens to live a normal life here," according to the anti-immigrant

Center for Immigration Studies.[25] Although the extent of and reasons for "self-deportation" are not clear from administrative data, the vast majority of unauthorized migrants are not fleeing back to their countries of origin. Even in restrictive contexts, such as Oklahoma, where anti-immigrant legislation has been passed, "most Latinos and immigrants—with the possible exception of unattached Latinos—have stayed" (Pedroza, Casas, and Santo 2012, 27). Mexican survey data also suggest that on the whole, rates of return migration have actually decreased (Rendall, Brownell, and Kups 2011).

Yet many undocumented and documented migrants still do return (despite the added border security) for a whole host of economic or social reasons (Massey, Durand, and Pren 2015). While this book focuses on those who have remained in the United States, many of the immigrant workers I initially surveyed undoubtedly eventually returned, propelled in large part by the failed promise of economic success and the exhaustion of dealing with ongoing labor exploitation and pervasive immigration enforcement. One such respondent with whom I kept in contact was Raúl, who had worked a series of low-wage service positions before becoming a skilled artisan for a company that churned out important cultural projects. He was also an avid runner and cyclist, and was taking English classes when we met. Above all, Raúl is an artist. His artist statement, which he shared with me, detailed his childhood growing up in a peri-urban industrial zone outside of Mexico City, not far from the pyramids of Teotihuacan. Raúl finished his education only through the ninth grade, though he became self-taught in a range of subjects. He began working at fifteen. Four years later, he took off to seek work north of the border.

Raúl counted himself among the lucky ones. He loved his job and was proud of his work, but there were issues. He was always aware that his position was uncertain. He had been one of the first to be let go when the company's contracts dried up, even though he had more experience than others, then was rehired when new work came in. And Raúl grew tired of being exploited over the years: "They [management] demand that I finish jobs in a certain amount of time, even if they added certain details to the plan at the end. If I didn't finish, they would use it as an excuse to not grant me a raise." For four years Raúl never received a raise, and his managers drove him and his other immigrant coworkers hard. Unlike his American-born counterparts, he never received guidance or consultation to plan pieces. Because he had talent, and spoke English, he was able to confront management more readily than the others. But his legal status kept him from pushing back too much. During his time at the company, his hours were cut permanently, his raise never materialized, and he suffered countless injuries that went unreported. Raúl stuck it out, however, because the job allowed him time after hours to work on his own art.

Then, in the year before his departure, Raúl and several of his also-unauthorized coworkers received one of the notorious No-Match Letters from the Internal

Revenue Service.[26] The letter directed him to resubmit his paperwork through his employer and threatened the company with a fine if he didn't and they continued to employ him. He and others had worked for years paying taxes with a valid Individual Taxpayer Identification Number (ITIN), but worked with Social Security numbers that were *chueco* (fake). The IRS had picked up on the discrepancy. Raúl's boss knew about each worker's status, and offered whatever support he could. Meanwhile, however, an overzealous human resources staff member held Raúl to account, at one point even aggressively approaching him to demand he pay the company's tax penalty. Raúl sought help from a local legal aid clinic, who advised him about the gray area of responding to such employer/employee audits. There was simply no good solution to his dilemma.

Raúl considered his options, recalling the times he had spent homeless and hungry following various clandestine crossings, once in the trunk of a car along with three immigrants. He thought also of his brother, now a US citizen, who lived nearby with his wife and US-born children. He also considered the deadlock in Congress, which he cynically felt was unlikely to actually pass the immigration reform rumored to be on the horizon. Raúl's friends told him to find another job, to wait it out, to consider the twenty years he had invested in this country. Surely there would be a political opening soon. Yet he didn't want to stick around and suffer the same fate as his friend, who lived nearby and had been picked up in an immigration raid in a Bay Area city that was otherwise known for its fervent immigrant activism and community policing.

Ultimately, Raúl decided to return to Mexico. His parents were ailing, and he had grown frustrated with the challenges of undocumented life. He had grown bitter about the way his job had treated him, despite years of loyalty and ongoing sacrifice. He longed now to live in a country that, despite its problems, was *his*. I had seen the public works projects to which the talented Raúl had dedicated countless hours. Looking on these impressive works, and the million-dollar contracts behind them, I reflected on the injustice of Raúl's case. Here were public monuments built by a taxpaying, underpaid worker who would never see a dime from the system he paid into. And still he was harassed by his employer and the federal government.

Nearly three years after our last meeting, I stood against the rail surrounding the massive cathedral in Mexico City's central square. The Mexican flag flew in the distance, throngs of faithful poured into mass, and laborers and people asking for charity mingled with the tourists, residents, and federal police. Eventually, Raúl emerged from the subway station, both of us ecstatic to meet again. As Raúl aptly described the long wait between our encounters: "The weeks and months had gone by so quick, but the days dragged on forever." Since his return, he had opened a store on his family's property, which he single-handedly managed and later had to close down. Life was not easy. He worked fourteen-hour shifts in a working-class neighborhood plagued with gang violence. Though the security situation was iffy, and he had recently witnessed a shooting, he had thus far managed to avoid paying extortion by doing his best to remain on good terms with all the various actors in the community. He would eventually go on to take a job as a truck driver.

Despite his struggles, Raúl was happy to be back and working for himself. He bemoaned his government's antiquated bureaucracy and corruption, but delighted in being a free citizen in a country that would never expel him. He had recently buried his father, and was now caring for his ill mother along with his siblings, who lived nearby. The United States would always have a special place in his heart. He told me that he longed for the Bay Area's running trails and the vibrant artist community he left behind. Weeks after we met, I would learn that he had closed the store, and eventually he picked up a truck route navigating the country's dangerous highway routes that he nonetheless enjoyed traversing.

Before he left the Bay Area, Raúl gave me a bronze triptych, which still hangs in my kitchen. The piece, titled *3 Days*, depicts a peasant, belongings in tow, walking toward, or perhaps away from, the iconic Aztec pyramids near Teotihuacan. The piece was inspired by an attempt to build a Walmart near Teotihuacan, a sacred site. The store was ultimately built, thanks in part to secret bribes made to shift zoning boundaries (Barstow and Bertrab 2012). The Bodega Aurrera, as Walmart stores are known in Mexico, is now the busiest store in town, displacing throngs of small shopkeepers and vendors and causing a spike in already-congested traffic. Raúl's work speaks to the connection between displacing these cultural and economic mainstays and workers like himself moving north to feed an insatiable global economy, as he had, and many others continue to do.

THE PURSUIT OF JUSTICE AND LESSONS LEARNED

As we have seen, the administrative procedure of rights enforcement is not cost-neutral and can lead to unintended consequences that compound the harms of the original injury. Given this, what are the lessons that workers learn from the claims process, and how can their experiences aid them in future claims? While research has long confirmed that individuals with previous claims experiences are more likely to claim again (Galanter 1974), it is not necessarily the case that those who file a claim walk away satisfied with the legal system or even see formally engaging the law as ultimately beneficial.

Indeed, the process of claiming itself can shape claimants' understanding of justice. Ellen Berrey, Steve G. Hoffman, and Laura Beth Nielsen (2012) refer to this contextual effect as "situated justice," highlighting the importance of both material and institutional contexts. Individual conceptions of justice vary and depend a great deal on claimants' age and social location within the polity and labor market. Many workers confess their "dashed hopes for fairness" (15) as well as their disappointment in certain government agencies, in the legal aid lawyers who counseled them against filing a claim, and/or in the for-profit attorneys who refused to take their cases. Incompetent lawyers, steep financial costs, the challenges of *pro se* litigation, the toll the claims process took on their personal lives, and the employee-employer power imbalances all irritated claimants.

In brief, standing up for one's rights can be simultaneously frustrating and empowering. Workers offered complex retrospective analyses of their experiences—positive and negative—with job loss and with the labor standards enforcement bureaucracy.

Enlightened and Empowered

On the positive side, there are workers who look back on their experience with pride for the grit and determination they showed. Many learned lessons about how to engage in their next job search, how to set boundaries with future employers from the start, and what mistakes to avoid if they ever found themselves engaging the legal bureaucracy again.

Consider Doris from chapter 4, who has taken away some valuable lessons despite admitting that the claims experience was emotionally trying.[27] In fact, she still harbors significant resentment toward her previous employer, who dismissed her after she took an extended lunch: "I think I'm more hurt than anything, that I don't feel that I did anything that wrong to get fired, and in my mind I still try to get . . . how . . . somebody . . . [can] just get rid of you like that. Especially in this economy . . . to fire you abruptly like that, and then to deny your unemployment, it almost seems cruel, and so I'm still trying to get through that."

However, she feels that she has learned to discern more carefully what she wants from her next job: "I want to work around people who are friendly and kind. I want to have flexibility with my schedule and hours, so I'm making up a list of things that I definitely want out of a job, and if I get into a situation, and it doesn't have those things, then I'll get out." She contrasts this ideal work environment to how she felt "trapped" in her previous position: "You go to work every day, you can only take a thirty-minute lunch, [and] some people can treat you any way they want because they're your bosses. You're a salaried employee, you're not exempt, so therefore you're in this box, and the people who are exempt get to be treated [differently] or have longer lunches." Having realized that "there is no loyalty anymore," she vows to be on guard with her future employers.

Similarly, when Lisette, a day care provider, lost her job after filing a claim for missed breaks, she looked past the financial and emotional burdens of the process to glean a valuable lesson: "I was pregnant, and it affected me a lot when they fired me. I became depressed, I didn't want to even get up or deal with the children I cared for."[28] Her employer refused her breaks, and as a result she developed severe back pain, wasn't eating regularly, and developed anemia: "The doctor said it was

I was not resting well. . . . . It was very painful. Emotionally and physically, it was very hard." She ultimately ran out of money and had to rely on support from her child's father, and a meager $160 biweekly unemployment check. Financial impacts aside, Lisette values her decision to file the claim: "I think it made me stronger. If I were to return to work in day care, I would not let them abuse me for so long. I'd put a stop to it right away. That is what I have learned. I don't want to wait any longer."

Even when a claim was an utter failure, some workers, such as Maite, found solace in their fight for justice.[29] Maite taught at a preschool that her daughter attended. She eventually left that position when, a week before school was set to resume in the fall, she was told that she would be required to work eight-hour shifts. When Maite first signed on, she had made an agreement with the director that she could work a shortened day in order to see to her own child care needs. Maite had in fact left a higher-paying teaching position in exchange for the convenience. Though Maite had a litany of complaints about the unprofessional way the preschool was run, she had not had any direct confrontations with the director up to this point. She was given two options: work the schedule the director was requesting or don't come back. Maite felt that she had no choice but to resign.

Maite thought it unjust that she was pushed out of her job and subsequently ignored when she tried to reason with management. As her calls went unanswered, and her efforts to communicate with management when she would go to pick up her child from the preschool were rebuffed, Maite filed a claim with the licensing agency. She sought help from the legal aid clinic, who asked to see her employment contract. Despite an uncooperative human resources department, she eventually secured a copy, at which point Maite discovered that her contract listed her position as a "temporary substitute" rather than a "permanent employee." Thanks in part to her husband's keen eye, Maite realized that her signature on this peculiar contract had been forged. The legal aid clinic immediately counseled her to get a private lawyer who specialized in fraud. Sadly, she quickly discovered that the retainer and fees required were far more than what she could pay: "[The lawyer] told me that he didn't know how much it would ultimately cost . . . that it would depend on how much time he had to put in. . . . He said it would take time to prove it wasn't my signature. So I decided to just leave it alone."

Maite ultimately summoned an apology from the company's president, who begged her not to prosecute the case further. "I know we violated your rights," Maite recalls him saying, "that it was unjust, but please just let me take care of this within the company." A slew of firings resulted, but Maite received no compensation. After considering all the costs she would have incurred had she pursued her claim, however, Maite is proud of her decision to first stand up for herself, then move on.

Resigned and Regretful

Other workers were left with a bitter taste in their mouths after their ordeals. Even some of those able to recover financially and physically or who had won a sizable settlement felt that the system had treated them unfairly.

For example Jose (from chapter 2), a cook who had worked in a kitchen for more than a decade, viewed his victory in the claims process as a hollow one.[30] He admitted to clashing often with his abusive manager, who eventually had him fired after a series of increasingly tense encounters. Jose sought help from the community law center as well as from the Mexican Consulate. In both cases, he was told that there was nothing to be done, given that managers have the right to reprimand, even harshly, their employees as they see fit. He complained to company higher-ups as well, to no avail. Eventually Jose found a private attorney through an ad, who told him to wait until he was fired, and that only then would they be able to build a viable case. All along the way, Jose kept detailed notes of his experiences and interactions, and on the day he was fired, he called his lawyer and filed a claim for his unjust termination and for a lingering workplace injury he had never reported. Though he won some compensation, he was unhappy with his final settlement, as he was struggling to live on his disability payments, which were only a third of his regular wages. Despite his best efforts to chronicle the abuse, he came away in a weaker position than before.

Workers placed an especially high premium on respect, lamenting the perceived humiliations they endured when they were merely trying to maintain their dignity (Lamont 2002). Take the case of Ben, a white male who returned to work at a national thrift store chain after retirement through a program designed for veterans.[31] After three years of employment, his manager accused him of stealing a laptop. Though the surveillance tape and inventory records showed no evidence of theft, and he produced a receipt for the computer, Ben was fired.

When we met, Ben was pursuing an appeal for an unemployment claim, which his company was contesting. Because the local legal aid center was unable to offer assistance, Ben sought help from a law student friend and another who was an attorney. Four months after filing his initial claim, Ben eventually received his first unemployment check. At sixty-eight, Ben feels lucky to have achieved that support, followed eventually by a new job. Yet he still wishes he had the money to have an attorney review his case again. Above all, he wants to be formally cleared of any wrongdoing: "I want my good name back and not to be accused of something [I didn't do]." Overall, he felt "humiliated," not empowered, by the whole ordeal, despite his access to several legally savvy friends.

If filing a claim empowered some workers to one day do it again, for others, the lessons learned from their claims experience made them more cautious. Yet for some, this newfound vigilance is itself empowering. Marcia was one such case, described in the previous chapter.[32] She was fired after four years despite never having received a write-up or warning. Worse, during these four years, Marcia regularly had to endure harassing comments from her male supervisor. Unlike Gloria, the woman who was sexually assaulted repeatedly at work, and Susana, whose manager exposed his genitals to her and her sister on a regular basis, the harassing behavior Marcia experienced was subtler and harder to prove. She directly confronted her supervisor and complained to her human resources representative on more than one occasion, to no avail. When she was ultimately fired, she attempted to file a claim. With no hard proof, though, she was told she had no case. Nonetheless, Marcia's family and friends encouraged her to fight. She eloquently recounts grappling with the decision: "We're really good at saying you should fight. . . . It's really easy to tell someone else to fight. But . . . when it came to me, I didn't know what to do. . . . At the end of the day, I decided it's my life. I was afraid of not having another job for the rest of my life." In this decision to *not* mobilize her rights, Marcia found her own sense of empowerment.

In sum, time and opportunity costs, the ability to reenter the labor market, and the impact on family and social networks all shape how workers reflect on their claims experience. For some, the lesson to be learned is: always speak up and defend your rights. For many others, the lesson is less inspiring: keep quiet or risk losing everything.

The gap between legal and lay justice is partly responsible for these divergent views of the worker mobilization process. The law defines a workplace violation differently than a worker might and gives wide latitude to employers. Moreover, while the bureaucrats and officers running the system see themselves as merely performing their duties, workers can be stressed and humiliated by the whole process. Aggrieved claimants and their attorneys don't always agree. Thus, ultimately for these respondents, in few cases does the destination seem worth the journey— an arduous trek through the claims-making process.

6

——

Conclusion

In the months and years since I conducted the interviews for this book, dozens of jurisdictions have passed much-needed expanded protections for low-wage workers. Cities and states have increased minimum wages, with some even going a step further and strengthening enforcement mechanisms for violating employers. The federal government has expanded overtime protections to previously unqualified middle-income employees. The Equal Employment Opportunity Commission effectively declared sexual orientation discrimination illegal in all states under Title VII of the Civil Rights Act. And just this month, the classification of independent contractors for high-profile companies such as Uber is being reevaluated. These are all welcome developments, but this book is meant to make us pause for a moment during this necessary push to expand the rights of low-wage workers. As we continue to demand stronger laws and expanded legal processes to hold employers accountable, we should not neglect to consider how workers fall into and out of the enforcement mechanisms already in place.

LAW ON THE BOOKS, LAW IN PRACTICE

This book has examined the ways in which the practical applications of labor laws contrast starkly with their original intent. In short, while many workplace protections exist, actually enforcing them poses many problems in our predominantly claims-driven system. For example, the protection against employer retaliation is a staple in many statutes. In practice, however, restrictions against employer retaliation mean little when employers can dismiss their at-will employees for any (or no) cause and when actually proving that a dismissal was due to retaliation is extremely difficult. Similarly, workers attempting to recover lost wages find that some claims are easier to advance (such as nonpayment of wages), while others (such as break violations) can be harder to prove without evidence of a clear and consistent pattern. To give yet another example, there are provisions in the workers' compensation realm for emotional distress and other psychological injuries. But to actually win such a "psych suit" requires that workers undergo extensive interrogations about the source of their distress, draining ordeals that are often rewarded with minimal financial payoffs.

This research has also highlighted cracks in the law for some ineligible workers, specifically nonemployees, who are often misclassified as independent contractors. Individuals who are hired by subcontractors to provide specific services, such as day laborers or other temp workers, may also lack certain protections. Often paid in cash by employers who fail to withhold the appropriate deductions and taxes, these workers can find themselves ineligible for key benefits such as workers' compensation and disability. Another way for a worker to fall through the legal cracks is to be excluded from an agency's jurisdiction; for instance, farm laborers and some small-business employees are not entitled to overtime. Until recently, this was the case for all domestic workers as well.

Even eligible employees may struggle to identify the right person to approach within their multilayered management hierarchy. For example, a janitor may have little face-to-face interaction with the lead supervisor who dispatches her to various sites throughout the city to clean throughout the night; or consider the recycling plant worker who applies for the position through a temp agency but reports directly to the processing site alongside other permanent employees. In both cases, identifying the first point of contact for filing a claim can be convoluted, as human resources departments are centralized offsite and workers may be assigned to multiple units and supervisors.

When workers do come forward to file claims, they make key decisions about which rights to pursue and which to let go. In this study, for example, there were workers who filed basic wage claims but refused to pursue action against ongoing unsafe workplace conditions and persistent sexual harassment. These workers understandably prioritized their immediate material well-being over broader, more difficult claims less likely to result in restitution. They also had insufficient time for, or interest in, engaging three agencies at three different government levels (that is, the local minimum-wage authority, the state-run workers' compensation system, and the federal EEOC). The path of least resistance is likely to be chosen. Workers' precarity and disjunctured bureaucracies allow "higher order" workplace violations not tied directly to employment and earnings to persist. In such scenarios, who could blame the aggrieved worker for feeling overwhelmed by the path before her and neglecting to pursue each time-consuming claim?

THEORIZING FROM THE BOTTOM UP

This book has attempted to complement existing studies that elucidate the process of rights enforcement from the perspective of elite actors such as bureaucrats and attorneys. These studies have crucially theorized the exercise of discretion, the logic of the courts, and the challenges of educating and empowering workers about their rights. However, by focusing on the perspectives of the workers themselves, a different set of concerns emerges. Specifically I have provided here a window into how workers navigate power at the workplace, how and when they learn about their rights and the resources to help them in mobilizing them, and the process of weighing when and how extensively to fight for justice. As such, the perspectives of workers themselves are crucial because they help illuminate the opportunities and pitfalls of labor law.

Admittedly this "bottom-up" approach is methodologically limited by its very nature, because by relying on nonexperts to recount their experience of the law, we are bound to encounter misunderstandings about the intent and application of the law. Yet these misunderstandings tell us much about the problems of the claims process. Many of the interviewees simply were unsure of the bureaucratic details of their cases. Some, for example, could not recall the exact name of the agency where their claim was filed, or even the specific type of claim they lodged. Workers sometimes also misunderstood the reasons for their claim's demise. Take, for example, the many workers who remained convinced that their attorneys had misguided them, or, even worse, intentionally deceived them for their own gain. Workers also often recounted their conviction that their settlements had been rigged and that they deserved more than they ultimately were awarded.

These misunderstandings can be interpreted as a failure of legal advocates to fully explain the labor standards bureaucracy to their clients. But from the perspective of the workers, who have little experience in these opaque processes, the misunderstandings seem inevitable. As they hand their claim over to experts, who do their best to shepherd that claim through the formal bureaucracy, it is not always apparent why and how decisions are made. Therefore, rather than arising from the particular actions of bureaucrats and advocates, the animosity many workers expressed to me was a direct reflection of their social position and marginality before the law. That is, given workers' precarious lives, lives in which the state and the law are rarely on their side, it is only rational for them to assume that the cards are not stacked in their favor.

WHAT DO WORKERS VALUE?

The perspectives of the workers in this book suggest the need for a broader understanding of how marginalized individuals conceptualize justice, as well as the impact this conceptualization has on their relationship to legal rights and their ultimate desire to mobilize them. According to Luc Boltanski and Laurent Thévenot (1999), a principle of equivalence is necessary for actors to initiate a claim in the realm of justice. The authors describe this notion as the process of making connections between different sets of people and objects, connecting stories, and finding a common good as a method of "unveil[ing] an injustice and ask[ing] for an atonement" (363). The process of seeking redress in this way requires proof and justification. These determinations are bound by the specific institutional space workers occupy. For example, in the labor market arena, individuals may evaluate their worth according to their (labor) price on the market, which gives an indication of their productivity and efficiency for capital. Ultimately, though, the authors argue that there may be other bases on which to engage a dispute, including a feeling of social obligation or other "affective relations." As confirmed by the experiences of many of the workers described here, this is a stark departure from the Rawlsian view of individuals as always "reasonable and rational" in their pursuits of justice (Rawls 2009; Turner 2014).

Workers' understanding of their rights, and their ultimate propensity to mobilize them, are tied not only to the overarching policies of the state and the principles embedded in the formal law, but also to the social institutions in which they are embedded (Albiston 2005a). Key to this process are workers' relationships with their employers, who may withhold and control access to certain information, who may or may not inspire loyalty, and who frame how their rights should be interpreted. Social networks (friends, family, and other contacts) can also shape how workers understand and mobilize their rights. While legal knowledge may indeed propel workers to pursue workplace change (Trautner, Hatton, and Smith 2013), other considerations may come into play during the course of a claim.

Workers decide whether to pursue or persist through a claim based not only on what they stand to gain but also on what they are likely to lose. As time goes on, many of those individuals choosing to fight for their claim must eventually reassess the logic of continuing to do so. Aside from the financial costs of retaining an attorney (if pro bono counsel is unavailable), workers must also consider the hours of work lost while attending meetings and hearings. In addition to wages, workers might also value scheduling priorities, peaceful relationships with employers and coworkers, and workplace perks that might vanish if they were to file a dispute. They might also consider time spent away from their families and the emotional toll that a legal dispute would cause. For undocumented workers, the threat of deportation and the challenge of finding a job without work authorization loom large.

During the claims-making process, workers must make determinations about how far to take a claim and how hard to fight based on the time and opportunity costs. Furthermore, they are forced to mute their own voices and trust an array of experts, who translate their painful subjective experiences into objective assessments of harm. While we tend to think of legal mobilization as an inherently empowering process, I found that many workers focused on what was missing or lost throughout the ordeal. A lack of access to key brokers and experts, issues with language and communication during appointments and proceedings, and the time, monetary, and emotional costs of endless wrangling all weighed heavily on them. The financial impacts of job loss were obviously of great concern during the claims process, but so too were the ripple effects on workers' families and broader social networks. Each of these factors contributed to how workers assessed their claims experience as either empowering or demobilizing. For some, the lesson to be learned was to always speak up and defend your rights; for many others it was to learn to remain quiet, as there is much to be lost.

The worker experience with the claims process is far from monolithic. Workers engage in legal mobilization selectively, sometimes opting to hold employers accountable for some forms of injustices but not others. Undocumented immigration status creates a contradictory dynamic, as workers are fearful of losing their jobs or being deported but also emboldened by their extreme precarity, which can give them the sense that they have little to lose. For some workers, self-preservation means defending their rights; for others it sometimes requires *disengaging* from the legal bureaucracy as a strategy for economic and emotional survival.

Despite all the challenges chronicled in these chapters, my intent has not been to paint these claimants as martyrs. In fact, as these interviews revealed, many of the workers I spoke with see themselves as agentic actors who are aware of what they have forgone or negotiated away, and what they have gained or preserved instead. Like the experts and defendants that they are up against, they are making strategic decisions about whether to move forward or stop fighting, even when they have imperfect information about their claim and its chances of success. And even for those workers who are left without a remedy and disillusioned with the legal system, they often devise a clear plan for how to deal with future harms by pursuing nonlegal strategies.

GATEKEEPING AND BROKERING RIGHTS

For the masses of workers protected under labor and employment law, there is no guarantee that they will see their day in court. Since William L. F. Felstiner, Richard L. Abel, and Austin Sarat (1980) proposed the model of "naming, blaming, and claiming," there has been an explosion of work evaluating how individuals navigate the dispute pyramid. This work has made clear the various steps of this elite space. To use these authors' terms, workers must first identify that they have in fact been grieved. Next they must come forth and file a claim (formally or not). If the employer (or opposing party) refuses to cooperate, a dispute will ensue. A portion of those workers filing claims will seek legal counsel to help fight their case, and an even smaller portion will actually proceed to court. Grievances can commence, end, and recommence, the worker all the while navigating among complicated management hierarchies, coworkers, agency staff, and attorneys.

While it is tempting to describe labor and employment law as a thoroughly broken system, a more nuanced portrayal would focus on those who benefit throughout the process, intentionally or not. The same actors standing at the gates of the dispute pyramid—employers, agencies, attorneys, insurers, and even coworkers and consumers—have distinct interests that shape how they engage in the labor standards enforcement system. Unpacking these incentives and disincentives is central to shattering the myth of an objective labor standards enforcement process.

Consider the state, which plays a dualistic role in the process of enforcing workers' rights. On the one hand, labor standards enforcement agencies are neutral sieves through which claims flow. Indeed, if you observe an administrative law hearing for a wage and hour claim or workers' compensation claim, or a mediation or superior court trial for a discrimination case, the commissioners and judges make clear that their job is to adjudicate the evidence for the benefit of both parties. For example, the California Labor Commissioner's stated mission "is to vigorously enforce minimum labor standards in order to ensure employees are not required or permitted to work under substandard unlawful conditions, and to protect employers who comply with the law from those who attempt to gain competitive advantage at the expense of their workers by failing to comply with minimum labor standards."[1] This protective role is at least the proclaimed ideal.

On the other hand, the state is a collection of enforcement bureaucracies with limited statutory tools and staff resources to hear and adjudicate workers' claims. Adjacent to the formal bureaucracy are also several ancillary actors, such as insurers and medical experts, who solicit or provide objective evidence. For example, in the field of workers' compensation, insurers rely on qualified medical examiners to assess the source and extent of a worker's injury. Their opinion is to be assessed separately from that of the worker's treating doctor, whose explicit goal is to help return a worker to health. The compensable part of a worker's disability is limited to the identifiable injury. Bureaucrats then use actuarial scales and occupational differentials with the goal of homing in on the value of a worker's labor productivity. During this process, a claimant's voice and holistic experiences can be lost amid the technocratic expertise.

Finally, attorneys can make or break a case. They can help workers determine whether their claim is worth pursuing and the chances of winning. They also help claimants gather the evidence necessary to bolster their claim, including records, eyewitness accounts, and other crucial documentation. Many of the workers I interviewed never made it past this first stage in the dispute pyramid once they realized that they were unable to secure legal counsel (either because none was available to take their case or because they could not afford to retain one). After an initial consultation with attorneys, others quickly realized that they were facing an uphill battle and that they ultimately had neither the means nor the emotional strength to head down that road. In addition to helping workers make this assessment, attorneys—even very good and well-intentioned ones—operate with limited resources that require them to restrict their caseload to only certain chosen claims. Time-intensive cases, those lacking a substantial monetary award, and those with a slim chance of prevailing are passed over. These structural constraints are often interpreted by claimants as a further offense perpetrated by a system that has shut them out.

THE NEED FOR ACCESSIBLE LEGAL COUNSEL

If bureaucrats and technocrats stand guard at the gates of the system of workers' rights enforcement, it falls largely to pro bono attorneys to shepherd the thousands of prevailing workers through. Attorneys and their staffs are the primary asset claimants have, especially if English is not their first language and if they are not "repeat players," those advantaged actors who over the course of filing many claims have gained a legalistic knowledge of the system and know how to best deploy it (Songer, Kuersten, and Kaheny 2000; Galanter 1974). Attorneys provide legal advice, mundane technical assistance, and routine but helpful referrals to other resources in the community where workers can get help for meeting their basic needs. These attorneys are saviors for workers, who desperately need someone to stand by their side, but they are also often the bearers of bad news, informing their clients when the law has no legal or practical tool to offer them in their quest for justice. Attorneys can be found in both nonprofit advocacy centers (Gordon 2007; Fine 2006; Cummings and Rhode 2010) and in the private bar, where plaintiff-side employment law offers much less lucrative options to new graduates. (Recently, some law schools have attempted to stem the steady "drift" away from notoriously unprofitable public interest law [Addington and Waters 2012]).

Nonprofit attorneys rely on foundation grants, private donations, and the various mechanisms of supporting pro bono counsel, such as IOLTA funding and in-kind services provided by lawyers in the private bar.[2] Given these limited sources of support, many legal aid clinics (in part due to funding restrictions) serve only applicants who meet low-income eligibility criteria. While this is a completely reasonable way to allocate scarce resources, it means that many middle-income workers are left ineligible for services. These restrictions notwithstanding, the clinic staff I saw worked generously and creatively to try and serve as many clients as possible. As a result, even several unemployed professionals—as opposed to low-wage workers—were included in our sample. Still, their claims tended to be of a qualitatively different nature than those of other low-wage workers, focusing especially on unjust termination and allegations of discrimination.

This research was conducted in arguably the most fertile region for pro bono labor and employment legal aid in the country, thanks in large part to the Legal Aid Society–Employment Law Center and its partner organizations. In areas lacking a robust pro-worker philanthropic community and/or a dense employment law community, however, such legal resources are rare. As a result, attorneys working there have a harder time advocating aggressively for their clients (Albiston and Nielsen 2014). Indeed, less than an hour or two from the San Francisco Bay Area, where the concentration of immigrant workers becomes quite dense in the agricultural regions of the Salinas Valley and the Central Valley, options for legal aid of any kind are scarce. In these remote regions, federal funds through the Legal Services Corporation (LSC) are often the only game in town. Worse, to gain access to these federal funds, clinics are prohibited from serving undocumented clients. While enough privately funded advocates are operating in large parts of California, the restrictions imposed by federal funds amount to writing a blank check to abusive employers in other parts of the country where these alternatives are not available.

Teaching clinics are another valuable legal resource, but to balance the pedagogical needs of a law school practicum with the practical needs of a low-income clientele can be challenging. For these clinics, a necessarily small caseload can disqualify cases that are too mundane or those that the clinic has insufficient resources to pursue. Moreover, workers often recounted their frustration over being passed from student to student and not allowed to see "the real lawyer." To be clear, the vast majority were grateful for the assistance they received. Of the 89 workers who granted me a follow-up interview, 60 affirmatively responded that they would return to the clinic if they had another workplace problem in the future. The average respondent also rated their experience in increasing their knowledge of workers' rights as a 3.8 on a scale of 1 to 5. However, of those who did not return to the clinic for future assistance in pursuing their claim, the vast majority were urged (or chose) to seek a private attorney.

By design, for-profit attorneys, crucial legal advocacy players especially for those cases that proceed to superior court, rely on the damages assessed to culpable employers to fund legal counsel. As a result, attorneys logically screen cases that offer little chance of recouping substantial fees and/or where limited evidence makes success a long shot. This creates a hierarchy of claims within the field whereby basic wage and hour claims are less attractive than high-impact (and clearly litigable) discrimination claims. Similarly, cases involving devastating injuries resulting from isolated, major incidents are far easier to make than those involving chronic injuries developed over a lifetime of precarious employment or psychological claims related to emotional distress. And when it comes to claimant parties, the more the merrier, as single-worker incidents are far less likely to garner interest from prospective attorneys. This leaves isolated workers at a further disadvantage.

The private bar, while a large source of support for legal aid centers, is not a silver bullet. These firms are often reluctant to work on cases that threaten corporate client interests, and as a result take on few cases in the areas of employment and labor, environmental justice, or consumer law (Selbin and Cummings 2015, 738). This has led some advocates to call for a reenvisioning of legal education and legal practice to focus on non-lawyers (Rhode 2013). There is in fact evidence from the United Kingdom that "nonlawyers generally outperformed lawyers in terms of concrete results and client satisfaction" (Moorhead, Paterson, and Sherr 2003; Rhode 2013, 249). And indeed, in administrative law contexts such as the California Labor Commissioner, non-lawyer advocates have been efficiently and competently accompanying clients to their hearings, often with stunning success. Nonetheless, many of the workers I interviewed valued professional legal representation highly, as employers undoubtedly do as well.

Employment and labor law suffers further from the disparity between the right to legal counsel in criminal versus civil law. While the Supreme Court has since 1963 upheld the right to counsel for individuals convicted of a crime, no such protection exists in the civil arena, which also includes a wide range of other areas of "poverty law" (Cummings and Selbin 2015) such as housing, health, and family law. Yet, as one advocate of "Civil Gideon" (an effort to provide access to counsel in civil, not just criminal, cases) poignantly explains, the two arenas (civil and criminal law) are inevitably intertwined: "Those who lose their employment or are denied unemployment benefits may be forced to rely on public benefits, and those who lose public benefits that had been providing access to preventative health care or ongoing treatment for chronic illnesses may require substantially more expensive emergency medical care that all taxpayers ultimately bear" (Pollock 2013, 6). Furthermore, civil litigants who cannot effectively protect their housing or employment interests in court may wind up in the criminal justice system as a result.

All of this goes to show that while an array of legal aid options exist for aggrieved workers, the apparatus has structural flaws that can foil a worker's legal mobilization.

THE INADEQUACY OF CLAIMS-DRIVEN ENFORCEMENT

The findings from this research have thrown the challenges of the current, mostly claims-driven system of labor standards enforcement into stark relief. There are, however, several models within the current system that place the burden of enforcement on the authorities rather than the victims. For example, the California Labor Commissioner's Bureau of Field Enforcement (BOFE) strategically targets noncompliant employers through agency-directed initiatives, as well as fielding complaints from workers and their advocates. In fiscal year 2013–14, BOFE conducted 3,792 inspections and issued 2,664 citations, focusing on low-wage industries such as agriculture (125), auto repair (253), car wash (201), construction (422), garment (135), restaurant (545), and retail (99). Nearly half of the citations issued were for workers' compensation violations (1,224). Less than 20 percent were for overtime (199), minimum wage (178), or rest and meal period (115) infractions. The rest focused largely on licensing and child labor violations. Overall, $41,204,039 in penalties were assessed, but, as is typical, only $11,403,380 was collected (Su 2015). These enforcement efforts, while welcome, pale in comparison to the number of cases brought before the California Department of Industrial Relations. In fiscal year 2012–13, the Division of Labor Standards Enforcement alone reported 35,093 wage and hour cases opened.[3]

Lack of agency coordination becomes especially problematic in a claims-driven enforcement regime, as the task is left primarily to workers and their advocates to sift through and triage claims across various agencies. Here again, California's efforts offer some positive models for joint enforcement. In 2013–14, for example, a joint Labor Enforcement Task Force between the Division of Labor Standards Enforcement, the Employment Development Department (which handles unemployment and state disability insurance), and the California Occupational Safety and Health Administration found that 40 percent of the 216 businesses inspected were out of compliance with all three agencies (California Commission on Health and Safety and Workers' Compensation 2014). Similarly, efforts targeted at low-wage, Spanish-speaking workers and carried out through federal partnerships with the Mexican Consulate also provide examples of cross-filing models (Bada and Gleeson 2015).

Ultimately, the problem with relying on a claims-driven system to hold employers accountable is not simply one of scale and efficiency but also one of authority. By relying on workers to bring a claim forward, legal scholar Kati L. Griffith (2012) argues, enforcement systems in effect deputize workers as private attorneys general who lack the proper expertise to fulfill their intended role (631). Rather than "police-patrol oversight," which would rely on widespread government inspections, this "fire-alarm oversight" approach relies on (often precarious) workers to pull the workplace "fire alarm" when necessary (see also McCubbins and Schwartz 1984). This is not to say that Congress did not anticipate this challenge in passing legislation to protect employees who do pull the alarm. In fact, the Fair Labor Standards Act and Title VII of the Civil Rights Act intended to preempt *sub-federal* laws that would otherwise discourage employees from coming forward. Both statutes provide incentives for these claims by allowing claimants to initiate private suits and requiring employers to pay attorneys' fees and costs when workers win, as well as providing anti-retaliation remedies (Griffith 2011a, 432–36).[4] (Yet, as my findings reveal, these incentives and remedies are dependent on a worker not only prevailing but also continuing to make her way through the claims process.) In the event of a victory, this legislation also requires that agencies make offending employers actually comply with a positive judgment, a difficult prospect when companies file bankruptcy, shut down, or simply disappear.

While it is unlikely that the imbalances in the claims-driven enforcement system will be eradicated, current state and local efforts to tie an employer's business operations to their workplace violation track record are encouraging. For example, emerging wage theft provisions in cities and counties across the country have used the revocation of business licenses as a tool with which to compel companies to comply with final judgments (National Employment Law Project 2011, 2012).

In this regulatory landscape, the challenge for undocumented workers is further complicated given their uncertainty about deportation. California law has addressed this fear explicitly in recent changes to the Labor Code, which revokes the business licenses of employers who use a worker's immigration status to threaten him or her. The new changes also allow a civil action to be brought against the offending employer (National Employment Law Project 2013). Similar protections are certainly needed across the country and should be expanded. In any case, the deeper structural issue remains the precarity of both low-wage workers and especially low-wage undocumented workers, who face the possibility of losing their jobs and have few or no other sources of support to meet their families' basic needs. Furthermore, even those who retain their jobs have limited time and resources to devote to advancing their claims, and the competing demands of everyday life are often likely to win out. As such, labor standards enforcement cannot rely solely on the efforts of precarious workers to hold employers accountable.

IMMIGRATION REFORM: NECESSARY AND INSUFFICIENT

The hurdles claimants face in navigating the labor standards enforcement bureaucracy are substantial regardless of legal status, but undocumented workers face specific and undeniable challenges. As of the writing of this book, the current political context in the United States has worsened for undocumented immigrants, given the hardened anti-immigrant rhetoric in the presidential election and the split June 24, 2016, Supreme Court decision in United States v. Texas, which effectively halted President Obama's attempt to provide deportation relief and work authorization to parents of US citizens and legal permanent resident children under the Deferred Action for Parental Accountability (DAPA) program. The injunction has also blocked relief for an expanded group of youth who are otherwise ineligible for the 2012 Deferred Action for Childhood Arrivals program.

For these still-undocumented workers, their legal status operates as a "precarity multiplier" (Gleeson 2014a). They are subject to deportation unless they qualify for one of the various narrow forms of relief reserved for individuals who assist with law enforcement, such as the U visa (Saucedo 2010; National Employment Law Project 2014). These "liminal legal statuses," however, hardly allow workers to immediately secure a higher-paying job in the formal economy that would transform their material reality (Abrego and Lakhani 2015). The yearly cap of 10,000 U visas has been reached every year since its creation in 2000. As of December 2014, only 116,471 undocumented immigrants and their family members had benefited from the U visa program (US Citizenship and Immigration Services 2014), compared to the estimated eight million undocumented workers currently in the US labor force.

For undocumented immigrants, a dialectical relationship may emerge between their legal precarity and their economic precarity. That is, if the labor standards enforcement process opens a path toward justice for undocumented workers, their legal status erects symbolic barriers. As my previous work has found (Gleeson 2010), these barriers can keep workers from filing a claim at all. And even for those who have crossed that legal threshold by initiating a claim, the consequences of workplace abuse (and an imperfect system in place to regulate it) can reify notions of subordinate inclusion (Agamben 1998; Chauvin and Garcés-Mascareñas 2014). Unlike the full legal inclusion that citizens apparently enjoy under the law, undocumented workers are relegated to a secondary category. However, unlike the "bare life" that Giorgio Agamben argues renders individuals subject to total political control and subordination, Sébastien Chauvin and Blanca Garcés-Mascareñas (2014) argue that in certain regimes (such as the labor market), undocumented workers should be understood as subcitizens rather than noncitizens altogether. That is, though they are often afforded some formal rights (if not full remedies), they also carry the "stigma of 'illegality'" all through their attempts to realize these rights (253).[5]

As demonstrated by the stories of workers such as Gloria, whose sexual assault at the hands of a manager destroyed her capacity to continue as an economic actor, the sidelining effects of labor exploitation not only harm workers and their families in a practical manner, but also challenge their sense of belonging. In a society so squarely intent on using economic rationales for justifying rights (Bosniak 2002; Baker-Cristales 2009; Gleeson 2015b), workers stripped of their labor capacity are left with few alternative rationales for asserting their worth. That is, in a context where the "hard work" of undocumented workers is hailed as their primary contribution to society (Gleeson 2010), losing access to work through either injury or dismissal can further marginalize them. This is true regardless of whether the law determines their claim to be valid and actionable.

The challenges of navigating the workers' rights bureaucracy also heightens workers' sense of peripheral belonging and shapes every decision they make along the way. In the not-uncommon case of the worker Yael, he could not, given the aggressive tactics of Immigration and Customs Enforcement (ICE), write off as empty his employer's threats to summon the police. With current discussions under way to dismantle sanctuary cities, and with tenuous Memoranda of Understanding in place to prevent immigration enforcement from interfering with labor standards enforcement efforts, the threat of deportation is a practical reality, even in progressive places like the San Francisco Bay Area.

More important to the everyday lives of the workers I interviewed for this book were the practical realities of managing poverty and the constant search for work; the legal ability to file a workplace claim often ranked far lower. This is not to say that work authorization would have no impact on earnings for undocumented workers, as clearly outlined by a recent Center for American Progress report, which estimates an 8.5 percent increase in earnings as a result of temporary work permits that would be made available by the currently sidelined, embattled Deferred Action for Parental Accountability program (Oakford 2014). However, this 8.5 percent increase should be understood within a context in which the median household income for unauthorized immigrants is more than 25 percent lower than that of US-born residents, in which the children of unauthorized immigrants are twice as likely to live in poverty, and in which more than half of unauthorized immigrants in the pre–Affordable Care Act era had no health insurance (Passel and Cohn 2009).

Further adding to the precarity of the undocumented is the ongoing decline in union power. Union membership has fallen to 11.1 percent overall, and only 6.6 percent for the private sector (Hirsch and Macpherson 2015). Mexican immigrants, many of whom are noncitizens and unauthorized, have the lowest levels of unionization (Milkman and Braslow 2011), and those who are unionized are represented by unions that are undeniably weaker than those reigning in years past (Rosenfeld 2014). As evidenced by the experiences of the sixty-two unionized workers in my sample, even union membership does not necessarily protect against workplace violations. While these unionized workers consistently reported fewer experiences of wage and hour violations, they reported shockingly similar levels of workplace injuries, verbal abuse, and sexual harassment as their nonunion peers.

Doubtless, there are key advantages to union membership, but not necessarily for the undocumented. One of the most robust benefits of a union contract is providing a more stable alternative to at-will employment by giving workers a structure within which to contest unfair dismissal. Undocumented union members certainly have access to these contract mechanisms, but under the 2002 Hoffman Plastics Supreme Court decision, they do not generally have a right to reinstatement. For the vast majority of nonunion, at-will undocumented workers, this right does not exist, either. As such, both at-will employment policies and employer sanctions fuel precarity for undocumented workers, significantly so for subcontracted and seasonal workers. Unauthorized status also prolongs the period over which workers endure violations such as sexual harassment and unsafe working conditions and shapes the factors that claimants weigh in negotiating settlements.

Therefore, in a context where wages and benefits are low, and job stability near-ly nonexistent, the necessity of immigration reform is inextricably linked to the necessity of revitalizing labor-capital relations and the systems structuring poverty and inequality more generally. The waning welfare state, which currently largely excludes undocumented immigrants (as well as DACA recipients under federal provisions of the Affordable Care Act), relegates the vast majority of undocument-ed workers to the market to meet their basic needs. While these workers are eli-gible to receive basic remedies under wage and hour, discrimination, and workers' compensation law, unemployment benefits are not an option, nor are most public benefits intended to keep individuals and their families out of poverty in the event of job loss or a reduction in hours. These realities should all be understood as the factors driving workers' decisions not only *whether* to file a claim but *how* to pursue it.

Having in this book outlined the history of labor standards enforcement and painted a detailed portrait of the claims process as it stands now, we should con-clude by briefly considering what the future holds for those undocumented work-ers who occupy a vital yet precarious position in our economy. The day after the next major immigration reform is handed down, there will be a new cohort of undocumented immigrants arriving in the United States who are ineligible for re-lief. That is, any legalization effort must also consider the ongoing flow of workers who will inevitably arrive. It is also unclear how those who do benefit from depor-tation relief, and a positive path to citizenship, will be able to translate their new status into educational investments and occupational mobility, especially later in life. While preliminary findings from the now three-year-old Deferred Action for Childhood Arrivals program are optimistic, they are likely limited of course to this relatively young and educated sample (Gonzales and Terriquez 2013; Gonzales, Terriquez, and Ruszczyk 2014; Patler and Cabrera 2015; Wong et al. 2013). Previ-ous evidence from the 1986 Immigration Reform and Control Act, the last major legalization program, suggest lasting negative effects of undocumented status that should temper our optimism about the emancipatory potential of future reforms (Powers, Kraly, and Seltzer 2004). In any case, worker and immigrant advocacy or-ganizations will play a pivotal role in any attempt to make these immigrant rights real (de Graauw 2016).

ON PRECARITY, AGENCY, AND THE PURSUIT OF JUSTICE

Over the last decade there have been a litany of reforms within the realm of in-dividual workers' rights. These include new bases for discrimination protections, expanded coverage for previously unprotected sectors, additional mechanisms to hold employers accountable, and innovations to protect undocumented workers. These also include a scaling back of benefits for workers' compensation beneficiaries, an expansion—and subsequent contraction—of unemployment benefits, and a mixed bag of decisions regarding the rights of workers to collectively bargain. In sum, the formal legal protections for workers' rights have expanded in important ways, even as they have also constricted in an era of increased "flexibilization" that has made workers more precarious (Fraser 2003). Irrespective of these advances and setbacks, coalitions of attorneys and other professionals have continued to advocate for workers' rights and attempted to hold the line for the most vulnerable employees. Groups such as the National Employment Law Project, Interfaith Worker Justice, Worksafe, the California Employment Lawyers Association, and the Coalition of Low-Wage and Immigrant Worker Advocates have worked tirelessly and effectively to this end.

While I have focused here on the experiences of individual workers navigating bureaucratic claims processes, these findings also have a bearing on how marginalized workers are being incorporated into collective mobilizations through unions and other worker centers. We know from the seminal work of Frances Fox Piven and Richard Cloward (1977) that bureaucratic forms of organizing can prove stifling, even when nominally in the service of positive reform. Social movement scholars such as Kim Voss and Rachel Sherman have identified key ingredients for combating bureaucratic conservatism in organized labor (Voss and Sherman 2000) and incorporating immigrants into collective mobilizing (Sherman and Voss 2000). Jennifer Chun's work highlights the importance of understanding how workers themselves conceive of their precarious employment relationships (Chun 2009) in going beyond the reliance on exclusionary models of leadership by elite professionals (such as attorneys and other technocratic experts) (Chun 2016). Similar bottom-up strategies have proven effective in a wide range of other democratic projects that foster local governance and decision making (see for example Fung 2009).

Beyond improvements in the individual workers' rights regime, coalitions have advanced alternative strategies beyond and outside the law to address the gaping hole between what the law says and what it does—or even to redefine what the law *should* do. Key examples from recent years include movements working to increase the minimum wage despite the ambivalence of federal and state legislators. The Fight for $15, which calls for a $15 minimum wage in the fast food industry, has perhaps become the most iconic of these movements for its attempt to organize a notoriously unorganizable sector. Other alternative labor strategies that rely on collective mobilization of precarious workers, such as the (now waning) OUR Walmart campaign, which nonetheless undoubtedly had some effect on the company's decision to announce a wage hike (Hopkins 2015), were energizing as well. The demands to expand key occupational safety and health provisions to farmworkers in California, as well as the victories of the Domestic Workers Bills of Rights in Massachusetts, California, and Hawaii, are other examples of invigorating critical movements (Appelbaum 2010).

Workers themselves have also developed alternative strategies of resistance that parallel the efforts made in the legal arena. For example, when a restaurant in Silicon Valley refused to pay its many outstanding judgments with the Labor Commissioner, a coalition of advocates (including the same attorneys who processed the wage claims through the formal bureaucracy) staged an ongoing protest that eventually shut the notorious employer down (Myllenbeck 2015; State of California Department of Industrial Relations 2014a). Similarly, there have been countless consumer boycotts against offending employers who have pending cases before various agencies. Most notably, the recent boycotts of Driscoll's (a berry grower that has underpaid its pickers in the United States and Mexico) (Luban 2015) and Amazon (following a 2015 *New York Times* exposé) (Kantor and Streitfeld 2015), have gained traction.

In other cases, mass protest has emerged as a way to advance perceived rights that the law does not recognize. For example, when a snacks factory in upstate New York recently chose to shut down and fire its workforce, workers and their advocates mobilized to protest a legal but (in their eyes) unfair action (Sayegh 2015). These attempts to pursue justice and restitution even when there was no identifiable violation reflect advocates' frustration with the current system of labor standards enforcement. They also reflect the frustrations of workers seeking, often unsuccessfully, to effect lasting change in an era of global capital. Driscoll's continues unfazed, and at last check Amazon is in no danger of going under.

What, finally, does this all mean for how we define and pursue social justice? Alfonso Gonzales (2013) offers a useful framework for understanding the failure of dominant (and heroic) efforts to defend immigrants' rights. The author argues that part of the explanation for these shortcomings lies in the myopic view of the neoliberal roots of migration and the entrenched nature of state violence; the democratic ideal, in other words, does not necessarily apply to all residents of the United States. An extension of this analysis must also recognize the weak legal and bureaucratic structures that regulate employer behavior—structures that are unable to alone address economic precarity for both undocumented immigrants and the other low-wage workers they labor beside. One answer is to break out of nation-bound models of inclusion, as advocated by Seyla Benhabib (2004), Linda Bosniak (2006), and Nancy Fraser (2009). But a move toward cosmopolitan rights does not alone guarantee equality. Transnational advocates, all of whom have their own interests, are also not in and of themselves a panacea. Together, an expanded rights regime, an empowered network of global workers and their advocates, and a persistent check on state and economic power will be required.

1. INTRODUCTION

1. Guy Standing's analysis has been deconstructed by a variety of critics who argue that the term is neither novel nor coherent, that it miscalculates the political implications of this new class formation, and that it ignores the empirical reality of the Global South (Paret 2016; Munck 2013; Breman 2013; Allen and Ainley 2011). See also Brown (2011) and Lee and Kofman (2012).

2. Based on analyses of Current Population Survey data, John Schmitt (2014) finds that only about one quarter of low-wage workers obtained health insurance from their employer in 2010, compared to 43 percent three decades ago (276). Although the Affordable Care Act created incentives for employers to provide workers with insurance, expanding Medicaid programs and federal subsidies is more likely to benefit these workers (283).

3. Labor standards enforcement processes have similarly promoted alternatives to administrative hearings and superior court litigation (Nielsen and Nelson 2005). In the case of unions, Nelson Lichtenstein (2002) argues that individualized grievance arbitration procedures, bogged down by seniority and precedent rules that have tamed more radical social movement tactics, have proven to be slow and ineffective.

4. Generally speaking, this phenomenon doesn't have to do with resources necessarily but rather with the types of claims these groups are likely to pursue (Miller and Sarat 1980). However, as Susan S. Silbey's (2005) ten-year-old but still very relevant review discusses, there is weak evidence that entire groups of people—women, people of color, workers— necessarily all engage the law in the same way.

5. As the entire field of critical race theory has established, racial inequality becomes inscribed not only in how the law is constructed, but also in how underrepresented racial minorities are able to mobilize the law. The diversity of undocumented workers across nationality (Passel and Cohn 2009) does not negate the racial inflections of this exclusion.

6. Michel-Rolph Trouillot (2001), adapting from Nicos Poulantzas, describes the reach of state power as producing "atomized" and "individualized citizens who all appear equal in a supposedly undifferentiated public sphere" (131). In the context of workplace protection, the creation of an individual rights regime decontextualizes workers from broader considerations of class struggle and race and gender inequality.

7. Source: US Census Bureau, 2011–13 Three-Year American Community Survey, DP02 and DP05, San Jose–San Francisco–Oakland, CA CSA, http://factfinder2.census.gov/.

8. However, none received funding from the Legal Services Corporation, which provides federal money for legal aid but expressly prohibits, with rare exceptions, organizations from serving undocumented clients. Clinic attendees had to meet low-income guidelines in order to qualify for services.

9. Where applicable, all interviews presented in this book have been translated into English by the author.

10. This is based on a series of reductive questions regarding nativity, citizenship status, legal permanent residence, and work authorization.

2. INEQUALITY AND POWER AT WORK

1. These include, in order of cost, Marin, San Francisco, San Mateo, (Honolulu), Santa Clara, and Santa Cruz counties.

2. Interview, June 2, 2012.

3. Interview, September 19, 2013.

4. Interview, October 5, 2009.

5. Interview, May 26, 2013.

6. Interview, October 3, 2013.

7. Interview, September 11, 2013.

8. Interview, May 20, 2013.

9. Interview, February 13, 2009.

10. Interview, September 19, 2013.

11. Interview, January 14, 2014.

12. Interview, September 23, 2013.

13. In 2014 California Governor Jerry Brown signed Assembly Bill 1897, which holds companies accountable for the workplace violations, even when they use labor contractors to locate and hire workers.

14. Interview, October 24, 2011.

15. Interview, February 13, 2009.

16. Interview, January 11, 2013.

17. Interview, November 17, 2013.

18. Interview, October 8, 2013.

19. Interview, December 20, 2011.

20. Interview, December 27, 2011.

21. Interview, January 4, 2012.

22. Interview, April 4, 2012.

23. Interview, April 2, 2012.

24. Interview, October 29, 2013.

25. Interview, October 22, 2013.

26. Interview, December 22, 2011.

27. Interview, June 6, 2013.

28. Interview, September 21, 2013.

3. THE LANDSCAPE AND LOGICS OF WORKER PROTECTIONS

1. For a useful compilation of reports on wage theft, see http://wagetheft.org/.

2. Anderson v. Mt. Clemens Pottery Co., 328 U.S.680 (1946).

3. For an overview of the DLSE claims process, see https://www.youtube.com/watch?v=eX6NZk6IxZc.

4. Data obtained through a public records request to the Division of Labor Standards Enforcement, March 10, 2014.

5. For example, in the biotech and nanotech industries, the health impacts of chemical exposure are poorly understood (see Leahy 2014).

6. http://www.coshnetwork.org/.

7. It is worth noting, however, that Matthew Hall and Emily Greenman found that undocumented workers are not more likely to work in the *most* dangerous settings, such as those with exposure to toxic materials, radiation, and disease, likely owing to enhanced security requirements and other gatekeeping mechanisms in these areas (2015, 431).

8. Additionally, there are also several other policies and laws that impact worker safety, such as standards enforced through the California Department of Pesticide Regulation.

9. In Texas, where employers are not required to carry workers' compensation insurance, a third of employers are nonsubscribers (Betts and Geeslin 2006).

10. This process becomes high-stakes, and is compounded by the fact that low-wage workers also often do not have access to private health coverage, leading them often to rely heavily on the (more expensive) services provided by the workers' compensation system (Baker and Krueger 1993).

11. California Labor Code Section 132a prohibits discrimination on the basis of a workers' compensation claim.

12. In the public sector, a federal employee may file a formal complaint only after attempting mediation. If there are no procedural errors, and the worker files on time, then the agency will conduct an investigation within 180 days, then give the worker the option to accept a decision based on this investigation or request a hearing, where an administrative judge hears the case. At several points throughout the process, the worker has the option to request a Notice of Right to Sue letter, where the case can be moved to district court. The agency's decision can be appealed to federal district court (if filed through the EEOC), and, in limited cases, subjected to a reconsideration (US Equal Employment Opportunity Commission 2015f).

13. There are important distinctions based on specific statutes, most notably age discrimination and Equal Pay Act cases (US Equal Employment Opportunity Commission 2015g). See http://www.eeoc.gov/eeoc/newsroom/wysk/abcs.cfm.

14. Interview, December 3, 2013.

15. While disparate impact theory does not rely on discriminatory motives, critics argue that the use of statistics is often inconsistent and ineffective for challenging the decisions that exclude underrepresented workers (Zuberi and Bonilla-Silva 2008).

16. These institutional environments significantly affect how workers perceive discrimination (Hirsh and Lyons 2010), the conditions under which discrimination occurs (Hirsh and Kornrich 2008), and the outcomes of charges (Hirsh 2008).

17. Interview, September 11, 2013.

18. Interview, September 25, 2013.

19. Alabama, Arizona, Arkansas, Florida, Georgia, Idaho, Indiana, Iowa, Kansas, Louisiana, Michigan, Mississippi, Nebraska, Nevada, North Carolina, North Dakota, Oklahoma, South Carolina, South Dakota, Tennessee, Texas, Utah, Virginia, Wisconsin, and Wyoming (National Right to Work Legal Defense Foundation 2015).

20. Of the 453 workers surveyed initially, 62 (13.6 percent) were union members, as were 19 (21.3 percent) of the 89 follow-up interviewees.

21. The Employee Free Choice Act, a national effort to make the process more efficient by switching over to "card-check," has been largely dead for eight years (Madland and Walter 2009).

22. However, more conservative political contexts have led to a narrowing set of protections for nonunion workers (O'Brien 2005).

23. Interview, May 31, 2013.

24. Interview, August 24, 2013.

25. Interview, September 21, 2013.

26. Interview, September 19, 2013.

27. Interview, October 3, 2013.

28. Typically the Office of Special Counsel (OSC) will take cases that involve workplaces with between four and fourteen employees. If an employer has fifteen or more employees, OSC will refer the case to the EEOC, while the EEOC will refer cases it does not have jurisdiction over to the OSC (Griffith 2011b, 1144).

29. Hoffman Plastic Compounds Inc. v. NLRB, 535 US 137 (2002).

30. Here and elsewhere in this manuscript, I use the terms *undocumented* and *unauthorized* interchangeably, following their usage by advocates, researchers, and the court.

31. The National Immigration Law Center, for example, has argued that the Social Security Administration databases on which the Basic Pilot / E-Verify program rely are riddled with errors, leading to the misidentification of many workers who should be authorized for employment. The adoption of the program, NILC also argues, imposes an undue burden and costs on small employers who have federal contracts and are thus required to participate in the program (National Immigration Law Center 2009).

32. http://www.catrustact.org/.

4. NAVIGATING BUREAUCRACIES

1. These interviews include 89 follow-ups with survey respondents and 24 interviews with injured workers recruited from Division of Workers' Compensation Injured Workers Workshops.

2. For overviews of each field, see for example Binder (2010) and Delgado and Stefancic (2001), respectively.

3. Beyond systematic bias, the arbitrary nature of rulings in some contexts can also derail a legal strategy. This is especially the case in the immigration and asylum law context (Schrag, Schoenholtz, and Ramji-Nogales 2009).

4. More broadly, the ongoing and widespread misclassification of these independent contractors (discussed in the previous chapter) can be understood as an attempt to negate the employment relationship (and thus liability) altogether (National Employment Law Project 2009).

5. Interview, December 12, 2011.

6. Interview, December 20, 2011.

7. Interview, January 9, 2014.

8. Interview, March 3, 2009.

9. Interview, June 4, 2013.

10. For example, one of the most common problems scholars and advocates have highlighted is that of the misclassification of independent contractors (National Employment Law Project 2009).

11. Interview, December 20, 2011.

12. Interview, January 28, 2012.

13. Interview, March 5, 2009.

14. Field notes, April 8, 2014.

15. Interview, January 3, 2014.

16. Interview, March 8, 2012.

17. Interview, September 17, 2013.

18. Interview, May 29, 2012.

19. Interview, January 24, 2012.

20. Interview, November 12, 2012.

21. Interview, June 14, 2013.

22. Interview, August 22, 2013.

23. Despite the public perception that unauthorized immigrants rely overwhelmingly on emergency room care, studies have confirmed that in fact immigrants are much less likely to use emergency rooms than native-born citizens (Cunningham 2006).

24. See: http://www.lep.gov/.

25. Interview, May 28, 2013.

26. Interview, January 4, 2012.

27. Interview, February 13, 2009.

28. Interview, December 12, 2011.

29. Interview, January 11, 2013.

30. Interview, September 23, 2013.

31. In 2013, California Senate Bill 462 limited the ability of prevailing employers to collect attorney fees unless the worker is found to have filed their claim in bad faith.

32. The pro bono bar is particularly important for low-income workers in navigating not only workplace claims, but also a range of related issues. Indeed, in the wake of a workplace dispute, there can be a snowball effect on a worker's housing security, family obligations,

and other financial obligations. The legal aid support available across these various arenas takes a number of forms, but the resources available rarely meet the need (Estreicher and Radice 2016).

33. Interview, April 5, 2012.

34. Interview, May 17, 2013.

35. Interview, June 7, 2012.

36. Interview, September 17, 2013.

37. This discrepancy is reflected in advocacy outreach material, which guides workers on how to communicate with their overburdened attorneys (Legal Aid Society—Employment Law Center 2015c).

38. Interview, October 8, 2013.

39. Interview, April 4, 2012.

40. Interview, November 22, 2013.

41. Interview, September 11, 2013.

42. Interview, January 11, 2013.

43. Interview, November 23, 2013.

44. Interview, November 12, 2013.

45. Interview, May 26, 2013.

46. This is not to say that there is no protocol for enforcing judgments against employers who have filed for bankruptcy (Legal Aid Society—Employment Law Center 2015a). However, workers join an often long line of creditors, and the process for getting in this line is burdensome.

47. Interview, May 28, 2013.

5. THE AFTERMATH OF LEGAL MOBILIZATION

1. Interview, October 24, 2011.

2. Interview, June 6, 2013.

3. Interview, June 4, 2013.

4. Interview, June 7, 2012.

5. Interview, November 13, 2012.

6. Interview, February 3, 2014.

7. Interview, January 11, 2013.

8. Interview, September 23, 2013.

9. Interview, October 24, 2011.

10. Interview, December 20, 2011.

11. Interview, July 16, 2013.

12. Interview, November 23, 2013.

13. Interview, January 14, 2014.

14. Interview, February 2, 2012.

15. Interview, April 5, 2012.

16. Interview, October 8, 2013.

17. Interview, July 17, 2009.

18. Interview, March 16, 2009.

19. Interview, October 22, 2013.

20. Interview, July 29, 2009.

21. Interview, February 13, 2009.

22. Interview, December 12, 2011.

23. Interview, October 21, 2011.

24. Interview, October 3, 2013.

25. One aspect of this restrictionist approach is efforts at the state and local level to beef up enforcement. This has been carried out in Alabama and Arizona, where undocumented individuals now fear any interaction with government agencies, even to carry out standard, necessary actions such as registering for public schools (a benefit notably afforded to *all* children regardless of legal status) (Serwer 2012). According to the Pew Hispanic Center, these anti-immigrant campaigns have led to net migration leveling off in recent years: "Of the 1.4 million Mexican immigrants and their children who returned to Mexico from the U.S. between 2005 and 2010 . . . most did so voluntarily." The study also notes that "anywhere from 5 to 35 percent [of Mexican return migrants] were sent back by U.S. authorities. . . . The other 65 to 95 percent returned to Mexico voluntarily" (Passel, Cohn, and Gonzalez-Barrera 2012).

26. While Raúl had received many such notices in the past, he wondered if this latest was the result of a long-overdue attempt to open a bank account in the United States.

27. Interview, April 5, 2012.

28. Interview, October 21, 2011.

29. Interview, June 20, 2013.

30. Interview, November 17, 2013.

31. Interview, December 3, 2013.

32. Interview, September 17, 2013.

6. CONCLUSION

1. http://www.dir.ca.gov/dlse/aboutdlse.html.

2. Interest on Lawyers Trust Accounts (IOLTA) funds are administered by each state and provide grants for access to justice, especially in the arena of civil legal aid. See http://www.iolta.org/what-is-iolta.

3. Response to public records request, March 4, 2014.

4. The current leadership of several of the labor standards enforcement agencies in California comes out of respected workers' rights communities, including California Labor Commissioner Julie Su and Department of Fair Employment and Housing Director Kevin Kish. Both have stellar records with respect to advancing the rights of immigrant workers in particular, and are expected to maintain their tough stance on retaliatory behaviors.

5. See also Abrego (2011).

REFERENCES

Early findings from the research in this book appeared in the following:

Abrego, Leisy J., and Shannon Gleeson. 2014. "Workers, Families, and Immigration Policies." In *Undecided Nation: Political Gridlock and the Immigration Crisis*, 209–28. Edited by Tony Payan and Erika de la Garza. Vol. 6 of *Immigrants and Minorities, Politics and Policy*. New York: Springer.

Gleeson, Shannon. 2014. "Navigating Occupational Health Rights: The Function of Illegality, Language, and Class Inequality in Workers' Compensation." In *The Nation and Its Peoples: Citizens, Denizens, Migrants*. Edited by John S. W. Park and Shannon Gleeson. New York: Routledge.

Gleeson, Shannon. 2015. "Between Support and Shame: The Impacts of Workplace Violations for Immigrant Families." In vol. 27 of *Research in the Sociology of Work: Immigration and Work*, 29–52. Edited by Jody Agius Vallejo. Bingley, England: Emerald.

Gleeson, Shannon. 2015. "Brokered Pathways to Justice and Cracks in the Law: A Closer Look at the Claims-Making Experiences of Low-Wage Workers." *WorkingUSA* 18 (1): 77–102.

Gleeson, Shannon. 2015. "Narratives of Deservingness and the Institutional Youth of Immigrant Workers." Special issue on "Complicating the Politics of Deservingness: A Critical Look at Undocumented (Im)migrant Youth," edited by Genevieve Negrón-Gonzales, Leisy Abrego, and Kathleen Coll, *Association of Mexican-American Educators Journal* 9 (3): 47–61.

Works Cited

Abrego, Leisy J. 2011. "Legal Consciousness of Undocumented Latinos: Fear and Stigma as Barriers to Claims Making for First and 1.5 Generation Immigrants." *Law and Society Review* 45 (2): 337–70.

———. 2014. *Sacrificing Families: Navigating Laws, Labor, and Love Across Borders*. Stanford, CA: Stanford University Press.

Abrego, Leisy J., and Roberto G. Gonzales. 2010. "Blocked Paths, Uncertain Futures: The Postsecondary Education and Labor Market Prospects of Undocumented Latino Youth." *Journal of Education for Students Placed at Risk* 15 (1–2): 144–57.

Abrego, Leisy J., and Sarah M. Lakhani. 2015. "Incomplete Inclusion: Legal Violence and Immigrants in Liminal Legal Statuses." *Law and Policy* 37 (4): 265–93.

ACLU Foundation. 2014. "American Exile: Rapid Deportations That Bypass the Courtroom." New York: American Civil Liberties Union. https://www.aclu.org/files/assets/120214-expeditedremoval_0.pdf.

Addington, Lynn A., and Jessica L. Waters. 2012. "Public Interest 101: Using the Law School Curriculum to Quell Public Interest Drift and Expand Students' Public Interest Commitment." *American University Journal of Gender, Social Policy and the Law* 21: 79–108.

Agamben, Giorgio. 1998. *Homo Sacer: Sovereign Power and Bare Life.* Stanford, CA: Stanford University Press.

Albiston, Catherine R. 2005a. "Bargaining in the Shadow of Social Institutions: Competing Discourses and Social Change in Workplace Mobilization of Civil Rights." *Law and Society Review* 39 (1): 11–50.

———. 2005b. "Rights Consciousness, Claiming Behavior, and the Dynamics of Litigation." In *Handbook of Employment Discrimination Research: Rights and Realities.* Edited by Laura B. Nielsen and Robert L Nelson. Dordrecht, the Netherlands: Springer.

———. 2010. *Institutional Inequality and the Mobilization of the Family and Medical Leave Act: Rights on Leave.* New York: Cambridge University Press.

Albiston, Catherine R., and Laura Beth Nielsen. 2014. "Funding the Cause: How Public Interest Law Organizations Fund Their Activities and Why It Matters for Social Change." *Law and Social Inquiry* 39 (1): 62–95.

Alexander, Charlotte, Zev J. Eigen, and Camille Gear Rich. 2016. "Post-Racial Hydraulics: The Hidden Dangers of the Universal Turn." *New York University Law Review* 91 (1): 1–58.

Allen, Martin, and Patrick Ainley. 2011. "The Precariat: The New Dangerous Class." *International Studies in Sociology of Education* 21 (3): 255–61.

Appelbaum, Lauren D. 2010. "Why a Domestic Workers Bill of Rights?" *UCLA Institute for Research on Labor and Employment Research and Policy Brief*, no. 6 (December). http://www.irle.ucla.edu/publications/documents/ResearchBrief6.pdf.

Armenta, Amada. 2015. "Between Public Service and Social Control: Policing Dilemmas in the Era of Immigration Enforcement." *Social Problems* 63 (1): 111–26.

———. 2016. "Racializing Crimmigration: Structural Racism, Colorblindness and the Institutional Production of Immigrant Criminality." *Sociology of Race and Ethnicity* (May).

Avalos, George, and Pete Carey. 2014. "Bay Area Apartment Rents Set Record." *San Jose Mercury News*, April 15. http://www.mercurynews.com/business/ci_25573285/bay-area-apartment-rents-set-record.

Bacon, David. 2008. "Workers Overcome Divisions After Mississippi Raid." Truthout.org, September 8. http://archive.truthout.org/article/workers-overcome-divisions-after-mississippi-raid.

Bada, Xóchitl, and Shannon Gleeson. 2015. "A New Approach to Migrant Labor Rights Enforcement: The Crisis of Undocumented Worker Abuse and Mexican Consular Advocacy in the United States." *Labor Studies Journal* 40 (1): 32–53.

Baker, Laurence C., and Alan B. Krueger. 1993. "Twenty-Four-Hour Coverage and Workers' Compensation Insurance." *Health Affairs* 12, supplement 1: 271–81.

Baker-Cristales, Beth. 2009. "Mediated Resistance: The Construction of Neoliberal Citizenship in the Immigrant Rights Movement." *Latino Studies* 7 (1): 60–82.

Bales, Kevin. 2012. *Disposable People: New Slavery in the Global Economy*. Berkeley: University of California Press.

Ballon, Daniel, Jordan Kwan, Clare Pastore, and Kevin Kish. 2009. "Voices from the Underground Economy: The Experiences of Workers and Advocates Seeking Meal and Rest Breaks in Low-Wage Industries." Los Angeles: USC Gould School of Law Access to Justice Practicum and Bet Tzedek Legal Services. http://www.bettzedek.org/wp-content/uploads/voicesfromtheunderground.pdf.

Barstow, David, and Alejandra Xanic Von Bertrab. 2012. "How Wal-Mart Used Payoffs to Get Its Way in Mexico." *New York Times*, December 17. http://www.nytimes.com/2012/12/18/business/walmart-bribes-teotihuacan.html.

Benhabib, Seyla. 2004. *The Rights of Others: Aliens, Residents, and Citizens*. Cambridge, England: Cambridge University Press.

Bernacki, Edward J., and Xuguang Grant Tao. 2008. "The Relationship between Attorney Involvement, Claim Duration, and Workers' Compensation Costs." *Journal of Occupational and Environmental Medicine* 50 (9): 1013–18.

Bernhardt, Annette. 2012. "The Role of Labor Market Regulation in Rebuilding Economic Opportunity in the United States." *Work and Occupations* 39 (4): 354–75.

Bernhardt, Annette, Heather Boushey, Laura Dresser, and Chris Tilly. 2008. *The Gloves-Off Economy: Workplace Standards at the Bottom of America's Labor Market*. Ithaca, NY: ILR Press.

Bernhardt, Annette, Ruth Milkman, Nik Theodore, Douglas Heckathorn, Mirabai Auer, James DeFilippis, Ana Luz González, et al. 2009. "Broken Laws, Unprotected Workers: Violations of Employment and Labor Laws in America's Cities." Center for Urban Economic Development, National Employment Law Project, and the UCLA Institute for Research on Labor and Employment. http://nelp.3cdn.net/319982941a5496c741_9qm6b92kg.pdf.

Bernhardt, Annette, Michael W. Spiller, and Diana Polson. 2013. "All Work and No Pay: Violations of Employment and Labor Laws in Chicago, Los Angeles and New York City." *Social Forces* 91 (3): 725–46.

Berrey, Ellen, Steve G. Hoffman, and Laura Beth Nielsen. 2012. "Situated Justice: A Contextual Analysis of Fairness and Inequality in Employment Discrimination Litigation." *Law and Society Review* 46 (1): 1–36.

Best, Rachel Kahn, Lauren B. Edelman, Linda Hamilton Krieger, and Scott R. Eliason. 2011. "Multiple Disadvantages: An Empirical Test of Intersectionality Theory in EEO Litigation." *Law and Society Review* 45 (4): 991–1025.

Betts, Albert, and Mike Geeslin. 2006. "Biennial Report of the Texas Department of Insurance to the 80th Legislature." Austin, TX: Division of Workers' Compensation. http://www.tdi.state.tx.us/reports/dwc/documents/wc2006.pdf.

Binder, Guyora. 2010. "Critical Legal Studies." In *A Companion to Philosophy of Law and Legal Theory*, 267–78. Edited by Dennis Patterson. Malden, MA: Blackwell.

Blasi, Gary, and Joseph W. Doherty. 2010. "California Employment Discrimination Law and Its Enforcement: The Employment and Housing Act at 50." Los Angeles: Center for Law and Public Policy (A Joint Center of UCLA Law and Rand). http://dfeh.ca.gov/res/docs/Renaissance/FEHA%20Study%20Executive%20Summary_FINAL.pdf.

Bloor, Michael. 2011. "An Essay on 'Health Capital' and the Faustian Bargains Struck by Workers in the Globalised Shipping Industry." *Sociology of Health and Illness* 33 (7): 973–86.

Bobo, Kim. 2008. *Wage Theft in America: Why Millions of Working Americans Are Not Getting Paid—and What We Can Do About It.* New York: The New Press.

Bohn, Sarah, Magnus Lofstrom, and Steven Raphael. 2013. "Did the 2007 Legal Arizona Workers Act Reduce the State's Unauthorized Immigrant Population?" *Review of Economics and Statistics* 96 (2): 258–69.

Boltanski, Luc, and Laurent Thévenot. 1999. "The Sociology of Critical Capacity." *European Journal of Social Theory* 2 (3): 359–77.

Bolton, Megan, Elina Bravve, Emily Miller, Sheila Crowley, and Ellen Errico. 2015. "Out of Reach 2015: Low Wages and High Rents Lock Renters Out." Washington, DC: National Low Income Housing Coalition. http://nlihc.org/sites/default/files/oor/OOR_2015_FULL.pdf.

Bonacich, Edna. 1972. "A Theory of Ethnic Antagonism: The Split Labor Market." *American Sociological Review* 37 (5): 547–59.

Bonilla-Silva, Eduardo. 2006. *Racism without Racists: Color-Blind Racism and the Persistence of Racial Inequality in the United States.* Oxford: Rowman and Littlefield.

Bonilla-Silva, Eduardo, and Gianpaolo Baiocchi. 2001. "Anything but Racism: How Sociologists Limit the Significance of Racism." *Race and Society* 4 (2): 117–31.

Borjas, George. 2013. "Immigration and the American Worker: A Review of the Academic Literature." Washington, DC: Center for Immigration Studies. http://www.hks.harvard.edu/fs/gborjas/publications/popular/CIS2013.pdf.

Bosniak, Linda. 2002. "Citizenship and Work." *North Carolina Journal of International Law and Commercial Regulations* 27: 497–521.

———. 2006. *The Citizen and the Alien: Dilemmas of Contemporary Membership.* Princeton, NJ: Princeton University Press.

Bradley, David H. 2015. "The Federal Minimum Wage: In Brief." Washington, DC: Congressional Research Service. http://www.fas.org/sgp/crs/misc/R43089.pdf.

Breman, Jan. 2013. "A Bogus Concept?" *New Left Review* 2 (84): 130–38.

Brown, Nina, ed. 2011. *Anthropology of Work Review, Virtual Issue: Precarity.* American Anthropological Association. http://onlinelibrary.wiley.com/journal/10.1111/(ISSN)1548-1417/homepage/virtual_issue__precarity.htm.

Brownell, Peter. 2011. "Supreme Court Decisions Regarding Workplace Remedies for Unauthorized Employees." *Law and Society Association Annual Meeting.* San Francisco, May 30.

Bureau of Labor Statistics. 2014. "National Census of Fatal Occupational Injuries in 2013 (Preliminary Results)." Washington, DC: United States Department of Labor. http://www.bls.gov/news.release/pdf/cfoi.pdf.

———. 2015a. "Local Area Unemployment Statistics, Unemployment Rates for States Annual Average Rankings Year: 2010." Washington, DC: United States Department of Labor. http://www.bls.gov/lau/lastrk10.htm.

———. 2015b. "Local Area Unemployment Statistics, Unemployment Rates for States Annual Average Rankings Year: 2013." Washington, DC: United States Department of Labor. http://www.bls.gov/lau/lastrk13.htm.

———. 2015c. "Unemployment Rates by State, 2010 Annual Averages." Washington, DC: United States Department of Labor. http://www.bls.gov/lau/maps/stseries.pdf.

———. 2015d. "Union Members—2014." Washington, DC: United States Department of Labor. http://www.bls.gov/news.release/pdf/union2.pdf.

Burnham, Linda, and Nik Theodore. 2012. "Home Economics: The Invisible and Unregulated World of Domestic Work." New York: National Domestic Workers Alliance. http://www.domesticworkers.org/sites/default/files/HomeEconomicsEnglish.pdf.

Burstein, Paul. 1991. "Legal Mobilization as a Social Movement Tactic: The Struggle for Equal Employment Opportunity." *American Journal of Sociology* 96 (5): 1201–25.

Calavita, Kitty, and Valerie Jenness. 2014. *Appealing to Justice*. Berkeley: University of California Press.

California Commission on Health and Safety and Workers' Compensation. 2014. "2014 Annual Report." Oakland: State of California, Department of Industrial Relations. http://www.dir.ca.gov/chswc/Reports/2014/CHSWC_AnnualReport2014.pdf.

California Department of Fair Employment and Housing. 2015. "Employment Flowchart." http://www.dfeh.ca.gov/Complaints_EmpFlowChart.htm.

"California Trust Act." 2015. http://www.catrustact.org/.

Carey, Pete. 2014. "Bay Area Home Prices Jump Year Over Year." *San Jose Mercury News*, April 16. http://www.mercurynews.com/business/ci_25577951/bay-area-home-prices-jump-year-over-year.

Carré, Françoise. 2015. "(In)dependent Contractor Misclassification." Washington, DC: Economic Policy Institute, June 8. http://www.epi.org/publication/independent-contractor-misclassification/.

Chauvin, Sébastien, and Blanca Garcés-Mascareñas. 2014. "Becoming Less Illegal: Deservingness Frames and Undocumented Migrant Incorporation." *Sociology Compass* 8 (4): 422–32.

Chen, Ming. 2013. "Doctrines of Deference Doing the Job in Workers' Compensation Claims." *Law and Society Association Annual Meeting*. Boston, May 30.

Cho, Eunice Hyunhye, Tia Koonse, and Anthony Mischel. 2013. "Hollow Victories: The Crisis in Collecting Unpaid Wages for California's Workers." New York: National Employment Law Project. http://alicelaw.org/uploads/asset/asset_file/1643/Hollow_Victories.pdf.

Chun, Jennifer Jihye. 2009. *Organizing at the Margins: The Symbolic Politics of Labor in South Korea and the United States*. Ithaca, NY: Cornell University Press.

———. 2016. "Building Political Agency and Movement Leadership: The Grassroots Organizing Model of Asian Immigrant Women Advocates." Special issue on "Building Citizenship from Below: Precarity, Migration, and Agency," *Citizenship Studies* 20 (3–4): 379–95.

City of San Jose. 2015. "Living/Prevailing Wage: Living Wage Determination." SanJoseCA. gov. https://www.sanjoseca.gov/index.aspx?NID=768.

Clermont, Kevin M., and Stewart J. Schwab. 2004. "How Employment Discrimination Plaintiffs Fare in Federal Court." *Journal of Empirical Legal Studies* 1 (2): 429–58.

Cohen, Lizabeth. 1991. *Making a New Deal: Industrial Workers in Chicago, 1919–1939.* Cambridge, England: Cambridge University Press.

Coile, Courtney C., Phillip B. Levine, and Robin McKnight. 2014. "Recessions, Older Workers, and Longevity: How Long Are Recessions Good for Your Health?" *American Economic Journal: Economic Policy* 6 (3): 92–119.

Colvin, Alexander J. S. Forthcoming. "Conflict and Employment Relations in the Individual Rights Era." *Advances in Industrial and Labor Relations*, no. 22.

Conti, Judy. 2014. "The Case for Reforming Federal Overtime Rules: Stories from America's Middle Class." Washington, DC: National Employment Law Project. http://www.nelp.org/content/uploads/2015/03/Reforming-Federal-Overtime-Stories.pdf.

Cooper, Laura J., and Catherine L. Fisk. 2005. *Labor Law Stories.* New York: Foundation Press.

Costello, Cathryn, and Mark Freedland. 2014. *Migrants at Work: Immigration and Vulnerability in Labour Law.* Oxford: OUP Oxford.

Coutin, Susan B. 2000. *Legalizing Moves: Salvadoran Immigrants' Struggle for US Residency.* Ann Arbor: University of Michigan Press.

Cox, Rachel, and Katherine Lippel. 2008. "Falling Through the Legal Cracks: The Pitfalls of Using Workers' Compensation Data as Indicators of Work-Related Injuries and Illnesses." *Policy and Practice in Health and Safety* 6 (2): 9–30.

Crenshaw, Kimberlé Williams. "Twenty Years of Critical Race Theory: Looking Back to Move Forward." *Connecticut Law Review* 43 (2011): 1253–352.

Cummings, Scott L. 2009. "Hemmed In: Legal Mobilization in the Los Angeles Anti-Sweatshop Movement." *Berkeley Journal of Employment and Labor Law* 30: 8–27.

———. 2012. "The Pursuit of Legal Rights—and Beyond." *UCLA Law Review* 59: 506–49.

Cummings, Scott L., and Deborah Rhode. 2010. "Managing Pro Bono: Doing Well by Doing Better." *Fordham Law Review* 78: 2357–442.

Cunningham, Peter J. 2006. "What Accounts for Differences in the Use of Hospital Emergency Departments Across U.S. Communities?" *Health Affairs* 25 (5): 324–36.

Curran, Barbara A. 1977. *The Legal Needs of the Public: The Final Report of a National Survey.* Chicago: American Bar Foundation.

Dababneh, Awwad J., Naomi Swanson, and Richard L. Shell. 2001. "Impact of Added Rest Breaks on the Productivity and Well-Being of Workers." *Ergonomics* 44 (2): 164–74.

De Genova, Nicholas. 2005. *Working the Boundaries: Race, Space, and "Illegality" in Mexican Chicago.* Durham, NC: Duke University Press.

de Graauw, Els. 2016. *Making Immigrant Rights Real: Nonprofits and the Politics of Integration in San Francisco.* Ithaca, NY: Cornell University Press.

Delgado, Richard, and Jean Stefancic. 2001. *Critical Race Theory: An Introduction.* New York: New York University Press.

Department of Industrial Relations. 2013. "A Report on the State of the Division of Labor Standards Enforcement." http://www.dir.ca.gov/dlse/Publications/DLSE_Report2013.pdf.

Department of Labor. 2010. "We Can Help." http://www.dol.gov/wecanhelp/.

Dietz, Miranda. 2012. "Temporary Workers in California Are Twice as Likely as Non-Temps to Live in Poverty: Problems with Temporary and Subcontracted Work in California." Berkeley: UC Berkeley Labor Center. http://laborcenter.berkeley.edu/pdf/2012/temp_workers.pdf.

Division of Workers' Compensation. 2012a. "Report of Subsequent Injuries Benefit Trust Fund in Compliance with Labor Code §4755(d)." http://www.dir.ca.gov/dwc/UEF/SIF_LC4755.pdf.

———. 2012b. "Report of Uninsured Employers' Benefits Trust Fund in Compliance with Labor Code §3716.1(c)." http://www.dir.ca.gov/dwc/UEF/UEF_LC3716_1.pdf.

Doussard, Marc. 2013. *Degraded Work: The Struggle at the Bottom of the Labor Market*. Minneapolis: University of Minnesota Press.

Dreby, Joanna. 2010. *Divided by Borders: Mexican Migrants and Their Children*. Berkeley: University of California Press.

Duncan, Grant. 2003. "Workers Compensation and the Governance of Pain." *Economy and Society* 32 (3): 449–77.

Edelman, Lauren B. 1992. "Legal Ambiguity and Symbolic Structures: Organizational Mediation of Civil Rights Law." *American Journal of Sociology* 97 (6): 1531–76.

Eliasoph, Ian H. 2008. "Know Your (Lack of) Rights: Reexamining the Causes and Effects of Phantom Employment Rights." *Employment Rights and Employment Policy Journal* 12 (2): 197–383.

Elwell, Craig K. 2014. "Inflation and the Real Minimum Wage: A Fact Sheet." Washington, DC: Congressional Research Service. http://www.fas.org/sgp/crs/misc/R42973.pdf.

Epp, Charles R. 2010. *Making Rights Real: Activists, Bureaucrats, and the Creation of the Legalistic State*. Chicago: University of Chicago Press.

Estreicher, Samuel, and Joy Radice. 2016. *Beyond Elite Law: Access to Civil Justice in America*. Cambridge, England: Cambridge University Press.

Ewick, Patricia, and Susan S. Silbey. 1998. *The Common Place of Law: Stories from Everyday Life*. Chicago: University of Chicago Press.

Fan, Z. Joyce, David K. Bonauto, Michael P. Foley, and Barbara A. Silverstein. 2006. "Underreporting of Work-Related Injury or Illness to Workers' Compensation: Individual and Industry Factors." *Journal of Occupational and Environmental Medicine* 48 (9): 914–22.

Fantasia, Rick, and Kim Voss. 2004. *Hard Work: Remaking the American Labor Movement*. Berkeley: University of California Press.

Farrell, Mary E. 2008. "Returning Injured Employees to Work While Complying with the ADA and FEHA." Keynote address at the California Division of Workers' Compensation 15th Annual Educational Conference, Los Angeles. http://www.dir.ca.gov/dwc/educonf15/keynotespeaker_presentation.pdf.

Felstiner, William L. F., Richard L. Abel, and Austin Sarat. 1980. "The Emergence and Transformation of Disputes: Naming, Blaming, Claiming." *Law and Society Review* 15 (3–4): 631–54.

Fine, Janice. 2006. *Worker Centers: Organizing Communities at the Edge of the Dream*. Ithaca, NY: ILR Press.

Fine, Janice, and Daniel Tichenor. 2012. "Solidarities and Restrictions: Labor and Immigration Policy in the United States." *The Forum* 10 (1): 1–21.

Fischer, Claude, Michael Hout, Martin Sanchez-Jankowski, Samuel R. Lucas, Ann Swidler, and Kim Voss. 1996. *Inequality by Design: Cracking the Bell Curve Myth*. Princeton, NJ: Princeton University Press.

Fishback, Price V. M., and Shawn E. Kantor. 2006. *A Prelude to the Welfare State: The Origins of Workers' Compensation*. Chicago: University of Chicago Press.

Fraser, Nancy. 2003. "From Discipline to Flexibilization? Rereading Foucault in the Shadow of Globalization." *Constellations* 10 (2): 160–71.

———. 2009. *Scales of Justice: Reimagining Political Space in a Globalizing World*. New York: Columbia University Press.

Freeman, Richard B., and Joel Rogers. 2007. "The Promise of Progressive Federalism." In *Remaking America: Democracy and Public Policy in an Age of Inequality*, 205–27. Edited by Joe Soss, Jacob S. Hacker, and Suzanne Mettler. New York: Russell Sage Foundation.

Fronstin, Paul. 2011. "California's Uninsured." Oakland: California Health Care Foundation. http://www.chcf.org/publications/2011/12/californias-uninsured.

Fung, Archon. 2009. *Empowered Participation: Reinventing Urban Democracy*. Princeton, NJ: Princeton University Press.

Galanter, Marc. 1974. "Why the 'Haves' Come Out Ahead: Speculations on the Limits of Legal Change." *Law and Society Review* 9 (1): 95–160.

Garcia, Ruben J. 2012a. *Marginal Workers: How Legal Fault Lines Divide Workers and Leave Them without Protection*. New York: New York University Press.

———. 2012b. "Ten Years after Hoffman Plastic Compounds Inc. v. NLRB: The Power of a Labor Law Symbol." *Cornell Journal of Law and Public Policy* 21: 659–75.

Glasmeier, Amy K. 2015. "Living Wage Calculator." Cambridge: Massachusetts Institute of Technology. http://livingwage.mit.edu/.

Gleeson, Shannon. 2009. "From Rights to Claims: The Role of Civil Society in Making Rights Real for Vulnerable Workers." *Law and Society Review* 43 (3): 669–700.

———. 2010. "Labor Rights for All? The Role of Undocumented Immigrant Status for Worker Claims-Making." *Law and Social Inquiry* 35 (3): 561–602.

———. 2012a. *Conflicting Commitments: The Politics of Enforcing Immigrant Worker Rights in San Jose and Houston*. Ithaca, NY: Cornell University Press.

———. 2012b. "Leveraging Health Capital at the Workplace: An Examination of Health Reporting Behavior among Latino Immigrant Restaurant Workers in the United States." *Social Science and Medicine* 75 (12): 2291–98.

———. 2014a. "Legal Status as Precarity Multiplier: Social and Economic Consequences of At-Will Employment and Unjust Termination for Unauthorized Workers." Paper presented at the Labor Employment Relations Association Annual Meeting, Portland, Oregon, June 1.

———. 2014b. "Navigating Occupational Health Rights: The Function of Illegality, Language, and Class Inequality in Workers' Compensation." In *The Nation and Its Peoples: Citizens, Denizens, Migrants*. Edited by John S. W. Park and Shannon Gleeson. New York: Routledge.

———. 2015a. "Brokered Pathways to Justice and Cracks in the Law: A Closer Look at the Claims-Making Experiences of Low-Wage Workers." *WorkingUSA* 18 (1): 77–102.

——. 2015b. "'They Come Here to Work': An Evaluation of the Economic Argument in Favor of Immigrant Rights." *Citizenship Studies* 19 (3–4): 400–420.

Gleeson, Shannon, and Roberto Gonzales. 2012. "When Do Papers Matter? An Institutional Analysis of Undocumented Life in the United States." *International Migration* 50 (4): 1–19.

Gleeson, Shannon, Ruth Silver Taube, and Charlie Noss. 2014. "Santa Clara County Wage Theft Report." San Jose, CA: Santa Clara County Wage Theft Coalition. http://www. sccgov.org/sites/owp/Documents/pub/WageTheftReportFinal-2014.pdf.

Golash-Boza, Tanya. 2015. *Deported: Policing Immigrants, Disposable Labor and Global Capitalism*. New York: New York University Press.

Golash-Boza, Tanya, and Pierrette Hondagneu-Sotelo. 2013. "Latino Immigrant Men and the Deportation Crisis: A Gendered Racial Removal Program." *Latino Studies* 11 (3): 271–92.

Gomberg-Muñoz, Ruth. 2011. *Labor and Legality: An Ethnography of a Mexican Immigrant Network*. New York: Oxford University Press.

Gonzales, Alfonso. 2013. *Reform without Justice: Latino Migrant Politics and the Homeland Security State*. New York: Oxford University Press.

Gonzales, Roberto G., and Veronica Terriquez. 2013. "How DACA Is Impacting the Lives of Those Who Are Now DACAmented." Washington, DC: Immigration Policy Center, American Immigration Council. http://www.immigrationpolicy.org/just-facts/ how-daca-impacting-lives-those-who-are-now-dacamented.

Gonzales, Roberto G., Veronica Terriquez, and Stephen P. Ruszczyk. 2014. "Becoming DACAmented: Assessing the Short-Term Benefits of Deferred Action for Childhood Arrivals (DACA)." *American Behavioral Scientist* 58 (14): 1852–72.

Gonzalez-Barrera, Ana, and Jens Manuel Krogstad. 2014. "US Deportations of Immigrants Reach Record High in 2013." Washington, DC: Pew Hispanic Center. http://www. pewresearch.org/fact-tank/2014/10/02/u-s-deportations-of-immigrants-reach-reco rd-high-in-2013/.

Gordon, Jennifer. 2007. *Suburban Sweatshops: The Fight for Immigrant Rights*. Cambridge, MA: Belknap Press.

Government Accountability Office. 2007. "Testimony Before the Subcommittee on Management, Investigations, and Oversight, Committee on Homeland Security, House of Representatives: Border Patrol, Costs and Challenges Related to Training New Agents (Richard M. Stana, Director of Homeland Security a.)." Washington, DC: Government Accountability Office. http://www.gao.gov/new.items/d07997t.pdf.

——. 2009. "Wage and Hour Division's Complaint Intake and Investigative Processes Leave Low Wage Workers Vulnerable to Wage Theft. Statement of Gregory D. Kutz, Managing Director, Forensic Audits and Special Investigations and Jonathan T. Meyer, Assistant Director." Washington, DC: Government Accountability Office. http://www. gao.gov/new.items/d09458t.pdf.

Greenstone, Michael, and Adam Looney. 2010. "Ten Economic Facts about Immigration." In *The Brookings Institution: The Hamilton Project*. Brookings.edu, September. http:// www.brookings.edu/research/reports/2010/09/immigration-greenstone-looney.

———. 2012. "What Immigration Means for US Employment and Wages." Brookings.edu, May 4. http://www.brookings.edu/blogs/jobs/posts/2012/05/04-jobs-greenstone-looney.

Griffith, Kati L. 2011a. "Discovering 'Immployment' Law: The Constitutionality of Subfederal Immigration Regulation at Work." *Yale Law and Policy Review* 29: 389–451.

———. 2011b. "ICE Was Not Meant to Be Cold: The Case for Civil Rights Monitoring of Immigration Enforcement at the Workplace." *Arizona Law Review* 53 (4): 1137–56.

———. 2012. "Undocumented Workers: Crossing the Borders of Immigration and Workplace Law." *Cornell Journal of Law and Public Policy* 21: 611–97.

Griffith, Kati L., and Tamara Lee. 2012. "Immigration Advocacy as Labor Advocacy." *Berkeley Journal of Employment and Labor Law* 33 (1): 73.

Grossman, Joanna L. 2003. "The Culture of Compliance: The Final Triumph of Form over Substance in Sexual Harassment Law." *Harvard Women's Law Journal* 26 (3).

Grossman, Jonathan. 2009. "Fair Labor Standards Act of 1938: Maximum Struggle for a Minimum Wage." Washington, DC: US Department of Labor. http://www.dol.gov/dol/aboutdol/history/flsa1938.htm.

Hacker, Jacob S. 2002. *The Divided Welfare State: The Battle Over Public and Private Social Benefits in the United States.* Cambridge, England: Cambridge University Press.

Hall, Matthew, and Emily Greenman. 2015. "The Occupational Cost of Being Illegal in the United States: Legal Status, Job Hazards, and Compensating Differentials." *Social Forces* 49 (2): 406–42.

Haney López, Ian F. 2000. "Institutional Racism: Judicial Conduct and a New Theory of Racial Discrimination." *Yale Law Journal* 109 (8): 1717–884.

Harper, Michael C., Samuel Estreicher, and Kate Griffith. 2015. *Labor Law: Cases, Materials, and Problems.* 8th edition. New York: Wolters Kluwer.

Harrington, Scott E., and Patricia M. Danzon. 2000. "Rate Regulation, Safety Incentives, and Loss Growth in Workers' Compensation Insurance." *Journal of Business* 73 (4): 569–95.

Hernández, Diana. 2010. "'I'm Gonna Call My Lawyer:' Shifting Legal Consciousness at the Intersection of Inequality." Special issue on "Interdisciplinary Legal Studies: The Next Generation," *Studies in Law, Politics and Society* 51: 95–121.

Higbie, Frank Tobias. 2003. *Indispensable Outcasts: Hobo Workers and Community in the American Midwest, 1880–1930.* Champaign: University of Illinois Press.

Hill, Laura, and Hans P. Johnson. 2011. "Unauthorized Immigrants in California: Estimates for Counties." San Francisco: Public Policy Institute of California. http://www.ppic.org/content/pubs/report/R_711LHR.pdf.

Hirsch, Barry T., and David A. Macpherson. 2015. "Union Membership and Coverage Database from the CPS." Georgia State University and Trinity University. http://www.unionstats.com/.

Hirsh, C. Elizabeth. 2008. "Settling for Less? Organizational Determinants of Discrimination-Charge Outcomes." *Law and Society Review* 42 (2): 239–74.

———. 2014. "Beyond Treatment and Impact: A Context-Oriented Approach to Employment Discrimination." *American Behavioral Scientist* 58 (2): 256–73.

Hirsh, C. Elizabeth, and Sabino Kornrich. 2008. "The Context of Discrimination: Workplace Conditions, Institutional Environments, and Sex and Race Discrimination Charges." *American Journal of Sociology* 113 (5): 1394–432.

Hirsh, Elizabeth, and Christopher J. Lyons. 2010. "Perceiving Discrimination on the Job: Legal Consciousness, Workplace Context, and the Construction of Race Discrimination." *Law and Society Review* 44 (2): 269–98.

Hopkins, Curt. 2015. "The Real Reason Walmart U-Turned on Wages." AlterNet.org, March 11. http://www.alternet.org/labor/real-reason-walmart-u-turned-wages.

Human Rights Campaign. 2015. "Support the Equality Act: What Is the Equality Act?" HRC.org. http://www.hrc.org/campaigns/support-the-equality-act.

Interfaith Worker Justice. 2015. "What Is Wage Theft?" http://wagetheft.org/wordpress/?page_id=1511.

Jayaraman, Saru, and Immanuel Ness. 2005. *The New Urban Immigrant Workforce: Innovative Models for Labor Organizing.* Armonk, NY: ME Sharpe.

Jobs with Justice. 2014. "Victory: Fired Immigrants Vindicated by NLRB." JWJ.org, November 13. http://www.jwj.org/victory-fired-immigrants-vindicated-by-nlrb.

Kalleberg, Arne L. 2000. "Nonstandard Employment Relations: Part-Time, Temporary and Contract Work." *Annual Review of Sociology* 26 (1): 341–65.

———. 2011. *Good Jobs, Bad Jobs: The Rise of Polarized and Precarious Employment Systems in the United States, 1970s–2000s.* New York: Russell Sage Foundation.

Kang, Jerry, Mark W. Bennett, Devon W. Carbado, Pamela Casey, Nilanjana Dasgupta, David L. Faigman, Rachel D. Godsil, Anthony G. Greenwald, Justin D. Levinson, and Jennifer Mnookin. 2012. "Implicit Bias in the Courtroom." *UCLA Law Review* 59 (5).

Kantor, Jodi, and David Streitfeld. 2015. "Inside Amazon: Wrestling Big Ideas in a Bruising Workplace." *New York Times*, August 15. http://www.nytimes.com/2015/08/16/technology/inside-amazon-wrestling-big-ideas-in-a-bruising-workplace.html.

Katz, Michael. 2010. "The American Welfare State and Social Contract in Hard Times." *Journal of Policy History* 22: 508–29.

Kazan, McClain, Satterley, Lyons, Greenwood, and Oberman: A Professional Law Corporation. 2015. "Assisting Injured Workers: A Manual on Workers' Compensation for Legal Services Programs." *Occupational Safety and Health Portal*, Oakland. http://www.kazanlaw.com/OSHPortal/solve/other_approaches/workers_comp_manual.php.

Kerwin, Donald M., and Kristen McCabe. 2011. "Labor Standards Enforcement and Low-Wage Immigrants: Creating an Effective Enforcement System." Washington, DC: Migration Policy Institute. http://www.migrationpolicy.org/pubs/laborstandards-2011.pdf.

Kobach, Kris W. 2007. "Attrition through Enforcement: A Rational Approach to Illegal Immigration." *Tulsa Journal of Comparative and International Law* 15: 155–63.

Kosanovich, Karen, and Eleni Theodossiou. 2015. "Trends in Long-Term Unemployment: Spotlight on Statistics." Washington, DC: US Bureau of Labor Statistics. http://www.bls.gov/spotlight/2015/long-term-unemployment/.

Krogstad, Jens Manuel, and Jeff S. Passel. 2015. "5 Facts about Illegal Immigration in the U.S." Washington, DC: Pew Research Center. http://www.pewresearch.org/fact-tank/2015/07/24/5-facts-about-illegal-immigration-in-the-u-s/.

Ku, Leighton. 2006. "Why Immigrants Lack Adequate Access to Health Care and Health Insurance." Washington, DC: Migration Policy Institute. http://www.migrationinformation.org/usfocus/display.cfm?ID=417.

Kugler, Adriana, Robert Lynch, and Patrick Oakford. 2013. "Improving Lives, Strengthening Finances: The Benefits of Immigration Reform to Social Security." Washington, DC: Center for American Progress. https://www.americanprogress.org/issues/immigration/report/2013/06/14/66543/improving-lives-strengthening-finances-the-benefits-of-immigration-reform-to-social-security/.

Lamont, Michele. 2002. *The Dignity of Working Men: Morality and the Boundaries of Gender, Race and Class.* Cambridge, MA: Harvard University Press.

Le, Van. 2015. "Mitt Romney Talks 'Self-Deportation'; More About What That Really Means." AmericasVoice.org, January 25. http://americasvoice.org/blog/mitt_romney_talks_self-deportation_more_about_what_that_really_means/.

Leahy, Stephen. 2014. "Exotic Nanomaterials Claimed Their First Major Workplace Injury." Motherboard.vice.com, May 20. http://motherboard.vice.com/read/exotic-nanomaterials-claimed-their-first-major-workplace-injury.

Lee, Ching Kwan, and Yelizavetta Kofman. 2012. "The Politics of Precarity: Views Beyond the United States." *Work and Occupations* 39 (4): 388–408.

Lee, Erika. 2003. *At America's Gates: Chinese Immigration During the Exclusion Era, 1882–1943.* Chapel Hill: University of North Carolina Press.

Lee, Stephen. 2009. "Private Immigration Screening in the Workplace." *Stanford Law Review* 61: 1103–46.

Legal Aid Society—Employment Law Center. 2004. "Do-It-Yourself Recovery of Unpaid Wages: How to Represent Yourself Before the California Labor Commissioner." LAS-ELC.org. https://las-elc.org/sites/default/files/self-help/Recovering_Unpaid_Wages.pdf.

———. 2009. "Do-It-Yourself Guide to Unemployment Insurance Benefits." LAS-ELC.org. https://las-elc.org/sites/default/files/self-help/Unemployment_Benefits.pdf.

———. 2015a. "Employer Bankruptcy, Sale, or Abandonment: Your Legal Rights." LAS-ELC.org. https://las-elc.org/factsheets/bankruptcy.pdf.

———. 2015b. "Undocumented Workers: Employment Rights." LAS-ELC.org. https://las-elc.org/fact-sheets/undocumented-workers-employment-rights.

———. 2015c. "Workers' Compensation Overview: Your Legal Rights." LAS-ELC.org. https://las-elc.org/factsheets/workers-comp-overview.pdf.

———. 2015d. "Your Legal Rights: State Disability Insurance (SDI) vs. Unemployment Insurance (UI)." LAS-ELC.org. https://las-elc.org/fact-sheets/state-disability-insurance-sdi-vs-unemployment-insurance-ui.

Leith, Lawrence H. 2014. "What Happens When Older Workers Experience Unemployment?" Washington, DC: Monthly Labor Review, US Bureau of Labor Statistics (October). http://www.bls.gov/opub/mlr/2014/beyond-bls/what-happens-when-older-workers-experience-unemployment.htm.

LEP.gov. 2015. "Limited English Proficiency (LEP): A Federal Interagency Website." http://www.lep.gov/.

Lichtenstein, Nelson. 2002. *State of the Union: A Century of American Labor.* Princeton, NJ: Princeton University Press.

Linder, Marc. 1998. *Void Where Prohibited: Rest Breaks and the Right to Urinate on Company Time.* Ithaca, NY: ILR Press.

Lippel, Katherine. 2007. "Workers Describe the Effect of the Workers' Compensation Process on Their Health: A Québec Study." *International Journal of Law and Psychiatry* 30 (4–5): 427–43.

Luban, Rachel. 2015. "Alleging Labor Abuses, U.S. and Mexican Workers Call for Boycott of Driscoll's Berries." InTheseTimes.com, April 18. http://inthesetimes.com/working/entry/17865/alleging_labor_abuses_u.s._and_mexican_workers_call_for_boycott_of_driscoll.

Lucas, Samuel R. 2008. *Theorizing Discrimination in an Era of Contested Prejudice: Discrimination in the United States.* Philadelphia: Temple University Press.

Luce, Stephanie. 2004. *Fighting for a Living Wage.* Ithaca, NY: Cornell University Press.

———. 2007. "The U.S. Living Wage Movement: Building Coalitions from the Local Level in a Global Economy." In *Labor in the New Urban Battlegrounds: Local Solidarity in a Global Economy,* 21–34. Edited by L. Turner and D. B. Cornfield. Ithaca, NY: ILR Press / Cornell University Press.

MacEachen, Ellen. 2000. "The Mundane Administration of Worker Bodies: From Welfarism to Neoliberalism." *Health, Risk and Society* 2 (3): 315–27.

Madland, David, and Karla Walter. 2009. "The Employee Free Choice Act 101: A Primer and Rebuttal." Washington, DC: Center for American Progress Action Fund, March 11. https://www.americanprogressaction.org/issues/labor/news/2009/03/11/5814/the-employee-free-choice-act-101/.

Marshall, Anna-Maria. 2003. "Injustice Frames, Legality, and the Everyday Construction of Sexual Harassment." *Law and Social Inquiry* 28 (3): 659–89.

———. 2005. "Idle Rights: Employees' Rights Consciousness and the Construction of Sexual Harassment Policies." *Law and Society Review* 39 (1): 83–124.

Martin, Philip. 2012. "Labor Relations in California Agriculture: Review and Outlook." *Giannini Foundation of Agricultural Economics* 15 (3): 5–8.

Massachusetts AFL-CIO. 2016. "Bust the Union Busters, Union Busting: A Multi-Million Dollar Industry to Take Away Your Rights." MassAFLCIO.org. http://www.massaflcio.org/bust-union-busters-0.

Massey, Douglas S., Jorge Durand, and Karen A. Pren. 2015. "Border Enforcement and Return Migration by Documented and Undocumented Mexicans." *Journal of Ethnic and Migration Studies* 41 (7): 1015–40.

Masson, Elizabeth J. 2004. "Captive Audience Meetings in Union Organizing Campaigns: Free Speech or Unfair Advantage." *Hastings Law Journal* 56: 169–92.

McCammon, Holly J. 2001. "Labor's Legal Mobilization: Why and When Do Workers File Unfair Labor Practices?" *Work and Occupations* 28 (2): 143–75.

McCann, Michael W. 1994. *Rights at Work: Pay Equity Reform and the Politics of Legal Mobilization.* Chicago: University of Chicago Press.

McCarthy, Allison L. 2009. "The May 12, 2008, Postville, Iowa Immigration Raid: A Human Rights Perspective." *Transnational Law and Contemporary Problems* 19: 293–315.

McCluskey, Martha T. 2003. "Efficiency and Social Citizenship: Challenging the Neoliberal Attack on the Welfare State." *Indiana Law Journal* 78: 783–878.

McCubbins, Mathew D., and Thomas Schwartz. 1984. "Congressional Oversight Overlooked: Police Patrols versus Fire Alarms." *American Journal of Political Science* 28 (1): 165–79.

Meissner, Doris. 2009. "Testimony of Doris Meissner Director, U.S. Immigration Policy Program Migration Policy Institute Hearing on 'Comprehensive Immigration Reform in 2009, Can We Do It and How?' Before the Committee on the Judiciary Subcommittee on Immigration, Border Security." Washington, DC: Migration Policy Institute. http://www.migrationpolicy.org/pubs/Testimony-04-30-2009.pdf.

Menjívar, Cecilia, and Leisy J. Abrego. 2009. "Parents and Children Across Borders: Legal Instability and Intergenerational Relations in Guatemalan and Salvadoran Families." In *Across Generations: Immigrant Families in America*, 160–89. Edited by Nancy Foner. New York: New York University Press.

———. 2012. "Legal Violence: Immigration Law and the Lives of Central American Immigrants." *American Journal of Sociology* 117 (5): 1380–421.

Merry, Sally Engle. 1990. *Getting Justice and Getting Even: Legal Consciousness Among Working-Class Americans*. Chicago: University of Chicago Press.

Migration Policy Institute. 2015. "U.S. Immigrant Population and Share Over Time, 1850–Present." Migrationpolicy.org. http://www.migrationpolicy.org/programs/data-hub/charts/immigrant-population-over-time.

Milkman, Ruth. 2002. "The New American Workplace: High Road or Low Road." In *Industrial Relations: Labour Markets, Labour Process and Trade Unionism*, 97–103. Edited by John E. Kelly. London: Routledge.

———. 2006. *L.A. Story: Immigrant Workers and the Future of the U.S. Labor Movement*. New York: Russell Sage Foundation.

———. 2011. "Immigrant Workers, Precarious Work, and the U.S. Labor Movement." *Globalizations* 8 (3): 361–72.

Milkman, Ruth, and Laura Braslow. 2011. "The State of the Unions 2011." New York: Joseph S. Murphy Institute for Worker Education and Labor Studies, Center for Urban Research, and NYC Labor Market Information Service, CUNY. https://www.gc.cuny.edu/CUNY_GC/media/CUNY-Graduate-Center/PDF/Centers/Center%20for%20Urban%20Research/LMIS/state_of_the_unions_2011_release_hires.pdf.

Miller, Richard E., and Austin Sarat. 1980. "Grievances, Claims, and Disputes: Assessing the Adversary Culture." *Law and Society Review* 15 (3–4): 525–66.

Miller, S. A., and Stephen Dinan. 2015. "Obama Budget Calls for Largest Federal Civilian Workforce Since Cold War." *Washington Times*, February 2. http://www.washingtontimes.com/news/2015/feb/2/obama-budget-calls-for-largest-federal-civilian-wo/.

Moorhead, Richard, Alan Paterson, and Avrom Sherr. 2003. "Contesting Professionalism: Legal Aid and Nonlawyers in England and Wales." *Law and Society Review* 37 (4): 765–808.

Munck, Ronaldo. 2013. "The Precariat: A View from the South." *Third World Quarterly* 34 (5): 747–62.

Murolo, Priscilla, A. B. Chitty, and Joe Sacco. 2001. *From the Folks Who Brought You the Weekend*. New York: The New Press.

Myllenbeck, Kristi. 2015. "Sunnyvale: Protesters Demand Wages from Crazy Buffet." *San Jose Mercury News*, March 13. http://www.mercurynews.com/my-town/ci_27693913/sunnyvale-protesters-demand-wages-from-crazy-buffet.

National Center for Transgender Equality. 2015. "Know Your Rights: Employment (General)." TransEquality.org. http://transequality.org/know-your-rights/employment-general.

National Conference of State Legislatures. 2015. "State Minimum Wages, 2015 Minimum Wage by State." Denver and Washington, DC. http://www.ncsl.org/research/labor-and-employment/state-minimum-wage-chart.aspx#1.

National Council for Occupational Safety and Health. 2015. "Campaigns: Temporary Workers." http://www.coshnetwork.org/node/381.

National Employment Law Project. 2009. "Independent Contractor Misclassification and Subcontracting." NELP.org. http://www.nelp.org/site/issues/category/independent_contractor_misclassification_and_subcontracting.

———. 2011. "Winning Wage Justice: An Advocate's Guide to State and City Policies to Fight Wage Theft." NELP.org. http://www.nelp.org/content/uploads/2015/03/WinningWageJustice2011.pdf.

———. 2012. "Winning Wage Justice: Summary of Research on Wage and Hour Violations in the United States." NELP.org. http://www.nelp.org/page/-/Justice/2012/WinningWageJusticeSummaryofResearchonWageTheft.pdf?nocdn=1.

———. 2013. "California's New Worker Protections Against Retaliation." NELP.org. http://www.nelp.org/page/-/Justice/2013/ca-worker-protections-against-retaliation.pdf.

———. 2014. "The U Visa: A Potential Immigration Remedy for Immigrant Workers Facing Labor Abuse." NELP.org. http://nelp.org/content/uploads/2015/03/UVisa.pdf.

———. 2015. "City Minimum Wage Laws: Recent Trends and Economic Evidence." NELP.org. http://www.nelp.org/content/uploads/City-Minimum-Wage-Laws-Recent-Trends-Economic-Evidence.pdf.

National Immigration Law Center. 2009. "Basic Pilot/E-Verify: Why Mandatory Employer Participation Will Hurt Workers, Businesses, and the Struggling U.S. Economy." NILC.org. http://www.nilc.org/immsemplymnt/ircaempverif/e-verify-facts-2009-01-29.pdf.

———. 2012. "The State of the States: E-Verify Laws 2012: State Laws and Executive Orders That Mandate E-Verify's Use." NILC.org. http://www.nilc.org/document.html?id=792.

National Labor Relations Board. 2015a. "1947 Taft-Hartley Substantive Provisions." NLRB.gov. https://www.nlrb.gov/who-we-are/our-history/1947-taft-hartley-substantive-provisions.

———. 2015b. "Appellate Court Decisions, 1974–2014." NLRB.gov. https://www.nlrb.gov/news-outreach/graphs-data/litigations/appellate-court-decisions-1974–2013.

———. 2015c. "Charges and Complaints." NLRB.gov. https://www.nlrb.gov/news-outreach/graphs-data/charges-and-complaints/charges-and-complaints.

———. 2015d. "National Labor Relations Act." NLRB.gov. https://www.nlrb.gov/resources/national-labor-relations-act.

———. 2015e. "What We Do: Investigate Charges." NLRB.gov. https://www.nlrb.gov/what-we-do/investigate-charges.

National Right to Work Legal Defense Foundation. 2015. "Right to Work States." NRTW.org. http://www.nrtw.org/rtws.htm.

Nelson, Robert L., Laura Beth Nielsen, Ryon Lancaster, John Donohue III, and Peter Siegelman. 2016. "Employment Discrimination Litigation." Chicago: American Bar Foundation. http://www.americanbarfoundation.org/research/project/45.

Ness, Immanuel. 2005. *Immigrants, Unions, and the New U.S. Labor Market.* Philadelphia: Temple University Press.

Nicholson, Valerie J., Terry L. Bunn, and Julia F. Costich. 2008. "Disparities in Work-Related Injuries Associated with Worker Compensation Coverage Status." *American Journal of Industrial Medicine* 51 (6): 393–98.

Nielsen, Laura Beth, and Robert L. Nelson. 2005. *Handbook of Employment Discrimination Research: Rights and Realities.* New York: Springer.

Nielsen, Laura Beth, Robert L. Nelson, and Ryon Lancaster. 2008. "Uncertain Justice: Litigating Claims of Employment Discrimination in the Contemporary United States." Chicago: American Bar Foundation Research Paper. http://ssrn.com/paper=1093313.

Oakford, Patrick. 2014. "Administrative Action on Immigration Reform: The Fiscal Benefits of Temporary Work Permits." Washington, DC: Center for American Progress. https://www.americanprogress.org/issues/immigration/report/2014/09/04/96177/administrative-action-on-immigration-reform/.

O'Brien, Christine Neylon. 2005. "The NLRB Waffling on Weingarten Rights." *Loyola University Chicago Law Journal* 37: 111.

Occupational Safety and Health Administration. 2014. "Reporting Fatalities, Hospitalizations, Amputations, and Losses of an Eye as a Result of Work-Related Incidents to OSHA." Washington, DC: United States Department of Labor. https://www.osha.gov/pls/oshaweb/owadisp.show_document?p_table=STANDARDS&p_id=12783.

———. 2015a. "OSHA Injury and Illness Recordkeeping and Reporting Requirements." Washington, DC: United States Department of Labor Employment Standards Administration Wage and Hour Division. https://www.osha.gov/recordkeeping/.

———. 2015b. "OSHA Law and Regulations." Washington, DC: United States Department of Labor. https://www.osha.gov/law-regs.html.

———. 2015c. "OSHA Training: Courses, Materials, and Resources." Washington, DC: United States Department of Labor. https://www.osha.gov/dte/index.html.

Orrenius, Pia M., and Madeline Zavodny. 2009. "Do Immigrants Work in Riskier Jobs?" *Demography* 46 (3): 535–51.

Paret, Marcel. 2016. "Politics of Solidarity and Agency in an Age of Precarity." *Global Labour Journal* 7 (2): 174–88.

Park, Lisa Sun-Hee. 2011. *Entitled to Nothing: The Struggle for Immigrant Health Care in the Age of Welfare Reform.* New York: New York University Press.

Parrish, Margarita, and Toni Schofield. 2005. "Injured Workers' Experiences of the Workers' Compensation Claims Process: Institutional Disrespect and the Neoliberal State." *Health Sociology Review* 14 (1): 33–46.

Passel, Jeffrey. 2006. "Size and Characteristics of the Unauthorized Migrant Population in the U.S." Washington, DC: Pew Hispanic Center. http://pewhispanic.org/reports/report.php?ReportID=61.

Passel, Jeffrey, and D'Vera Cohn. 2009. "A Portrait of the Unauthorized Migrants in the United States." Washington, DC: Pew Hispanic Center. http://pewhispanic.org/files/reports/107.pdf.

Passel, Jeffrey S., D'Vera Cohn, and Ana Gonzalez-Barrera. 2012. "Net Migration from Mexico Falls to Zero—and Perhaps Less." Washington, DC: Pew Hispanic Center. http://www.pewhispanic.org/2012/04/23/net-migration-from-mexico-falls-to-zero-and-perhaps-less/.

Patler, Caitlin, and Jorge Cabrera. 2015. "From Undocumented to DACAmented: Benefits and Limitations of the Deferred Action for Childhood Arrivals (DACA) Program, Three Years Following Its Announcement." Research and Policy Brief 27. Los Angeles: UCLA Institute for Research on Labor and Employment.

Pedroza, Juan, Juane Casas, and Jonathan Santo. 2012. "Mass Exodus from Oklahoma? Immigrants and Latinos Stay and Weather a State of Capture." *Journal of Latino/Latin American Studies* 4 (1): 27–41.

Pender, Kathleen. 2014. "$1 Million City: S.F. Median Home Price Hits 7 Figures for 1st Time." SFGate.com, July 17. http://www.sfgate.com/business/networth/article/1-million-city-S-F-median-home-price-hits-7-5626591.php.

Perea, Juan F. 2011. "The Echoes of Slavery: Recognizing the Racist Origins of the Agricultural and Domestic Worker Exclusion from the National Labor Relations Act." *Ohio State Law Journal* 72: 95–138.

Piven, Frances Fox, and Richard Cloward. 1977. *Poor People's Movements*. New York: Pantheon.

Pollock, John. 2013. "It's All About Justice: Gideon and the Right to Counsel in Civil Cases." *American Bar Association Human Rights Magazine* 39 (4). http://www.americanbar.org/publications/human_rights_magazine_home/2013_vol_39/vol_30_no_4_gideon/its_all_about_justice.html.

Portes, Alejandro, Donald Light, and Patricia Fernández-Kelly. 2009. "The U.S. Health System and Immigration: An Institutional Interpretation." *Sociological Forum* 24 (3): 487–514.

Powers, Mary G., Ellen Percy Kraly, and William Seltzer. 2004. "IRCA: Lessons of the Last U.S. Legalization Program." Migrationpolicy.org, July 1. http://www.migrationpolicy.org/article/irca-lessons-last-us-legalization-program.

Quinlan, Michael. 2004. "Workers' Compensation and the Challenges Posed by Changing Patterns of Work: Evidence from Australia." *Policy and Practice in Health and Safety* 2 (1): 25–52.

Quinlan, Michael, and Claire Mayhew. 1999. "Precarious Employment and Workers' Compensation." *International Journal of Law and Psychiatry* 22 (5): 491–520.

Quinn Mills, Daniel. 1996. "The Changing Social Contract in American Business." *European Management Journal* 14 (5): 451–56.

Rawls, John. 2009. *A Theory of Justice*. Cambridge, MA: Harvard University Press.

Rendall, Michael S., Peter Brownell, and Sarah Kups. 2011. "Declining Return Migration from the United States to Mexico in the Late-2000s Recession: A Research Note." *Demography* 48 (3): 1049–58.

Restaurant Opportunities Center of New York. 2009. "Burned: High Risks and Low Benefits for Workers in the New York City Restaurant Industry." New York: Restaurant Opportunities Center of New York, Restaurant Opportunities Center United, New York City Restaurant Health and Safety Taskforce, and New York City Restaurant Industry Coalition. http://www.scribd.com/full/26629052?access_key=key-1b9hjjqk5mxqz0jm018d.

Restaurant Opportunities Centers United and Rosemary Batt. 2012. "Taking the High Road: A How-To Guide for Successful Restaurant Employers." New York: Restaurant Opportunities Centers United and Cornell University ILR School. http://rocunited.org/wp-content/uploads/2013/04/reports_taking-the-high-road_version-jan-23-2012.pdf.

Rhode, Deborah L. 2013. "Reforming American Legal Education and Legal Practice: Rethinking Licensing Structures and the Role of Nonlawyers in Delivering and Financing Legal Services." *Legal Ethics* 16 (2): 243–57.

Robinson, William, and Xuan Santos. 2014. "Global Capitalism, Immigrant Labor, and the Struggle for Justice." *Class, Race and Corporate Power* 2 (3). http://digitalcommons.fiu.edu/classracecorporatepower/vol2/iss3/1.

Rosenfeld, Jake. 2014. *What Unions No Longer Do.* Cambridge, MA: Harvard University Press.

Rudolph, Linda, Kathy Dervin, Allen Cheadle, Neil Maizlish, and Tom Wickizer. 2002. "What Do Injured Workers Think About Their Medical Care and Outcomes After Work Injury?" *Journal of Occupational and Environmental Medicine* 44 (5): 425–34.

Sarathy, Brinda. 2012. *Pineros: Latino Labour and the Changing Face of Forestry in the Pacific Northwest.* Vancouver: UBC Press.

Sassen, Saskia. 2014. *Expulsions: Brutality and Complexity in the Global Economy.* Cambridge, MA: Harvard University Press.

Saucedo, Leticia M. 2009. "The Three Theories of Discrimination in the Brown-Collar Workplace." *University of Chicago Legal Forum* 2009 (1), article 10: 345–79. http://chicagounbound.uchicago.edu/uclf/vol2009/iss1/10/.

———. 2010. "Immigration Enforcement versus Employment Law Enforcement: The Case for Integrated Protections in the Immigrant Workplace." *Fordham Urban Law Journal* 38 (1): 303–25.

Sayegh, Briggette. 2015. "Demonstrators March through Liberty to Protest Ideal Snacks Layoffs, Working Conditions." TWCnews.com, May 18. http://www.twcnews.com/nys/watertown/news/2015/05/18/hundreds-rally-outside-of-ideal-snacks-facility.html.

Scherzer, Teresa, Reiner Rugulies, and Niklas Krause. 2005. "Work-Related Pain and Injury and Barriers to Workers' Compensation Among Las Vegas Hotel Room Cleaners." *American Journal Public Health* 95 (3): 483–88.

Schmidt, Janet. 1980. "Workers' Compensation: The Articulation of Class Relations in Law." *Critical Sociology* 10 (1): 46–54.

Schmidtz, David, and Robert E. Goodin. 1998. *Social Welfare and Individual Responsibility.* New York: Cambridge University Press.

Schmitt, John. 2014. "Can the Affordable Care Act Reverse Three Decades of Declining Health Insurance Coverage for Low-Wage Workers?" In *What Works for Workers?: Public Policies and Innovative Strategies for Low-Wage Workers,* 273–304. Edited by Stephanie Luce, Jennifer Luff, Joseph A. McCartin, and Ruth Milkman. New York: Russell Sage Foundation.

Schrag, Philip G., Andrew I. Schoenholtz, and Jaya Ramji-Nogales. 2009. *Refugee Roulette: Disparities in Asylum Adjudication and Proposals for Reform.* New York: New York University Press.

Secunda, Paul M. 2009. "The Contemporary Fist Inside the Velvet Glove: Employer Captive Audience Meetings under the NLRA." *Florida International University Law Review* 5: 385–410.

SEIU Local 521. 2015. "Grievances." SEIU521.org. http://www.seiu521.org/members/rights/grievances/.

Selbin, Jeffrey, and Scott L. Cummings. 2015. "Poverty Law: United States A2—Wright, James D." In *International Encyclopedia of the Social & Behavioral Sciences (Second Edition)*, 733–40. Oxford: Elsevier. http://www.sciencedirect.com/science/article/pii/B9780080970868861322.

Serwer, Adam. 2012. "'Self-Deportation': It's a Real Thing, and It Isn't Pretty." *Mother Jones*, January 23. http://www.motherjones.com/mojo/2012/01/romneys-self-deportation-just-another-term-alabama-style-immigration-enforcement.

Sherman, Rachel, and Kim Voss. 2000. "Organize or Die: New Organizing Tactics and Immigrant Workers." In *Organizing Immigrants: The Challenge for Unions in Contemporary California*, 81–108. Edited by Ruth Milkman. Ithaca, NY: Cornell University Press.

Shierholz, Heidi. 2013. "Roughly One in Five Hispanic and Black Workers Are 'Underemployed.'" Washington, DC: Economic Policy Institute. http://www.epi.org/publication/roughly-hispanic-black-workers-underemployed/.

Shor, Glenn. 2006. "Low-Wage Injured Workers and Access to Clinical Care: A Policy Analysis." Berkeley: Center for Occupational and Environmental Health, University of California. http://coshnetwork6.mayfirst.org/sites/default/files/coeh-shor.pdf.

Silbey, Susan S. 2005. "After Legal Consciousness." *Annual Review of Law and Social Science* 1: 323–68.

———. 2008. "Legal Consciousness." In *The New Oxford Companion to Law*, 695–96. Edited by Peter Cane and Joanne Conaghan. Oxford: Oxford University Press.

Songer, Donald, Ashlyn Kuersten, and Erin Kaheny. 2000. "Why the Haves Don't Always Come Out Ahead: Repeat Players Meet Amici Curiae for the Disadvantaged." *Political Research Quarterly* 53 (3): 535–37.

Spieler, Emily A. 1994. "Perpetuating Risk? Workers' Compensation and the Persistence of Occupational Injuries." *Houston Law Review* 31: 119–264.

Standing, Guy. 2011. *The Precariat: The New Dangerous Class*. London: Bloomsbury Academic.

———. 2014. *A Precariat Charter: From Denizens to Citizens*. London: Bloomsbury Academic.

State of California Department of Industrial Relations. 2011. "Division of Labor Standards Enforcement Rest/Meal Periods." dir.ca.gov. http://www.dir.ca.gov/dlse/restandmealperiods.pdf.

———. 2014a. "Labor Commissioner Cites Ten Northern California Buffet Restaurants $16 Million for Wage Theft Violations." dir.ca.gov. http://www.dir.ca.gov/DIRNews/2014/2014-109.pdf.

———. 2014b. "Workers' Compensation in California: A Guidebook for Injured Workers, Chapter 5. Temporary Disability Benefits." dir.ca.gov. http://www.dir.ca.gov/InjuredWorkerGuidebook/Chapter5.pdf.

———. 2015a. "DWC Glossary of Workers' Compensation Terms for Injured Workers." dir.ca.gov. http://www.dir.ca.gov/dwc/wcglossary.htm.

———. 2015b. "FAQ: Workers' Compensation." dir.ca.gov. https://www.dir.ca.gov/dlse/FAQ-Workers%20Compensation.pdf.

———. 2015c. "How to File a Wage Claim." dir.ca.gov. http://www.dir.ca.gov/dlse/howtofilewageclaim.htm.

———. 2015d. "Industrial Welfare Commission Wage Orders." dir.ca.gov. http://www.dir.ca.gov/IWC/WageOrderIndustries.htm.

State of California Employment Development Department. 2015. "Unemployment Insurance (UI) Tax." edd.ca.gov. http://www.edd.ca.gov/payroll_taxes/unemployment_insurance_tax.htm.

Stone, Deborah. 1984. *The Disabled State*. Philadelphia: Temple University Press.

Strunin, Lee, and Leslie I. Boden. 2004. "Family Consequences of Chronic Back Pain." *Social Science and Medicine* 58 (7): 1385–93.

Su, Julie A. 2013. "A Report on the State of the Division of Labor Standards Enforcement." dir.ca.gov. http://www.dir.ca.gov/dlse/Publications/DLSE_Report2013.pdf.

———. 2015. "2013–2014 Fiscal Year Report on the Effectiveness of the Bureau of Field Enforcement." dir.ca.gov. http://www.dir.ca.gov/dlse/BOFE_LegReport2014.pdf.

Theodore, Nik, Beth Gutelius, and Linda Burnham. 2013. "Home Truths: Domestic Workers in California." New York, Oakland, and Chicago: National Domestic Workers Alliance, Data Center, and the Center for Urban Economic Development, University of Illinois, Chicago. http://www.domesticworkers.org/sites/default/files/HomeTruths.pdf.

Trautner, Mary Nell, Erin Hatton, and Kelly E. Smith. 2013. "What Workers Want Depends: Legal Knowledge and the Desire for Workplace Change Among Day Laborers." *Law and Policy* 35 (4): 319–40.

Travis, Jeremy. 2005. *But They All Come Back: Facing the Challenges of Prisoner Reentry*. Washington, DC: Urban Institute.

Trouillot, Michel-Rolph. 2001. "The Anthropology of the State in the Age of Globalization: Close Encounters of the Deceptive Kind." *Current Anthropology* 42 (1): 125–38.

Tucker, Philip. 2003. "The Impact of Rest Breaks upon Accident Risk, Fatigue and Performance: A Review." *Work and Stress* 17 (2): 123–37.

Turner, Brian. 2014. "Three Theories of Justice: Preliminary Reflections." In *The Spirit of Luc Boltanski: Essays on the "Pragmatic Sociology of Critique,"* 29–48. Edited by Simon Susen and Bryan S. Turner. New York: Anthem Press.

Uchitelle, Louis. 2007. *The Disposable American: Layoffs and Their Consequences*. New York: Vintage Books.

US Citizenship and Immigration Services. 2014. "USCIS Approves 10,000 U Visas for 6th Straight Fiscal Year." USCIS.gov. http://www.uscis.gov/news/uscis-approves-10000-u-visas-6th-straight-fiscal-year.

US Department of Labor. 2015a. "Summary of the Major Laws of the Department of Labor." DOL.gov. http://www.dol.gov/opa/aboutdol/lawsprog.htm.

———. 2015b. "The Occupational Safety and Health (OSH) Act." DOL.gov. http://www.dol.gov/compliance/laws/comp-osha.htm.

US Equal Employment Opportunity Commission. 2000. "IV. Background." EEOC.gov. http://www.eeoc.gov/eeoc/mediation/report/chapter4.html.

———. 2008. "Sexual Harassment Verdict Upheld in Favor of EEOC Against Ag Industry Giant Harris Farms: Ninth Circuit Court Affirms Latina Farm Worker's Jury Award of Over $1 Million." EEOC.gov. http://www.eeoc.gov/eeoc/newsroom/release/4-25-08.cfm.

———. 2011. "G. Alcoholism and Illegal Use of Drugs." EEOC.gov. http://www.eeoc.gov/facts/performance-conduct.html#alcohol.

———. 2013. "Jury Awards $240 Million for Long-Term Abuse of Workers with Intellectual Disabilities." EEOC.gov. http://www.eeoc.gov/eeoc/newsroom/release/5-1-13b.cfm.

———. 2015a. "50th Anniversary of the EEOC: The Law." EEOC.gov. http://www.eeoc.gov/eeoc/history/50th/thelaw.cfm.

———. 2015b. "Charge Statistics: FY 1997 through FY 2014." EEOC.gov. http://eeoc.gov/eeoc/statistics/enforcement/charges.cfm.

———. 2015c. "EEOC Litigation Statistics, FY 1997 through FY 2014." EEOC.gov. http://www.eeoc.gov/eeoc/statistics/enforcement/litigation.cfm.

———. 2015d. "History of the EEOC Mediation Program." EEOC.gov. http://www.eeoc.gov/eeoc/mediation/history.cfm.

———. 2015e. "How to File a Charge of Employment Discrimination." EEOC.gov. http://www.eeoc.gov/employees/howtofile.cfm.

———. 2015f. "Overview of Federal Sector EEO Complaint Process." EEOC.gov. http://www.eeoc.gov/federal/fed_employees/complaint_overview.cfm.

———. 2015g. "What You Should Know: ABC's of the EEOC." EEOC.gov. http://www.eeoc.gov/eeoc/newsroom/wysk/abcs.cfm.

———. 2015h. "EEOC Wins Jury Verdict of Over $17 Million for Victims of Sexual Harassment and Retaliation at Moreno Farms: Florida Farm Managers Subjected Women Workers to Coerced Sex, Groping and Verbal Abuse, Then Fired Them for Objecting, Federal Agency Charged." EEOC.gov. http://www.eeoc.gov/eeoc/newsroom/release/9-10-15.cfm.

———. 2016a. "The E-RACE Initiative." EEOC.gov. http://www.eeoc.gov/eeoc/initiatives/e-race/.

———. 2016b. "Youth at Work." EEOC.gov. http://www.eeoc.gov/youth/.

Valenzuela, Abel. 2003. "Day Labor Work." *Annual Review of Sociology* 29 (1): 307–33.

Valenzuela Jr., Abel, Nik Theodore, Edwin Melendez, and Ana Luz Gonzalez. 2006. "On the Corner: Day Labor in the United States." Los Angeles: UCLA Center for the Study of Urban Poverty. http://www.urbaneconomy.org/sites/default/files/onthecorner_daylaborinUS_39p_2006.pdf.

Voss, Kim, and Rachel Sherman. 2000. "Breaking the Iron Law of Oligarchy: Union Revitalization in the American Labor Movement." *American Journal of Sociology* 106 (2): 303–49.

Wage and Hour Division. 2008. "Fact Sheet #17G: Salary Basis Requirement and the Part 541 Exemptions Under the Fair Labor Standards Act (FLSA)." Washington, DC: United States Department of Labor. http://www.dol.gov/whd/overtime/fs17g_salary.htm.

———. 2014a. "Fact Sheet #13: Am I an Employee?: Employment Relationship Under the Fair Labor Standards Act (FLSA)." Washington, DC: United States Department of Labor. http://www.dol.gov/whd/regs/compliance/whdfs13.pdf.

———. 2014b. "EMPLEO Reaches 10 Years Helping Immigrant Workers and Their Employers: Labor Outreach and Assistance Partnership Keeps Growing as It Celebrates First Decade." Washington, DC: United States Department of Labor. http://www.dol.gov/whd/media/press/whdpressVB3.asp?pressdoc=Western/20140613_2.xml.

———. 2015. "Minimum Wage Laws in the States: January 1, 2015." Washington, DC: United States Department of Labor. http://www.dol.gov/whd/minwage/america.htm.

Waldinger, Roger D., and Michael I. Lichter. 2003. *How the Other Half Works: Immigration and the Social Organization of Labor.* Berkeley: University of California Press.

Weber, Max. 1978. *Economy and Society.* 2 vols. Berkeley: University of California Press.

——. 2009. "Bureaucracy." In *From Max Weber: Essays in Sociology*, 196–244. New York: Routledge.

Weil, David. 2014. *The Fissured Workplace : Why Work Became So Bad for So Many and What Can Be Done to Improve It.* Cambridge, MA: Harvard University Press.

Wong, Tom K., Angela S. García, Marisa Abrajano, David FitzGerald, Karthick Ramakrishnan, and Sally Le. 2013. "Undocumented No More: A Nationwide Analysis of Deferred Action for Childhood Arrivals, or DACA." Washington, DC: Center for American Progress. https://www.americanprogress.org/issues/immigration/report/2013/09/20/74599/undocumented-no-more/.

Working Partnerships USA. 2015. "Silicon Valley Rising." San Jose, California. http://silicon valleyrising.org.

Worksafe!, A California Coalition for Worker Occupational Safety Health Promotion. 2010. "A Broken System." Oakland. http://www.worksafe.org/2010/01/broken-wc-system.html.

Wright, Erik Olin. 2004. "Basic Income, Stakeholder Grants, and Class Analysis." *Politics and Society* 32 (1): 79–87.

Zatz, Marjorie S., and Nancy Rodriguez. 2015. *Dreams and Nightmares: Immigration Policy, Youth, and Families.* Berkeley: University of California Press.

Zatz, Noah D. 2008. "Working Beyond the Reach or Grasp of Employment Law." In *The Gloves-off Economy: Workplace Standards at the Bottom of America's Labor Market*, 31–64. Edited by Annette Bernhardt, Heather Boushey, Laura Dresser, and Chris Tilly. Ithaca, NY: ILR Press.

Zlolniski, Christian. 2006. *Janitors, Street Vendors, and Activists: The Lives of Mexican Immigrants in Silicon Valley.* Berkeley: University of California Press.

Zong, Zie, and Jeanne Batalova. 2015. "Frequently Requested Statistics on Immigrants and Immigration in the United States." Migrationpolicy.org, February 26. http://www.migration policy.org/article/frequently-requested-statistics-immigrants-and-immigration-united-states.

Zuberi, Tukufu, and Eduardo Bonilla-Silva. 2008. *White Logic, White Methods: Racism and Methodology.* Lanham, MD: Rowman and Littlefield Publishers.

INDEX

Abel, Richard L., 2, 127
Affordable Care Act, 39, 91, 135, 136, 139n2
African Americans: surveyed respondents, 18; unemployment rates, 5
Agamben, Giorgio, 134
age discrimination, 29, 65, 106, 141n13
Age Discrimination in Employment Act (1967), 65
agriculture, farm labor, 7, 16, 43, 64, 68–69, 92, 124, 137–38
Alabama: no minimum wage statute, 8; restrictionist approach, 145n25
Alexander, Charlotte, 87
Amazon, boycotts, 138
American Federation of Labor, 4, 68
Americans with Disabilities Act (1990), 64, 65, 96
arbitration, 13, 43, 44, 71, 139n3
Arizona: Legal Arizona Workers Act (2008), 73; restrictionist approach, 145n25
Asian immigrants, 4
Asians/Pacific Islanders, surveyed respondents, 18
attorneys, 78–79, 122, 125; claims-making role, 16, 93–97, 128–29; discrimination lawsuits, 68; legal aid/workers' rights clinics/nonprofit, 17, 21, 89, 93–97, 99, 129–31; private/for-profit, 12, 94–96, 103, 120, 121, 128–29, 130–31; right to, 131; union membership and, 103; workers' compensation, 63, 65, 94, 97; workers' dissatisfactions with, 97, 99, 119, 125

at-will employment, 39, 83; claims-making, 96; laws in practice and on the books, 123–24; precarity, 22, 36–38, 67; retaliation by employer, 64; undocumented immigrants, 7; unfair termination, 41–42, 109; unions and, 36–38, 135. *See also* independent contractors

"bad jobs," 1–2, 38–39
bankruptcy, employers declaring, 33, 76, 98, 99, 133, 144n46
Basic Pilot/E-Verify program, 73, 74, 94, 142n31
benefits: "bad jobs," 2, 39; nonemployees, 124; pensions, 4; public, 6, 65, 131, 136; retirement, 5–6, 17, 74; undocumented immigrants, 73–74; vacation, 26, 39, 46. *See also* insurance; Social Security; workers' compensation
Benhabib, Seyla, 138
Berkeley, minimum wage, 56
Berman claim, 59
Bernhardt, Annette, 56
Berrey, Ellen, 16, 118
Best, Rachel Kahn, 66
bias: bureaucracies, 14, 21, 78–79; claims-making process, 9
Blasi, Gary, 14
Bobo, Kim, 56
Bodega Aurrera, 118
Boltanski, Luc, 126
Bosniak, Linda, 138

Employment Development Department,
California, 29, 72, 132
enforcement, rights, 118; discrimination laws, 65.
See also immigration enforcement; labor
standards enforcement
Epp, Charles R., 53
Equal Employment Opportunity Commission
(EEOC), 80, 96, 141n12, 142n28;
discrimination claims, 1, 11, 14, 65–66, 68, 73,
123; sexual harassment claims, 87, 101, 102;
wage and hour claims, 99
Equal Pay Act, 141n13
equivalence, principle of, 126
E-Verify program, 73, 74, 94, 142n31
*Expulsions: Brutality and Complexity in the
Global Economy* (Sassen), 5
eyewitness testimony, claims-making, 79

Fair Employment Practices Agencies (FEPAs), 65
Fair Labor Standards Act (FLSA), 8, 12, 55, 58, 132
family: claims-making and, 22, 77, 80–81, 105,
112–14; in countries of origin, 84–85, 114–15;
family leave, 54; information source, 80–81;
job loss/abuse and, 101–4, 108, 110, 112–15, 126
Fantasia, Rick, 69
farm labor, 7, 16, 43, 64, 68–69, 92, 124, 137–38
federal labor standards, 1, 7–9, 11, 14, 53–61, 74,
123; enforcement, 54, 73–75, 89, 130, 132,
140n6, 141n12
Felstiner, William L. F., 2, 127
feminism, 1, 3, 10. *See also* women
Fight for $15, 70, 137
"fire-alarm oversight," 132
firing. *See* termination, unfair
"fissured workplace," 79
food-related work: farm labor, 7, 16, 43, 64,
68–69, 92, 124, 137–38; food processing, 1, 7;
food service, 3, 20, 137
forestry replanting work, 60
Fraser, Nancy, 138

Garcés-Mascareñas, Blanca, 134
Garcia, Ruben J., 53–54
gatekeepers, claims-making, 22–23, 77, 77fig,
86–91, 127–29
gender identity: employment discrimination, 65,
66. *See also* sexual orientation; women
Genetic Information Nondiscrimination Act
(2008), 65
globalization, 4
Gompers, Samuel, 4

Gonzales, Alfonso, 138
Greenman, Emily, 141n7
grievance process, 9; prison, 9; union, 43, 49,
70–71, 139n3. *See also* claims-making
Griffith, Kati L., 132
guest worker programs, 4, 70

Hall, Matthew, 141n7
health, 8, 25, 104, 105–6; Affordable Care Act,
39, 91, 135, 136, 139n2; deaths on the job, 60;
emergency room care, 31, 64, 91, 131, 143n23;
"independent medical reviewers" (IMRs),
90; insurance, 5–6, 29, 30, 39, 57, 61, 74, 106,
108, 111–12, 139n2; after job loss and injuries,
104, 109–12; medical examiners (QMEs),
90–91, 97, 128; occupational health clinic, 31,
44, 64, 110, 114; older workers, 106–7; OSHA,
8, 52, 59–61; psychological, 91, 98, 104, 113–15,
124; sick leave, 26–27, 39; stress of claims-
making, 98–99, 112; tech industries, 141n5.
See also disability; injuries, workplace; safety
"high-road employment," 5, 56
"high-skilled" workforce, 6
Hoffman, Steve G., 16, 118
Hoffman Plastic Compounds Inc. v. the National
Labor Relations Board, 73, 135
hospitality industry, 28, 38, 86
hostile work environment, 40, 67, 82
hours, work, 8, 25, 68; rest and meal breaks, 57,
124, 132; standards, 55–59; wage and hour
claimants, 57–59, 68, 84, 99
housing: California Department of Fair
Employment and Housing (DFEH), 14, 27,
30–31, 65, 101, 145n2; eviction from, 102;
recession affecting, 5; San Francisco Bay
Area, 24, 103, 104
human resources departments, 44–46; contract
fraud, 120; and discrimination, 9, 46; dispute
resolution, 13, 42–43, 44, 46; and injuries,
30–32, 44; and No-Match Letters, 117;
offsite, 124; and sexual harassment, 9, 45;
termination through, 29, 103; and workers'
compensation, 45, 63–64
humiliation, 62, 98, 121, 122

immigrants, 3–12, 16–20; deaths on the job, 60;
immigrant labor unions, 69–70; legalization
program, 73; pliability, 7; population rise, 6;
racist policies toward, 4, 11–12; restrictionist
policies, 4, 6, 55, 116, 145n25; return
migration, 21, 23, 104, 115–18, 145n25;